# VIOLENCE AND AGGRESSION

## A Physiological Perspective

# VIOLENCE AND AGGRESSION

*A Physiological Perspective*

## K. E. MOYER

A PWPA Book

PARAGON HOUSE PUBLISHERS

NEW YORK

Published in the United States by
Paragon House Publishers
2 Hammarskjold Plaza
New York, New York 10017

A Professors World Peace Academy Book

Designed by *Paul Chevannes*

**Library of Congress Cataloging-in-Publication Data**

Moyer, Kenneth E. (Kenneth Evan), 1919–
  Violence and Aggression.

  "A PWPA book."
  Bibliography:
  Includes index.
    1. Violence—United States.   2. Aggressiveness
(Psychology)   I. Title.
HN90.V5M68   1985      j303.6'2      86-4987
ISBN 0-943852-15-3
      0-943852-19-6 (paperback)

# Contents

## BOOKS BY K. E. MOYER

Moyer, K. E. *The Psychobiology of Aggression.*

Moyer, K. E. *The Physiology of Hostility.*

Moyer, K. E. (Ed.) *The Physiology of Aggression and Implications for Control.*

Crabtree, J. M. & Moyer, K. E. *Bibliography of Aggressive Behavior: A Readers Guide to the Research Literature.*

Moyer, K. E. & Crabtree, J. M. *Bibliography of Aggressive Behavior: A Readers Guide to the Research Literature,* Volume II.

Moyer, K. E. *Neuroanatomy: Text and Illustrations.* Available in Spanish Translation.

Moyer, K. E. *You and Your Child—A Primer for Parents.*

# BIOGRAPHICAL INFORMATION

In a book of this nature, it is important for the reader to know something about the author.

Professor Moyer studied for his doctorate at Washington University in St. Louis, receiving the degree in 1951. He has taught at Carnegie-Mellon University for the past thirty-five years. He has been on the council of the International Society for Research on Aggression since 1976. In 1974 he founded the international journal *Aggressive Behavior* and served as its Editor-in-Chief for four years. His publications include eight books, twenty-five chapters in books by other authors, five entries in four different encyclopedias, and seventy-one articles in scientific journals.

The paper, "Kinds of Aggression and their Physiological Bases," has been so frequently quoted that it was designated as a *Citation Classic* by the Institute for Scientific Information, indicating that it has had a major impact on the field.

Organizations in many countries including France, Italy, Hungary, the Netherlands, Brazil and others have invited Dr. Moyer to lecture.

His biography may be found in: *Who's Who in the World; Who's Who in America; American Men of Science,* and *World Who's Who in Science from Antiquity to the Present.*

He is a fellow in the American Association for the Advancement of Science and the Psychopharmacology division of the American Psychological Association.

To the best of friends
Bob and Millie
and
Dave and Arlene

# Preface

In 1966 thirty-two people died at the hands of three unhappy, unreasoning, unfortunate, deranged young men. Richard Speck, apparently under the combined influence of alcohol and unnamed drugs, engaged in an orgy of violence in a nurse's residence in Chicago. He did not know his victims; he could not remember the incident, but he stabbed, slashed and strangled eight young women in the prime of their lives.

Charles Whitman, with the heat of fury in his brain, shot his wife and mother-in-law. He then proceeded to fulfill the angry fantasies he had previously disclosed to a psychiatrist. After shooting the receptionist at the top of the clock tower of the University of Texas, he systematically and with deadly accuracy shot anyone he could bring into the sights of his high-powered rifle. When his furor was finally terminated by the heroic efforts of the police, fourteen passersby were dead and thirty-one lay injured.

Three months later, five women and two children in Mesa, Arizona were forced to lie head to head in the form of a cartwheel on the floor of a beauty parlor. Robert Smith, a high school senior, coolly and without apparent motive shot them through the head. Even as this book is being written, a report has come in that James Huberty went "hunting for humans" in San Diego. He set a new record in senseless killing. He went into a MacDonalds hamburger stand and began shooting customers and employees. He killed twenty-one people and wounded seventeen more, men, women, and children between the ages of eight months and seventy-four years.[15]

The impact of the 1966 senseless, violent acts forced me to reconsider my priorities. Up until that time, I had the usual citizen's concern about the apparent increase in brutal behavior in the American scene. As did most people, I read with increasing dismay the news media's portrayal of meaningless murders, savage sexual assaults and robberies in which the opportunity to inflict pain on the victim seemed more important to the perpetrator than the money gained. I worried about it; I knew little about the problem; and I did nothing constructive. It was obvious that something needed to be done, but it was not clear what, and it was even less evident what I, as an individual, could do.

When a college professor is faced with a problem, he or she is prone (sometimes wisely, and sometimes not) to devote his or her time to study and to thought rather than to action. Since I had not the slightest idea of what actions might be taken to reduce the level and intensity of aggressive interactions among people, I was moved to do what I knew how to do: to study, to think, to research, and attempt to integrate the diverse materials on the subject into some meaningful pattern. The hope, of course, was that from these activities would come understanding, and from understanding, some implications for intelligent action.

This book attempts to provide some understanding of the incredibly complex problem of aggressive behavior. The understanding achieved here does imply actions that can be taken now and it indicates directions in which we may look for further methods of modifying behavior in order to reduce the level and intensity of aggression in our lives. It is also hoped that a better understanding of aggressive behavior will contribute in some measure to a better understanding of behavior in general, and provide some insight into humankind's most complex problem—humans.

There are now several hundred books that deal with some aspect of violence and aggression. Why do we need another? There are a number of reasons.

First the area is of the utmost import. If we do not in some way solve the problem of international aggression, it will not matter which of the various theories provides the best explanation of the facts at hand.

Second, our lack of understanding of how hostile tendencies should be handled may result in great unhappiness for ourselves and for others. Wife-beaters and child-abusers deal with their hostile impulses in a less than adjustive manner.

Third, there is a clear need for a new look at the problem of aggressive behavior because there has been a recent surge of experimental information on the physiological bases of aggression. Most of it has not yet been incorporated into the older theoretical systems which have had a profound influence on our thoughts and on our behavior.

Fourth, we must come to grips with the problems associated with hostile behaviors. As the second chapter will show, violence is one of civilization's major scourges. It must be dealt with and ways must be found for reducing the various forms of hostility. Different theories lead to quite different courses of action.

In addition to the plethora of books, there are literally thousands of studies on aggressive behavior. A recent book by Moyer and Crabtree[414] lists 3,636 items from 1975–1981. An earlier book by Crabtree and Moyer[116] lists 3,460 references earlier than 1975.

Fortunately, the entire Moyer and Crabtree book had been

entered into the memory of the Carnegie-Mellon Dec-20 computers. This permitted a search of the data bank for any number of items. Thus, one could ask the computer for a search of alcohol and the full reference for all items having alcohol in the title would be printed. A word stem could be entered and the computer would print out full references for all items containing that word stem, thus *murd* would catch all of the items for *murder, murderer, murdered, murderess, etc.*

The data bank was searched for 138 items considered to be important to this volume. This included such items as: brain, rape, ethical, and sex. This procedure yielded 2,592 items, although many of them appeared in more than one category. It was then necessary to go through the cited items to select the most relevant and incorporate them into the book. In spite of this effort, I am under no illusions that I have found all references relevant to this work, or even all those that are very important to the concepts under discussion. Even with some of the most sophisticated computer techniques, it is still possible to miss some important references.

Since this book is not an organized annotated compilation of the world's literature on aggression, it was necessary to select the most relevant studies for inclusion and discussion. The result is the bibliography at the end of the book.

With such an abundance of literature it was difficult to decide what not to include. Clearly, one cannot cover everything about everything, and even the most casual reader will see large areas of the literature that *should* have been included. Most of the material is related in some way to the explication of a particular model of aggressive behavior, other items have been left out.

It is expected that the readers of this book will have widely different professional vocabularies. This problem is met, in part, by the glossary at the end of the book.

One need not be sophisticated in neuroanatomy to follow the line of reasoning of this volume. It is useful to have some general landmarks, to know the occipital lobe is at the back of the brain, and the frontal lobes, reasonably enough, are at the front. For most people, it is sufficient to have a general idea of where things are.

The figures have been labeled for greatest convenience. Each diagram is numbered and each structure or each drawing is numbered. When a structure is to be located, the drawing number is given first and the structure number is second. Thus, (2-5) indicates the location of the temporal lobe (5) on figure number (2).

# Acknowledgments

I am grateful to many people for help on this book. Maureen Taylor did much of the word processing on the early chapters. Carol Thomas struggled valiantly with the computer to wrest from it the final formatting of the manuscript.

I particularly appreciate the help of Dr. Diane McGuiness who went through the manuscript word by word and made many important suggestions. This is a better book for her efforts.

Robert and Cathy Noblick and Professor Robert Johnson also read the entire volume and offered comments from the point of view of the layperson. Their efforts have been most helpful.

Others have been helpful in many ways, but I, alone, am responsible for the errors that may have found their way into this volume.

# CHAPTER

# I

# Four Cases*

## Mr. Jarvis

A Mr. Jarvis, because he has a headache, comes home from work early. He notices that there is an unfamiliar car in the driveway. He does not pay much attention to it, but he does wonder. As he enters the house, he hears a man's voice as well as the voice of his wife. He is unable to tell what is being said, but he is aware of heavy breathing. Although he has never had any hard evidence, he has suspected for some years that his wife has had an affair, or perhaps several. As he climbs the stairs to the bedroom he cannot make out what is being said, but it becomes quite clear what is being done. He kicks in the locked door. His wife screams and jumps out of bed. The plumber does not move. He appears to be paralyzed with fear. By this time Jarvis is in a towering, overwhelming rage. He goes for his gun that is kept in the top drawer of the dresser. In his haste he pulls the drawer all the way out and everything falls to the floor. He swears fluently and dives for the gun which slid under the bed. The plumber makes no attempt to get his clothes but runs for the door. Jarvis gets the gun in his right hand and sticks out his left foot to trip the plumber whose speed propels him over the landing and down the steps. As the

---

*These four cases are fictional. However, they are representative of cases one might find in the daily newspaper.

1

intruder falls, Jarvis gets up with the gun. He is shaking all over with the palsy of intense rage. His wife continues to scream while cowering in the corner. The plumber is getting up by the time Jarvis gets to the top of the stairs. Jarvis fires shot after shot and misses time after time. Just before the gun is empty, a bullet hits the plumber almost by accident. The plumber dies instantly.

## Mr. Speleni

Speleni has been in the same line of work for many years. He enjoys it and he believes, with reason, that he is very good at it. He is currently working under a new contract and is in the preliminary phase that he considers to be of the utmost importance. Speleni sits quietly having a martini, glancing at his quarry Dr. Milton. He does not know what Milton has done to merit the attention of Jack Speleni and he really doesn't care very much. In the course of several days, he has developed a good fix on the general habits of Dr. Milton. He knows when Milton has his hospital rounds. He knows generally when Milton goes to his home about half a mile from the bar. Tonight Speleni plans to meet him about half way. He leaves the bar about fifteen minutes before Milton usually does. When he gets outside, he pauses to put the silencer on his .38. He walks a ways up the street and stops in the shadows near a street light. His preliminary work has paid off; Dr. Milton is right on time. As Milton walks into the glare of the street light, Speleni steps out and fires two shots into his victim's chest at pointblank range. Since Speleni is a thorough man and does not want to leave anything to chance, he puts another round in Dr. Milton's head as he goes down. Speleni walks calmly away taking the cumbersome silencer off his weapon and goes home to his family, secure in the thought that he will now be able to get his wife the station wagon she has been wanting so that she can better take the children all the places that they must go.

## Tom Hayduke

Tom Hayduke has had his National Guard uniform for just a week. He is the youngest member of his company and perhaps the regiment. He wears his uniform with pride. Actually, he has not had an opportunity to wear it outside the home. When the opportunity comes he will be ready.

He sees himself, after a hurricane, shoving looters around, and if necessary, shooting them. He sees himself as a hero helping the victims of a flood. He, in his thinking, is as tough on the *forces of evil* as necessary. Tom's opportunity to confront *evil* comes all

2

too soon. Strikers who are sure they have been wronged have become progressively more disorderly and have been smashing windows in the plant, and trampling lawns, flower beds and gardens in the vicinity of the plant. An enormous demonstration has been planned for Sunday with reinforcements of the same union from nearby towns. The governor is concerned about the possibility that violence will get out of hand. He calls Tom and the rest of his company out to preserve order. The strikers become more and more angry and upset as they march from the center of town. They begin to shout profanity at the guards, the available symbols of authority. Tom, standing in a large doorway becomes more frightened as the crowd becomes more unruly. As he is jostled against the door he begins to shake. His stomach is churning, his mouth is dry, and his palms begin to sweat. He backs up against the door and puts the clip into his rifle. He backs up in terror, and when someone throws a rock that breaks the window in the side of the doorway, and some of the strikers are pushed against him by the press of the crowd, he fires six shots at random into the crowd. Four men die.

## Jack Ronnal

A teller (first window) at the First National Bank does a good job. His customers find him courteous and pleasant. The bank manager believes that Jack is careful and meticulous in his work. He is very seldom short or over in his daily balance. Those who know him, if they really knew him, would agree that he is vicious and depraved. He has, contrary to everyone's opinion, been involved in a series of heinous crimes. His procedure has been to observe an attractive young woman in a supermarket. He follows her home and keeps her under surveillance to find the pattern of her behavior. He must sometimes observe several potential victims before he finds one that has all the necessary characteristics: attractive, living alone, and in an apartment that is not secure. As he gets closer and closer to his ultimate goal, he becomes progressively more sexually excited. He finally gains entry to the apartment, then terrorizes his victim with threats he is all too ready to carry out. When she cowers before him, he rapes her with an unsatisfactory result. His sexual arousal increases as he beats her in the face and head with his heavy flashlight, and he has an orgasm as he stabs her repeatedly. The next morning he is courteous, friendly and pleasant to his customers.

Most people would agree that in all of the above cases a murder was committed, perhaps different degrees of murder, but murder nonetheless. Most would also agree that the behavior of each murderer was aggressive. However, it is obvious that the behaviors are very different. One of the problems with research on aggression and theorizing about it is that the same terms, at times, mean different things to different people. And, of course, that different terms may mean the same thing to different people.

The behavior of Mr. Jarvis, the irate husband, was the result of an overwhelming, perhaps uncontrollable rage reaction. In many cultures, including some portion of our own, the murder would be considered justifiable. All during this rage reaction, changes were going on in the brain and body of Mr. Jarvis. That rage reaction is controlled in part by complex but relatively specific neural mechanisms and involves specific activity in the autonomic nervous system that contributes to the fight-or-flight reaction. In Jarvis's case, the rage reaction caused an increase in heart rate, increase in blood pressure and sweating palms, among other things.

These mechanisms of brain and body also involve those portions of the brain that relate to learning and memory. It is obvious that learning and memory are involved. The entire sequence of finding the gun, aiming and pulling the trigger must have been enabled by neural systems not specifically related to the mechanisms of rage.

The case of Mr. Speleni, the contract killer, is very different. Speleni knows no rage during the murder. He has no antipathy toward Dr. Milton. In fact, he feels that he might like Milton if he knew him better. If Speleni has any reaction at all, it is probably mild excitement, in some measure like stage fright. In this case there is no involvement of the neural system for rage, and thus the activity in the brains of Jarvis and Speleni are quite different.

Hayduke of the National Guard is highly emotional and his entire body is racked with fear. The shaking, the mounting blood pressure, the blurred vision, and all of the turbulent reactions from the region of his gut are the result of intense fear generated by the situation. On the surface, the reactions of Jarvis and Hayduke appear to be very similar. However, there is evidence that the involvement of the autonomic system in fear and rage can be differentiated. There is also good evidence that there are separate parts of the brain involved in rage and fear.

Jack Ronnal is, of course, very different from the other three. It is clear that the type of victim is different and is critical to the behavior he displays. He, as with the other two, has a high level of arousal, but his perception of his own feelings is quite different. It is probably the case that the pattern of his autonomic reaction is also very different. The brain mechanisms that are active during this encounter differ from the other three. Ronnal also has activity in the endocrine system which was not the case in the other three murderers. There is some probability that he is

4

showing a periodic increase of the male hormones called andro-gens. There is also the possibility that this man's outrageous behavior could be controlled by reducing the androgen level in his blood stream through use of androgen-blocking agents.

It must be made clear, however, that a *cure* from the manipu-lation of physiological mechanisms is by no means certain. He may be operating under the pressure of a high androgen level, but his sexual expression obviously shows a behavior pattern far beyond the norm. This behavior pattern also reflects learned behavior. Both learned and physiological factors contribute to his behavior and any therapy for Ronnal must be based on the interactions of both of these variables. If, in fact, his bizarre reaction is due primarily to an intense and pathological hatred of women, his behavior will be changed only partially by hormone therapy.

## Summary

You have just read the essence of this book. The major points made in this short chapter are summarized below:

1. There are a number of different kinds of aggression which can be identified and considered separately. When this point is not recog-nized, only confusion results.

2. Each kind of aggression, except that shown by the contract killer, has a separate identifiable neural mechanism which is active during the response.

3. Each kind of aggression, except that shown by Speleni, involves that part of the nervous system which controls body processes and provides different activation patterns that produce the various feel-ings associated with emotion.

4. There is a kind of aggression (that shown by Speleni) that does not involve an emotional response. The behavior is the result of a learning experience just as eating corn flakes for breakfast is the result of learning. The brain is, of course, involved in this kind of response but the neural mechanisms are diffuse and cannot be specifically located.

5. The specific neural systems that underlie each type of aggression always and in all instances interact with brain traces laid down during experience. This is the case even if the aggression systems are directly activated by brain stimulation.

## Where Do We Go From Here?

In the next chapter, the nature and the magnitude of the problems associated with aggressiveness will be discussed. The informa-tion associated with the theory of aggression in this book has a quite different implication than do the more traditional theories. In Chapter III, a bio-experiential model will be presented.

The mechanisms involved in each kind of aggression can be more or less sensitive to activation. A variety of manipulations can alter the threshold of the systems underlying each behavior. This material will be discussed in Chapter IV.

Chapter V provides information about some of the physical disorders of humans that result in an increase in aggressive behavior.

Chapter VI deals with the issues on which theoretical positions differ. It also includes the predictions made by the bio-experiential model.

There are a variety of ways to reduce the probability of the expression of an aggressive response. Those involving learning and neural mechanisms are considered in Chapter VII. Those involving hormonal and pharmaceutical techniques will be covered in Chapter VIII.

Chapter IX deals with the limitations of physiological methods in the reduction of aggression.

Chapter X is a more detailed discussion of one particular problem, that of territory.

# CHAPTER

# The Problem of Violence and Aggression

In the United States today there is considerable legitimate concern about the problem of violence and aggressive behavior. After two years of study, the National Commission on the Causes and Prevention of Violence has concluded:

> Violence in the United States has risen to alarmingly high levels. Whether one considers assassination, group violence, or individual acts of violence, the decade of the 1960s was considerably more violent than the several decades preceding it and ranks among the most violent in our history. The United States is the clear leader among modern, stable democratic nations in its rates of homicide, assault, rape, and robbery, and it is at least among the highest in incidence of group violence and assassination.

> This high level of violence is dangerous to our society. It is disfiguring our society—making fortresses of portions of our cities and dividing our people into armed camps. It is jeopardizing some of our most precious institutions, among them our schools and universities—poisoning the spirit of trust and cooperation that is essential to their proper functioning. It is corroding the central political processes of our democratic

society—substituting force and fear for argument and accommodation (p. XV).[430]

More recently, Dr. Max Siegel [525] in his presidential address to the American Psychological Association made the following assessment:

.... The specter of violent crime lurks everywhere. . . . We are faced with ghastly statistics: Someone is murdered every 23 minutes. A woman is raped every 6 minutes. As I speak, two people will be robbed in this country, and two more will be shot, stabbed, or seriously beaten. And these data may well be doubled, since less than half of violent crime is reported. . . . The evidence is clear. Next year, it is likely that 18,000 Americans will be murdered (a 50% increase from just one decade ago) and three million more will be robbed, assaulted, or raped. Twenty-five million or more households will be burglarized.

Six hundred years before the birth of Christ the prophet Ezekiel had the same concerns when he wrote " . . . the land is full of bloody crimes and the city is full of violence." (Ezekiel VII:23). Every sixty-eight seconds between the years of 1820 and 1945, one person has died at the hands of another as a result of violence ranging from murder to war.[63,467]

Thus, it appears that people's hostility toward one another, and their concern about that behavior, is as old as life itself. Aggressive behavior is not new. What is new is the dramatic increase in destructive capacity. On the international scene, as we have often been told, it is now possible to create a nuclear winter that will make the planet uninhabitable for people and animals that do survive the bomb blast. At the level of the local tavern, the temporary loss of habits of hostility-control caused by alcohol can result in death because of the availability of the lethal handgun. Only a technologically advanced civilization could provide its politicians with a hydrogen bomb and every second home with a gun.[433]

There may have been a time in human development when our tendencies to hostility were adaptive for the individual and for the species. Attempts at tracing the evolutionary development of behavior patterns are at best conjectural. However, it is possible to hypothesize a number of selective pressures which might have favored the breeding of aggressive individuals with the result that the perpetuation of the species was enhanced.[359,360,245]

There is a vast amount of evidence indicating that aggressive

8

behavior has been a useful method for the dispersal of animal populations. Adequate dispersal prevents the exploitation of the resources to such an extent that the species survival is threatened by starvation. Wynne-Edwards[639] provides information to show that, in most animals, density dependent control mechanisms are applied before starvation begins to affect the group. According to Wynne-Edwards, those species manifesting "territoriality" will permit only a limited amount of encroachment on their home range. Beyond that, intense aggressive behavior is elicited. The population density is limited to a safe level by this mechanism and once the territory is established, the individuals or family groups may engage in normal life-sustaining activities without the constant stress of competition for the resources. Chapter IV will show that such an oversimplified view of territoriality is not justified.

Strong males with aggressive tendencies are able to drive off weaker competitors and take the prerogative of mating with the available females.[385] The characteristics of strength are thus perpetuated in the species with a resulting increase in its capacity to deal with predators and other environmental hazards. There is also obvious advantage to a species which has the strength and the tendency to fight in defense of the young.

Due to the aggressive tendencies of the stronger animals, males generally, a dominance hierarchy is set up in many animal societies that results in an overall reduction in the level of aggression in that society. Social stability is achieved because each animal learns the relative aggression potential of other members of the group. Social interactions are then subject to influence by postures and gestures of threat rather than overt physically damaging attack. This type of hierarchical social system has been described in considerable detail for the baboon,[148] the rhesus monkey,[541] and a number of other species.

Another advantage of aggressiveness to the species is suggested by Lorenz.[359,360] The tendency to aggressiveness enhances the survival probability of stronger individuals with a resulting increase in life span. They can then live long enough to accumulate experience. The tendency to aggression also puts them in a position of dominance where they can function as group leaders. The accumulated experience then facilitates group survival. There is experimental work to indicate that younger individuals tend to imitate the older more dominant animals more than they do other colony members.

Aggression may also be valuable because, in addition to spacing the population out, it places a limit on the overall population size. The population limitation is accomplished directly in that one animal may kill another, and indirectly through stress effects.

## Non-Adaptive Aspects of Aggression

Many investigators have emphasized that intraspecific aggression is ritualized and that aggressive displays take the place of actual fighting. As a result, relatively little physical damage is done to the combatants. However, particularly in crowded conditions, fights are frequently fatal. Darling,[127] in his study of red deer, refers to these fatalities as "fratricidal accidents." Under conditions of increasing population pressure, the frequency and intensity of the fighting of the stags increases. They fight both in season and out, and may attack and kill juveniles and females, neither of which is the usual target of the stag's hostility.

Southwick[541] also points out that severe fighting will occur in monkey groups if the established hierarchy is disrupted because of population changes resulting from the addition of strangers or the removal of dominant animals.

Carpenter suggests that aggressive behavior in primates is, under normal circumstances, of low intensity; "However, at high intensities of excitement in primates the aggressive behavior is all-out and full charge. Kill or be killed is its design characteristic." Also, like the red deer, the aggressive animal may displace its attack behavior from the instigator to other animals.[96]

One result of the intense fighting in nonhuman primate populations is a reduction in the number of males and the exclusion of others from reproductive groups. Similar results have been reported for a number of other animals, including the wild Norway rat,[89] the house mouse,[79] the red deer,[127] and the hippopotamus[604].

The stress associated with increases in intense fighting appears to produce a population reduction in two ways. First, the defeated animal may die from the effects of the stress even though it has not been wounded or has received only superficial wounds. Second, the capacity of the females to reproduce and care for the young is reduced by the stress effects. Death resulting from the stress of defeat has been described in the rat;[38] the ruffled grouse,[6] and the mouse.[89] Death may be quite sudden or may develop over days during which the victim becomes progressively weaker, refusing food, and withdrawing from social contact. Barnett[38] offers several hypotheses for the physiological basis for this phenomenon but recognizes that no completely satisfactory explanation is currently available.

Excessive population size is also prevented because the increased pressure of numbers with its increase in aggressive

10

behavior and social stress results in a reduction in fertility, birthrate, and survival of the young.[38] Maternal behavior is disrupted; litters are abandoned or killed; and fetuses are reabsorbed.[79,89,352] (Reviews of this phenomenon may be found in the following references:)[102,103,576]

## Aggression, Adaptation, and Humans

Whether all or any of the so called advantages of aggressive behavior apply to humans is, of course, open to question. However, even though expressions of hostility may at one time have enhanced the survival of the species *Homo sapiens*, there seems to be little doubt that our very existence is now in jeopardy if those tendencies are not reduced. Further, if one is concerned with the quality of life of the species as well as its simple existence, means must be found to bring hostility to heel. Hostility, if expressed, brings frustration and unhappiness to the victim. The energizing, strength-conferring, physiological concomitants of angry feelings are much less likely to be of survival value to today's individual who is enmeshed in the restraints of a complex civilization. In general, difficulties are better resolved through careful thought rather than blindly beating against the battlements of the problems.

Whether aggressive behavior should be simply "regulated" rather than "eliminated" as suggested by Carpenter[96] may very well depend on the type of aggression under consideration and on the methods of regulation or elimination. One of the important concerns of this book will be an analysis of the implications of the bio-experiential theory for the inhibition of hostility, or perhaps in some selected types of aggression, its elimination.

An understanding of aggressive behavior is becoming progressively more important because of the relatively high level of expressed hostility in our society. Whether humans in their current "civilized" state have better control over their aggressive tendencies than they did during the decline of the Roman Empire is, perhaps, unknowable. Some progress may have been made in that we no longer demand and approve gladiatorial games and vast spectacles of organized cruelty. However, the concentration camps of the Nazi era and the Vietnam war with its My Lai 4 incident convincingly demonstrate that there is a capacity for terror lurking beneath the varnish of humankind's civilized exterior. When the inhibitions to hostility are lowered, whether physiologically through the use of alcohol,[636] for example, or psychologically by such processes as "deindividuation",[644] violent behavior frequently results.

Projections beyond the next ten years must be tentative at

11

best, but there appears to be good reason to believe that interpersonal aggression in the long run is going to increase. In spite of the recent FBI statistics that violent crime in the United States is declining, other factors may reduce the importance of those minor gains. A "population explosion" now seems inevitable. According to Paul Ehrlich,[159] one of the more visible of the population biologists, "The battle to feed all of humanity is over. In the 1970s the world will undergo famines—hundreds of millions of people are going to starve to death in spite of any crash program embarked upon now." His predictions are valid. The world bank came to quite similar conclusions in 1984. Also in 1984, a group of nineteen Nobel Prize winners and one hundred environmental and arms control organizations attending a conference on "The Fate of the Earth" came to the following conclusion, " . . . that an exploding global population and the nuclear arms race are both threats to the future. . . . What nuclear war could do in 50 to 150 minutes, an exploding population assaulting Earth's life support systems could do in 50 to 150 years."

It is obvious that the population growth rate of approximately 1.8 percent per year (the 1.8 figure is from the 1983 Advance Report on World Population Statistics of the United States Census Bureau) cannot continue indefinitely. At that rate, the world population will double by the beginning of the next century. Several authors have calculated the absurd consequences of a theoretical continuation of such a birthrate.[21,159,565] In five hundred to six hundred years, each individual would have one square yard of the surface of the earth to call his own, and in 6000 years, the mass of people would exceed that of the known universe.

The population problem will, of course, be solved. The death rate will, in time, begin to exceed the birthrate. How soon that will happen will depend on a multiplicity of factors including the various methods of birth control and technical advances in food production. If we can place any faith in the pessimistic prognosis of Ehrlich,[159] it is unlikely that any or all of the possible projected solutions are going to be sufficiently effective to prevent a massive population increase within the life span of the reader of this book. This massive population increase must, inevitably, result in mass starvation. It is also highly likely that there is going to be an aggression explosion which accompanies the population explosion.[98]

There is little doubt that overcrowding in many animal societies results in a population reduction as a direct or indirect result of increases in interanimal hostility. Obviously, it does not follow that an increase in population density in humans will necessarily lead to an increase in aggression just because it does so in animals. However, unless some measures are taken to prevent it, the extreme crowding will provide the type of environment which breeds violence. The report of the commission on the causes and prevention of violence leaves little doubt that violent crime (homicide, rape, robbery, and assault) in the United States today is concentrated in the areas of high population density. *"Violent crime in the United States is primarily a phenomenon of large cities. This is a fact of central importance."*[430] The likelihood of being a victim of a violent crime is eleven times greater if one lives in a city of over 50,000 than if one lives in a rural area.

According to another estimate, a Chicagoan living in the area of greatest population density in the inner city faces a risk each year of one in seventy-seven of being assaulted. In the less dense, "better" areas of the city the risk is only one in 2,000. For individuals living in the rich suburbs, however, the risk is down to one in 10,000.[430]

A drastic increase in population density is most likely to result in conditions which favor an increase in aggressive behavior. These conditions will be dealt with in more detail later in the book, but at least deserve to be mentioned here. Tinbergen [579] has suggested that humans already live at a far higher density than their evolutionary development has prepared them for. As the population pressures increase, the amount of inter-individual and inter-group contact will increase. The increase in actual contacts, plus the developments in long distance communication, combine to provide for the possibilities of continuous external provocations to aggression.

As the population level exceeds available resources to maintain it, physical deprivation will substantially increase with a resulting increase in aggressive tendencies. When the have-nots encounter deprivation or the threat of deprivation through production deficits or inequitable distribution, they are prone to violence against the haves. Food riots are a part of the history of the human race[578] and if the population prophets are correct, worldwide deprivation is going to occur on a scale not yet experienced in the history of the species.

The pressure of ever-rising numbers will also bring frustration of many of people's needs. Although we need not accept all of the premises of the frustration-aggression theorists, there is little doubt that frustration inclines people to hostility. There is also little doubt about the frustration potential of population pressure. The red-faced angry driver caught in a traffic jam unable to find a parking space is already a well-recognized urban phenomenon. In the foreseeable future, the availability of simple walking space is going to be limited. Each individual's "personal space"[240] will be more frequently violated and he will be less able to escape from the general press of humanity. The constant threat of too much closeness and the decreased opportunity to avoid it may very well lower the threshold for hostile behavior. As the number of social contacts increases, the amount of information to be processed by each individual increases and when the population density approaches that in the large metropolitan area, the excessive input results in a frustrating information overload which requires adaptive mechanisms to deal with it. As Milgram indicates,[395] "Overload characteristically deforms daily life on several levels, impinging on role performance, the evolution of social norms, cognitive functioning, and the use of facilities." The frustration of humans' need for privacy, the simple desire to be alone,[619] is going to be progressive and people are going to become more and more restricted in their attempts to satisfy these basic unlearned needs, as well as those derived from the culture in which they live. Frustrated people become angry people, and the hostility of one person frustrates the needs of another. Thus, the potential for an ever mounting spiral of aggression is not at all unlikely.

When the social organization of a group of animals breaks down because of an influx of strangers or because of the pressure of numbers, aggressive behavior becomes frequent, diverse and extensive.[505] In a study of the rhesus macaque in India, Southwick[541] has shown that the amount of aggressive behavior varies directly with the population density. Those monkeys living in the neutral forest habitat showed only one-fourth the amount of aggression found in the group concentrated in a city temple area at Aligarh. The greatest frequency and intensity of aggressive behavior (fifty times greater than the forest group) was found in a captive group which was crowded into an area of 1,000 square feet. Social changes in the captive group had an even greater effect on the amount of aggressive behavior than did environmental changes. The introduction of social strangers to the captive group increased the amount of agonistic behavior from four to ten times that found in the socially stable group.[541]

Carpenter[97] described the persistent fighting in a Santiago Island rhesus colony during the socially disorganized early stages of the development of the colony. The expressed hostility was so great that many of the individuals, particularly infants and younger juveniles, were killed and some animals were completely excluded from the colony and driven into the sea.

There is considerable evidence that a similar mechanism operates in disorganized communities of humans.[185] In the

14

United States, those areas which have the fastest population growth also have the highest rate of violent crime.[461] It is well-recognized that there is an exceptional amount of social disorganization evident in urban areas of highest population density. Evidence of social pathology include delinquency of various kinds and illegitimacy[98] and violent crime is significantly more prevalent in those sections of the cities in which there is low income, poor housing, high mobility, and where anonymity replaces the binding forces of mutual recognition and friendship.[229,247,261]

There is reason to believe that when the population pressures increase sufficiently, the same kinds of variables which operate to produce the anomie of the central city will contribute to the breakdown of the social forces which bind the rest of society into a reasonably cohesive, aggression-controlled body. Unless drastic measures are taken, we can look forward to the time when violent crime escapes from the bonds of the urban ghetto and becomes rampant in the land.

As explained in detail later, there are individuals who are physiologically prone to violent behavior. Frank Ervin[172] estimates that there are at least half a million persons known to have brain disorders which result in intense feelings of anger and recurring physical assault on others without reasonable provocation, although this estimate may be high. He also suggests that there are a number of people with this type of brain disorder who have not been diagnosed. As the population grows there will be an increase in the absolute number of these biologically violence-prone individuals, and because of the crowding and increase in contact, the number of available victims and innocent provocateurs will also increase. The result will be a significant rise in the number of incidents of senseless mass murder and irrational attack.

As the population pressures grow, the cauldron of violence, hostility, and aggressive behavior will seethe and boil more furiously unless measures are taken to deal with that specific problem. The possibilities for the inhibition of aggression will be considered in Chapters VII and VIII, but it should be mentioned here that although an increasing population density increases the likelihood of a more violent society because it magnifies most of the situational precursors to violence, that end result is not inevitable. Milgram[395] suggests several ways in which the city dweller attempts to cope with the information overload and its attendant stressful effects. These involve the production of synthetic privacy through such devices as an unlisted phone number and a variety of social screening devices.

Siegel[526] has described the techniques used by defensive

15

societies in their attempts to control aggressive tendencies within the society, and the reactions of the individuals to external threats. These include behavioral controls, training in self-restraint, and training for submission to authority. There are also possibilities for the physiological reduction of hostile impulses and these have many ethical problems associated with them. What is eminently clear, however, is that there is already an overwhelming need for methods of reducing the amount of individual and collective aggression of human beings, and that need is going to increase steadily as the almost inevitable rise in population continues. The more that is known about the mechanisms underlying aggression, the greater the probability that it will be possible to contribute to the inhibition of hostile behavior in order to protect humankind from destruction. Thus, these are eminently practical reasons for the study of aggressive behavior.

There are also good theoretical reasons for the study of aggression. Aggression is a definable category of behavior which, like most organized behaviors, is determined by an interwoven complex of internal, external, and experiential factors. As more is learned about the determinants of aggression, it may be possible to develop models which will be useful in attempts to understand other complex behaviors and behavior tendencies as well as the interactions among the various subsets of definable behaviors.

# CHAPTER

# A Bio-Experiential Model

The preview of mechanisms that influence aggressive behavior reveals an urgent need to revise our theories of aggression and the way in which we think about hostility and violence. In order to accomplish this task, the vast reservoir of that information on aggression must be organized so that one can see relationships among the many parts. The development of a model or a theory provides the necessary integration, but the theory must be stated so that it can make predictions about other relationships. It must also show that the predictions from that model differ from those of other models, thus furthering our understanding of the relevant phenomena. In this chapter the *bio-experiential* model will be developed. In the next two chapters, additional aspects of it will be considered. I want to begin by establishing some very precise definitions of the terms that are used in developing the model.

## Definitions

There are, indeed, several types of behavior that come under almost any definition of aggressive behavior. As a consequence of the common confusion about aggression, it is necessary to define it clearly and also to define the different kinds of aggression that come under the general definition of the phenomenon. A definition is, of course, never wrong, but it can be more or less confusing. Any attempt at precision requires a definition of terms. When the terms to be used are in the common domain they mean different things to different people, although they may

17

have a core of agreement. One is then faced with two possible solutions to the definition problem. New words can be created and rigorously defined, or the ones in common usage can be redefined. In the first approach there will be no confusion about the meaning as a result of the reader's idiosyncratic experience. However, neologisms are not readily learned or accepted and the reader must constantly engage in a translation procedure that interferes with the smooth thought processes. Therefore the lesser of two evils has been chosen and the more common words have been used, with an attempt to make an explicit statement regarding the connotations to be assigned to them.

There have been a number of attempts to define *aggression* and the terms relating to aggressive behavior.[87,152,304,403] The following definitions do not quite agree with any of them. However, these terms provide an understanding from which further concepts may be developed.

1. **AGGRESSION.**   Aggression in overt behavior involving intent to inflict noxious stimulation or to behave destructively toward another organism. Aggressive behavior may be direct or indirect. Under conditions of aversive stimulation or frustration, aggressive destructive behavior may be directed toward inanimate objects. The important variable is the intent, or the perceived intent, of the behaving individual. A small boy who vigorously attacks but is unable to injure a larger boy is behaving aggressively. The poor marksman who shoots at his wife but misses her is aggressive whether she is injured or not.

2. **INTENT.**   Intent is also included in this definition in order to exclude from the concept of aggression those accidental acts that may result in noxious stimulation to some organism. Intent implies goal direction, is always a private event, and can only be inferred from behavior. In humans, intent can frequently be inferred from verbal behavior. One can ask humans if they intended to produce noxious stimulation and frequently (although obviously not always) infer intent from their answer.

Since some of this volume will be devoted to animal experiments as they teach us something about humans, the problem of the handling of the concept of intent is also of importance here. An elephant walking through the veldt may, without awareness, step on a field mouse. The behavior may result in noxious stimulation to the mouse. However, in this text the elephant would not, in that instance, be considered aggressive. One can infer agressive intent in an animal if it persists in destructive behavior toward the same or similar stimulus object at different times. With this approach it is possible to operationally define intentional behavior. Destructive acts can be defined without much difficulty. Whether the animal really intends to produce noxious stimulation is, of course, unknowable. There are many conditions under which humans and animals behave destructively toward inanimate objects. However, in the sense that the term is used here few of them involve aggression. The person who rakes up leaves in the fall and burns them is engaged in destructive but not aggressive behavior. However, the frustrated driver who kicks a flat tire is aggressive. Destructive behavior toward inanimate objects is only considered aggressive if frustration or aversive stimulation is involved. Frustration is here considered to be any condition that blocks or prevents the fulfillment of intent as it has been operationally defined above.

3. **SYMBOLIC AGGRESSION.** Much of the behavior of humans is symbolic and the expression of aggression may also be symbolic rather than physical. Individuals may produce noxious stimulation through sarcasm, gossip, or character assassination. Others may be hurt by destroying their property. All of these behaviors are considered aggressive.

4. **HOSTILITY AND HOSTILE BEHAVIOR.** These terms are the equivalent to aggression and aggressive behavior and will be used interchangeably in this book.

5. **FANTASY AGGRESSION.** Covert behavior, in which individuals imagine situations in which they engage in hostile behavior, is called fantasy aggression. This may involve the planning or rehearsal of a specific aggressive act, or it may involve ruminations unrelated to any intentions to overt behavior.

6. **THREAT.** Behavior that attempts to communicate the intent to behave aggressively. In humans, threats may be verbal or involve postures and gestures. In animals threats usually involve species-specific postures and gestures.

7. **ANGER.** An aroused state involving particular autonomic and muscle tone patterns. During anger, the individual's threshold for aggression is lowered.

8. **VIOLENCE.** A form of human aggression that involves inflicting physical damage on persons or property. Violent behavior is frequently intense, uncontrolled, excessive, furious, sudden and, at times, seemingly purposeless.[126]

Popular usage of the term aggression includes some behaviors that are specifically excluded from the definition as it is used here because it is felt that quite different physiological mechanisms are involved. People who work hard toward the achievement of a particular goal are not considered to be aggressive unless their behavior includes the intent to do injury to others along the way. Assertiveness (that is, the positive statement or affirmation of a point of view) is not considered aggressive unless an intent to demean or otherwise hurt another person is involved. The examples cited in Chapter I make it clear that humans manifest several kinds of aggressive behavior. In those cases, the motivations differ. The emotional states are also different as are the internal processes going on in the brain.

## Contrasting Arousal and Human Aggression

When dealing with animals, it is possible to provide operational definitions of the different kinds of aggression using the specific behavior patterns and the types of stimuli that elicit the aggressive behavior. For example, a predatory cat slinks low to the ground and pounces on a rat if given the opportunity. The behavior is quite similar from cat to cat and in the same cat from one trial to another. The cat will attack a live rat but not a dead one, or a stuffed one. It will not attack a styrofoam block about the size of a rat. Unfortunately, these valuable indicators are of little use when applied to human beings.

The outstanding capacity of humans for learning and for symbol manipulation permits them to interchange the object of their aggressive intent and to substitute one object or type of object for another much more readily than is possible for animals. The object against which the aggressive behavior is directed may be more than once or twice removed from the original eliciting stimulus and mechanisms such as repression may make it difficult for the individual himself to recognize the original target of his hostility.

It is also not possible to differentiate among the various kinds of aggression in humans on the basis of the response patterns as it is in animals.* Except for the possibility of a few expressive movements that may have an innate basis,[161] humans have few automatically elicited behavior patterns. Even the expressive movements are readily subject to modification and control through the learning process. There are many ritualistic aspects

---

*The classification of aggressive behaviors in animals includes predatory, inter–male, fear-induced, maternal, irritable, sex-related, and instrumental.

to certain aggressive behaviors in humans, but these are culturally determined and may vary from one cultural group to another. The use of tools by humans further complicates any attempt to differentiate the different kinds of aggression on the basis of response patterns. A knife may be used in a confrontation between rival males (inter-male aggression); in an attack on a frustrator (irritable aggression); in a sadistic assault on a victim during a sexual frenzy (sex-related aggression); or during a paroxysm of fear when cornered by a bully (fear-induced aggression).

In spite of our inability to define operationally the various kinds of aggression in humans, it is important to recognize that different kinds do exist. Thus, a particular physiological manipulation may alter the tendency to hostility in one individual but have no effect on another. This may well be due to the fact that the substrates of the aggressive behavior may be different in the two individuals. Although their behaviors are the same, they may reflect a different type of aggression.

It seems likely that the following aggression types do exist. Instrumental aggression, one of the most important in humans, is aggression that has been learned, and has no strong emotional component. Mr. Speleni, the contract killer, typifies instrumental aggression. Irritable aggressive behavior occurs when the individual is frustrated, or under stress. Its most extreme form is homicidal rage. Mr. Jarvis typifies that state. In sex-related aggression the same stimulus elicits both the sexual and the aggressive response. The brutal rape-murder by Jack Ronnal, the bank teller, exemplifies this type of aggression. Finally, Tom Hayduke's terrified murder of the strikers as a member of the National Guard shows fear-induced aggression.

The preceding discussions have dealt with the classes of aggression in their pure form as much as possible in order to clarify the distinctions among them. There is every reason to believe, however, that the different kinds of aggression interact with each other, and differently with other motivation states.

There is no theoretical reason why behavior should not be under the influence of more than one set of physiological processes. It is, in fact, probably the most common state of affairs. The possible interactions among the different kinds of aggression and other motivational states are extremely complex, and a detailed model is needed that attempts to specify the possible behavior outcomes of various simultaneous motivational influences. The tendency to sex-related violence may be inhibited by processes that activate physiological mechanisms associated with fear. However, sex-related aggression may be facilitated by an increase in arousal level or those processes relating to irritable aggression. The different intensity levels of the various motivational states may have different influences on a particular behavior tendency. The mechanisms involved in the interactions among motivational states are also extremely complex. Some of the factors involved in the process of fear are particular patterns of muscle tone. These may be directly incompatible with the muscle tension patterns required for rape, and may have a direct autonomic effect resulting in loss of erection. The sensory mechanisms may also be influenced by the central processes involved in the fear reaction, so that some types of stimuli are more effective in eliciting attention from the individual than others. There may also be direct inhibiting and facilitating interactions among the central processes themselves. The potential complexity of the possible interactions soon exceeds the information-processing capacities of the human mind. Thus it seems likely that further progress in our understanding of these interactions will come from a computer-modeling approach to the problem.

## Basic Premise

The basic premise of the model proposed here is that there are in the brains of animals and humans neural systems that, when activated by the presence of a relevant target, result in aggressive or destructive behavior towards that target. In the case of humans, the actual aggressive behavior may be controlled, but the individual will have the appropriate feelings of hostility. It should be emphasized that, although these neural systems exist and are innately organized, aggression is not necessarily inevitable, nor is it uncontrollable. The activity of these neural systems is constantly being modulated by input from other neural systems, including changes in the nervous system produced by learning and by a variety of changes in the blood chemistry. The factors that determine whether the neural systems for aggression are activated and whether or not that activity results in overt aggressive behavior are discussed later.

As the term is used here, neural system refers to a complex of neurons involving several brain levels. Although each neuron in the system has many possible connections, the system tends to function as a unit. Other things being equal, when neurons within the system are activated, there is greater probability that other neurons in the system will be activated in preference to those not so included. Thus, because of some innate mechanism there is less synaptic resistance (broadly defined) among neurons

22

within a particular system than among neurons in general. There is now abundant evidence to support that premise. (See Figure 1.)*

## Brain Stimulation

Some of the most fundamental work in the stimulation of the brain has been done by John Flynn at Yale. He has worked with cats and has enlarged techniques that were developed in the early 1940s. It must be emphasized that data obtained through the use of animals can never be directly applied to humans. However, because there are many similarities between humans and animals, animal work does permit the generation of hypotheses and educated guesses as to the kinds of processes that may exist in humans. Many of these hypotheses can also be tested in humans.

It is possible to implant an electrode in specific areas deep in an animal's brain. The electrode can then be attached to a plug that is cemented to the skull. The plug can then be attached to a stimulation source, making it possible to stimulate the depths of the brain of an animal or human that is awake and free to move around.

When the experiment is finished for the day, the subject can be returned to its home cage none the worse for the experience. The cats are, of course, operated on under general anesthesia and feel nothing. Although the electrode (a very thin wire that is insulated except for the tip) does pass through brain tissue, there are no behavioral changes resulting from the implant. Very small electrical currents are used in the stimulation procedures. Although the cats may engage in a series of quite complex behaviors during the stimulation, they do not show any indication of pain.

The cats used by Flynn, like many house cats, were non-predatory and would not normally attack rats or other small animals. Some, in fact, would live with a rat for months and not molest it. If an electrode implanted in the cat's *lateral hypothalamus* (3-2) is electrically activated, the animal will ignore the experimenter, but will immediately attack and kill an available rat. The kill will be quite precise, resulting from a bite in the neck

---

*Explanation of diagrams of the nervous system. Each drawing is given a number in the center of the page above the label. The various structures within the diagram are also given numbers located in the righthand margin. This system provides immediate access to any structure. All references to the nervous system are given two location numbers. An example is (1-5). The 1 refers to the name of the drawing and the 5 refers to the particular structure. In this example the (1) indicates the first drawing (Lobes of the brain) and the (5) indicates the structure, in this case, the temporal lobe.

region of the spinal cord in the typical predatory behavior of that animal. However, if the electrode is located toward the center of that structure, and the cat is stimulated in the presence of the rat, it will ignore the rat, turn, and attack the experimenter. The attack on the experimenter will be well-directed. The cat appears as though it intends to do the experimenter harm, and in fact, it will.[158]

One particularly interesting experiment was done by Robinson and his colleagues.[472] They used a small rhesus monkey as a subject and implanted an electrode in the *anterior hypothalamus* (3-6). They put the animal in a restraining chair and activated the electrode. The monkey did not become aggressive towards inanimate objects, nor did it become aggressive towards humans. The subject was then put in a cage with another monkey that was larger and dominant to the experimental animal, and with the dominant monkey's female consort. When stimulated in this situation, the experimental monkey vigorously and immediately attacked the dominant monkey. It did not attack the female. It attacked only the dominant male monkey. This appeared to be a valid primate attack because the dominant monkey reacted by counterattacking just as viciously as it usually would if attacked by a submissive animal. The scenario was repeated a number of times with the result that the dominance relationship changed. The stimulation-induced attacks were so intense that the formerly dominant animal ultimately became submissive to the experimental monkey.

This experiment shows first that the particular brain stimulation used resulted in one specific kind of aggression, which I have called "inter-male," that is, the specific tendency for one male animal to attack another. Second, this experiment demonstrates that aggressive behavior is stimulus-bound. That is, even though the neural system specific to a particular kind of aggression is well-activated, the behavior does not occur unless an appropriate target is available. The animal does not attack the walls or inanimate objects. This monkey, although stimulated repeatedly in the presence of other targets, only attacked the male animal. It was not even aggressive toward the female which, of course, was a relatively similar stimulus.

The experiments cited above are not isolated findings. There have now been hundreds of studies that have used direct brain stimulation to produce a wide variety of effects. Brain stimulation, depending on the location of the electrode, can produce a wide variety of behaviors including drinking, eating, sexual responses, gnawing on wood, as well as several kinds of aggression.

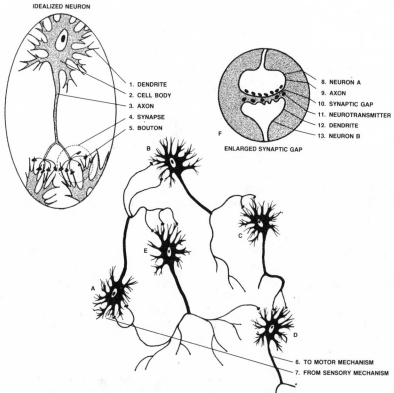

IDEALIZED NEURON

1. DENDRITE
2. CELL BODY
3. AXON
4. SYNAPSE
5. BOUTON

8. NEURON A
9. AXON
10. SYNAPTIC GAP
11. NEUROTRANSMITTER
12. DENDRITE
13. NEURON B

ENLARGED SYNAPTIC GAP

6. TO MOTOR MECHANISM
7. FROM SENSORY MECHANISM

FIGURE 1. It must be remembered that this is a schematic and a poor substitute for the incredibly complex mechanism that it represents. At the top is an idealized neuron, the building block of the nervous system. The nerve impulse travels from the dendrites (1–1) to the axon (1–2) to end at the bouton. Between the first and second neuron is a space so that the neurons do not touch. That space is called the synaptic gap (1–10). The bouton contains chemicals that are released when the nerve impulse reaches them. These chemicals, called neurotransmitters (1–11) cross the synaptic gap (1–10). The effect of the transmitters may either increase the probability that the second neuron will fire, or it may contribute to the inhibition of that neuron and will prevent it from being activated. There are thousands of boutons (1–5) on each nerve. Whether a nerve will fire (be activated) will depend on the balance between the activating or inhibiting mechanisms.

A neural system is made up of thousands of neurons that tend to operate together. This may be because each neuron in the system has more connections with the next one and a greater number of boutons, than do cells not in the system.

Each neuron has many connections to those not in the system but those cannot be activated without the help of more nerve cells. In the diagram, neurons ABC and D may be considered as a part of a system. The thicker lines represent more powerful connections. Neuron B sends connections to E, that is not in the system. E sends connections to A and to D, but E cannot activate or inhibit those neurons without the help of other neurons.

Since impulses cross the synapse by way of chemicals called neurotransmitters, it is not surprising that certain chemicals can influence the activity within a system. These chemicals may be normally within the body as hormones, or external to the body such as alcohol.

25

# Stimulation in Humans

Ervin et al.,[174] spell out some of the difficulties met when attempting to interpret brain stimulation in humans. In spite of these problems, however, the data are useful. He considers the many problems with the interpretation of brain stimulation as follows:

> Electrical stimulation of discrete regions of the *subcortex* in waking humans provides a wealth of titillating anecdotal material. To relate this material to the problem of cerebral organization in psychopathological states is conceptually difficult. A few of the more obvious difficulties in interpretation should be noted:

1. A synchronous electrical discharge is quite different from the exquisitely patterned afferent volley of physiologic signals.

2. In a complex neural aggregate the electrical input may activate excitatory and inhibitory; afferent, efferent, and integrative; or cholinergic and adrenergic systems indiscriminately. (In simplest terms, Ervin is saying that electrical stimulation may cause many different types of neurons to fire at once. These may include the neurons from the senses that bring information to the senses, motor nerves that go from the central nervous system to the various muscles of the body, and the many kinds of neurons that function to integrate the various parts of the nervous system. The stimulations may also activate neurons that use different kinds of chemicals (transmitters) to activate other neurons.)

3. The instantaneous state of cerebral organization—i.e., all the other influences acting on the object structure at the time of stimulation—is unknown.

4. At best, the site stimulated is part of an integrated system, so that the stimulus is like a rock thrown in a pond—perhaps influencing by waves a distant lily pad. The stimulation of a structure says what it *can* do under certain circumstances, not what it *does* do normally.

5. It should be further emphasized that ablation is not the reciprocal of stimulation in other than very simple input or output systems.[174] (It is essential to keep these interpretation problems in mind. However, there is still much to be learned from the studies of brain stimulation.)

Animal work has generated a large number of hypotheses regarding physiological bases of aggression in humans. It is obvious that one cannot do neatly controlled experiments on humans to test those educated guesses. However, there are a number of reasons for using direct brain stimulation in humans.

These include finding the brain focus for epilepsy, the exploration of brain areas to reduce intractable pain, the location of the extent of a brain tumor, and during surgery for Parkinson's disease. Careful observation of the patients can provide valuable information. As a result of many studies, there is now good evidence that humans, for all of their encephalization, have not escaped from the neural determinants of their aggressive behavior. There are now several hundred people who have electrodes implanted in their brains. As with the animal experiments, the electrodes are attached to small sockets cemented to the skull. These patients can be brought into the laboratory, plugged in, and precise areas deep in the brain can be electrically stimulated.

A case reported by King[313] is particularly instructive. This patient was a very mild-mannered woman who was a generally submissive, kindly, friendly person. An electrode was implanted in the area of her brain called the *amygdala* (4-5 & 6-3). Dr. King stimulated this patient in the amygdala with a current of four milliamperes and there was no observable change in her behavior. (One cannot tell when one's brain is stimulated; there are no receptors that can indicate it, thus, the patient was unaware of the stimulation.) When the amperage was increased to five milliamperes, she became hostile and aggressive. At one time during a pause between stimulations she said, "I wanted to get up from this chair and run. I wanted to hit something; tear up something—anything. Not you, just anything. I wanted to get up and run. I had no control of myself." Later during stimulation she said in an angry voice, "Quit holding me. I'm getting up. You'd better get somebody else if you want to hold me! I'm going to hit you!" At that point she raised her arm as if to strike. The experimenter then wisely turned down the current.

It was possible to turn this woman's anger on and off with a simple flick of a switch because the electrode was located in a part of the neural system for hostility. She indicated having felt anger. She also reported being concerned about the fact that she was angry. She did not report pain or other discomfort. She was simply "turned on" angry. Similar findings have been reported by other investigators.[257,511]

One of the best-reported cases is that of Julia.[379,377,378] Julia was a twenty-two-year-old girl with a history of brain disease that evidently began with an attack of encephalitis before she was two years old. She was subject to seizures and showed severe temper tantrums, which were usually followed by intense remorse. On twelve different occasions Julia seriously assaulted people without apparent provocation. When other treatments failed, electrodes were implanted in the *temporal lobe* (1-5) of Julia's brain. In one instance, stimulation of the *hippocampus*

27

(6-4), while she was talking to her psychiatrist, resulted in gradually increasing EEG and clinical abnormalities. Over a period of several seconds after the termination of the stimulation, she lost responsiveness to the examiner and suddenly began to furiously attack the wall with her fist. In another instance stimulation was applied to the *amygdala* (4-5 & 6-3) while she was playing a guitar and singing for her psychiatrist. After a buildup lasting a few seconds, she lost contact, stared ahead blankly, and was unable to answer questions. Then, during a storm of electrical activity from an area below the cortex, she swung her guitar just past the head of the psychiatrist and smashed it against the wall.

As with animals, brain stimulation in humans can result in a variety of conscious states and behaviors. Although our interest in this section is on eliciting anger, it should be noted that brain stimulation has produced a wide variety of emotional and motivational states in humans, ranging from sheer terror through rage to what has been described as drunken euphoria. It should be recognized that these moods and feeling states are not simply the aftermath of memories evoked by stimulation of the cortex. Penfield has reported that memories can be evoked by stimulation of the temporal cortex, but came to the conclusion that electrical stimulation could not evoke such emotions as anger, joy, pleasure, or sexual excitement, and that there were no specific *cortical* mechanisms directly associated with those emotional states.[445] Sem-Jacobsen[511] has listed the following mood changes that have occurred during stimulation of subcortical locations: relaxed, feeling of well-being, sleepy, restless, anxious, tense, sad, irritable, depressed, unhappy, angry, afraid, and an orgastic response. Feelings of loneliness and positive expressions of love have also been noted.[137] Heath,[254] discussing twelve years of experience with brain stimulation in humans, had indicated that the emotional and feeling changes that have occurred on stimulation have been fairly consistent from one patient to another.

Both fear and anger have been produced by brain stimulation. Fear is perhaps more frequently found, and at times both fear and anger have been evoked from the same anatomical location with approximately the same stimulus parameters.[253,254,257,261] This is not surprising as might first appear. It has been shown repeatedly with animals that the stimulated brain generally reacts only to appropriate stimuli in the environment. When brain-stimulation-induced aggression is evoked, an animal seldom attacks inappropriate targets. Brain stimulation studies in humans are carried out in as friendly an environment as is possible, so it is uncommon that there are appropriate targets for aggression, except as the patient may misinterpret the situation. At the same time, however, the entire operative situation may cause anxiety or fear. The patients are justifiably fearful and concerned when their brains are to be stimulated. If there is already natural ongoing activity in the neural system for fear it should require less intense electrical stimulation to elicit an overt response. Thus, a fear reaction may be evoked even though the electrode is not placed directly in the neural system for fear. Further, with the proximity of the neural systems for fear and anger, it would not be unlikely that an electrode could be placed near enough to both systems that either one could be activated with a given stimulation. Which reaction would be evoked would depend on the state of activity in the two systems, or the "neurological set," as explained later.

An anger reaction, in association with anxiety, has been produced by stimulation in the *hippocampus* (6-4) with Levarterenol Bitartrate and by electrical stimulation in the *posterior hypothalamus* (5-4).[439] Intense rage accompanied by pain has resulted from stimulation in the front part of the *mesencephalon* (2-10)[260] and in the posterior hypothalamus (5-4).[254] In these situations, the rage may be a consequence of the pain, since there is abundant evidence for a pain-aggression interaction. However, it is also true that not all pain produces hostile behavior.

# Neural Modulation

The neural systems that underlie hostile behavior are modulated by other portions of the brain that send either facilitating or suppressing signals to those systems. The complex of neurons that are responsible for the various kinds of aggression receive connections from many different portions of the brain. Some of these inputs produce changes that facilitate actions in the system, thus increasing the probability that neural activity will occur, and that hostile behavior will ensue. On the other hand, if the input is inhibitory, there will be a decrease in the probability of aggressive behavior occurring. There have been a number of studies in animals that have shown these effects.[158,367,613]

In many instances the facilitating neural input comes from other complex circuits that are associated with other mechanisms. Even though the studies have not yet been done to demonstrate increases in neural sensitivity in this neural system by the activation of neural substrates of other complex behaviors, one can draw such an inference from certain behavior studies.

A number of different states increase the tendency for the subject to manifest irritable aggression in the presence of an appropriate stimulus. These include aversive stimulation, particularly pain;[596] a variety of deprivation states, such as food deprivation,[129,503] sleep deprivation,[333] morphine deprivation in addicted rats;[66] and frustration produced by withdrawal of reinforcement.[24,306,577]

All the preceeding conditions function as stressors and, if long continued, may produce endocrine changes that may influence the sensitivity of the aggression system (see the following discussion); however, the relatively rapid onset of aggression after some of these stressors implies a neural facilitation.

All of the studies that relate to the decrease in sensitivity of the aggression systems by neural inhibition lead to the conclusion that the inhibitory neural influences may also be related to the activation of other motivational or motor-predispositional systems. These mechanisms may function in a manner similar to what has been called the reciprocal inhibition mechanism in muscle control. Thus, the intense activation of the neurological substrate for the euphoric or fear response may be neurologically incompatible with the simultaneous activity of the irritable aggression system because the activation of one system involves the inhibition of the other.

As in animals, the stimulation of the deep structures of the brain of humans results in emotional and motivational states that generally do not outlast the duration of the stimulus. However, there is an increasing number of reports that indicate that stimulation in some areas results in delayed as well as prolonged effects. This implies that neurohumoral rather than neuroelectric processes are involved. One patient with electrodes implanted in the brain for the purpose of relieving intractable pain was stimulated at various points over a one-and-a-half-hour period. No changes in mood or in amount of pain were observed. *Amygdala stimulation* (4-5 6-3) did result in a sharp rise in blood pressure that lasted for almost an hour after the termination of the stimulation. At the end of the session the patient was returned to the ward. After a twenty-minute delay, this mild-mannered, courtly and dignified man who had no history of brain damage or behavioral disturbance became extremely angry and would attack without provocation anyone close enough. He was incontinent and climbed on his bed and threw feces at anyone within range. He was finally sufficiently restrained to be given an injection of chlorpromazine (one of the major tranquilizers), after which he calmed down and went into a deep sleep. When he awoke, he had total amnesia for the incident. Later, stimulation of the opposite amygdala resulted in a very similar reaction, although of shorter duration. The patient's death from unrelated causes twelve days after treatment permitted the investigators to check the electrodes' locations. They were placed as intended, in the right and left amygdala.[174] Unfortunately, the report does not indicate the specific location of the electrodes within the amygdala, which would have been more informative. Other cases of a similar nature are reported in the same paper and in Mark et al.[378] and Stevens et al.[554] Prolonged and delayed effects have also been reported for euphoric responses, relaxation, and pain relief. (See preceding references, Heath & Mickle[261] and Sem-Jacobsen & Torkildesen.)[512] There are suppressor areas for aggressive behavior in the brain of humans, as there are in the brains of animals, and there is good reason to believe that those suppressor areas are associated with other motivational systems. Heath[255] described the reaction of a psychomotor epileptic patient to *septal* (2-5) stimulation. The patient was exhibiting agitated, violent psychotic behavior when the septal stimulation was introduced without his knowledge. His behavioral state changed almost instantaneously from disorganization, rage, and feelings of persecution to happiness and euphoria. He described the beginnings of sexual motive state and was unable to explain the sudden shift in his behavior when he was directly questioned about it. Heath goes on to point out that the case described is not unique, but has been repeated in a large number of patients in his laboratory.

The aggression-suppression effects of brain stimulation may also have a relatively prolonged effect. Sem-Jacobsen and Torkildesen[512] report that stimulation in the middle of the *frontal lobes* (1-1) had a calming effect on a violent manic patient. A similar effect resulted from stimulating the *central area of the temporal lobe* (1-5). When both points were stimulated in rapid succession the calming, antihostility effect was greater and of some duration. Peterson, in a discussion of the Sem-Jacobsen and Torkildesen paper, also reports that actively disturbed and antagonistic patients become quite placid and talk well after about fifteen minutes of stimulation in the *frontal lobes* (2-1) of the brain. This period of calmness may last for a day or even longer. There is no indication in any of the reports that the investigators were dealing with a general "arrest" phenomenon, that is, a blocking of all behavior. The patients reacted normally but their mood level and affective tone was shifted in a more positive direction. Although the physiological basis for the effect is not clear, there is some evidence that the brain stimulation effects can extend over a period of months. One patient with psychomotor seizures, who also exhibited assaultive behavior, was given several periods of electrical stimulation to an undesignated area in the right amygdala. The results were said to produce long-lasting and gratifying improvement in his mood and thought

31

content. The results were so favorable that the electrodes were removed and the patient was able to hold a good job and was relatively free in regard to both seizures and violence for a period of a year.[563]

Brain chemistry modulates neural sensitivity. There are a significant number of changes in blood chemistry that produce changes in the brain, depending on which neural systems are activated or deactivated. These vary as widely as the testosterone level in the blood stream, or the hormonal changes characteristic of the premenstrual period. Other factors, such as a deficiency in the blood-sugar level, also increase feelings of irritability and at times, overt physical aggressive behavior. Some individuals have behavioral allergies that produce an increase of aggressive tendencies when specific allergens enter the blood stream. Each of these sensitizers will be considered in some detail below.

## Learning and the Manifestation of Aggressive Behavior

The importance of learning and experience to aggressive behavior of all kinds cannot be underestimated. Aggressive behavior, like all other basic behaviors, is strongly influenced by experience. An animal can be readily taught to overeat[629] or undereat[343,384] through the use of reinforcement, regardless of the state of deprivation. Similarly, animals can be taught to exhibit or inhibit aggressive behavior.

It is possible to increase the probability of occurrence of any aggressive or destructive response, no matter what its initial motivational source, if that response is followed by a positive reinforcement. The *Law of Effect* operates just as effectively to facilitate motor responses that are labeled aggressive as to facilitate those that are not. In the classification system outlined in Chapter I, aggressive behavior, so determined, is referred to as instrumental aggression.

In many circumstances, aggressive behavior is rewarded and, as with other learning situations, the aggressive response shows a greater probability of occurring. In areas of poverty, the environment is particularly suited for the learning of hostile responses. McCandless puts it well as he describes the fertile field for the learning of aggression by a poor child:

He has learned that he had better grab while the grabbing is good, because if he doesn't, one of his brothers and sisters, or his parents, or his peers, will grab instead. Reason has never won a street fight nor enabled him to get the biggest share of the can of beans, nor served to keep his father from beating his mother when he got drunk . . . Without immediate action and intense drive, the child may not survive the tooth-and-claw existence that for him is almost routine . . . When one is battling for survival—for his fair share of the limited supply of food in the window cooler or ice box, for his turn with the local call girl who will let the boys go as far as they want—intense emotion facilitates and spurs action. Standing back, thinking, and suppressing result in failure to reach the goal. Striking out, yelling, and pushing cause others to stand back so that you can go ahead. [386]

Techniques utilizing the principles of learning are most important. Over the long run, civilization must depend primarily on learning as the *major* technique for the inhibition of interpersonal and international aggression.

Any positive reinforcement can be used to increase the tendency to behave aggressively. However, there is also evidence that the opportunity to express aggression can be used to reinforce new learning.

It would appear that the aggressive act is only reinforcing when the relevant neural system for that particular kind of aggression is either active or highly sensitized. Thus, non-mouse-killing cats will learn a Y-maze in order to obtain a rat to kill if the system in the brain for predation is stimulated during the learning process. However, performance quickly deteriorates when trials are given in the absence of the brain stimulation.[470] Predatory rats will learn a maze to obtain a mouse, whereas nonkiller rats will not.[424]

The opportunity to behave aggressively can be used to reinforce learning if that opportunity is provided in situations that normally elicit aggression. Tail shock produces "reflexive" aggression in monkeys. These animals will also learn a chain-pulling response in order to obtain a canvas-covered ball that they may bite.[24] If pigeons are rewarded with food for pecking a key, they will learn the response quickly. If the reward is suddenly terminated, the birds will behave aggressively. During this period, they will also learn to peck a key that produces another bird that can then be attacked.[23]

Although aggressive behavior may be positively reinforced when the relevant neural system is functioning, activity in the neural system itself may be either positively or negatively reinforcing, depending on the kind of aggression involved. There is as yet relatively little hard data available on this concept. There is little doubt that activity in the neural system for aggression that is produced by aversive stimulation has negative reinforcement value. The monkey, which will learn a response for the opportunity to bite a ball under the stress of tail shock, will certainly learn a response to terminate the tail shock and the resultant neural activity.

Although the evidence is complex and difficult to interpret, some inferences may be drawn from studies that use brain stimulation to induce aggressive behavior. If an animal will work to terminate the stimulation activating a neural system that produces aggressive behavior, one might infer that the activity in that system is associated with negative affect. If the animal will work to turn the aggression-inducing stimulation on, positive affect might be inferred. Both kinds of evidence exist. Monkeys will lever-press to terminate brain stimulation that appears to produce irritable aggression.[451] In another study, monkeys pressed a bar to receive stimulation that produced inter-male aggression.[472] However, there are other interpretations possible. These systems may be functionally discrete even though they are anatomically proximal. Thus, the affective state generated by the stimulation may be irrelevant to the manifest behavior. More definitive information in this problem must come from work with humans who can provide verbal reports on the affective states that accompany the different kinds of aggression.

Just as aggressive behavior can be facilitated by reward, it can be inhibited by punishment. Predatory aggression can be readily suppressed by punishment of the attack response.[422] In spite of the fact that noxious stimulation produced irritable-aggressive behavior,[596] it can also, if sufficiently intense, inhibit aggressive tendencies. Aggressive behavior is suppressed in monkeys if the punishing shock is more intense than the shock that elicited the fighting.[598] The negative reinforcement in defeat during inter-male aggression results in a decrease in aggressive tendencies.[295,327] Miller et al.[397] have clearly shown that it is possible to manipulate social hierarchies in monkeys by punishing a dominant animal in the presence of a subordinate, and Ulrich indicates that when a monkey is severely bitten by an opponent, there is an obvious decrease in the aggressiveness of the bitten subject.

In an established colony where animals have a frequent opportunity to interact, it is easy to see that the preceding learning mechanisms could account for the development of dominance hierarchies. A given animal could easily learn to respond to the cue complex of one animal in the colony with aggressive responses but to another with avoidance, submission, or aggression-inhibitory responses. One would certainly expect these learned responses to interact with the other internal states of the organism such as the activity of particular aggression systems. If an animal is punished in the presence of the cues associated with food, it will be inhibited, regardless of the amount of deprivation (and presumed activity in the neural systems for hunger or consummatory behavior). One would expect no less of an influence of learning on the manifestations of aggression. As Plotnik et al.[451] and Delgado[136,140] have shown, the brain-stimulation-induced aggressive behavior of monkeys is related to the animal's prior experience. The effect of lesions involving the aggression systems are also influenced by the animal's earlier learning.[477,535,536] It is more rare for the activity of the aggression systems to be so intense that they appear to override well-established habit patterns, although this has been reported in monkeys.[472]

An extensive series of experiments has shown that an individual may learn aggressive behavior through a simple observation of another person behaving aggressively. (See Bandura[32] for a complete review of this material.) In a classic experiment of this type, nursery school children were permitted to observe the behavior of an adult solving a problem. The behavior of the adult included the punching of an inflated Bobo doll as well as other responses that were irrelevant to the solution of the problem. When the observing children were put into the situation and given the problem to solve, they imitated many of the behaviors of the adult model, including the irrelevant aggressive reponses of hitting the inflated doll.[34] A number of theories have been suggested to explain why modeling occurs.[32] However, further consideration of these theories is beyond the scope of this book.

There is little experimental evidence on the neural mechanisms involved in learned inhibition of aggressive responses. It could, according to this model, occur at any one of several levels. As indicated previously, the inhibition may occur at the level of the integrating aggression system itself. For example, the subjective feeling of anger in the human (which would be indicative of activity in the system for irritable aggression) would be replaced by a sufficiently intense fear such that the irritable aggression system would be inhibited and the individual would no longer have the subjective experience of anger. The inhibition could also occur at the muscular level, producing the extreme tension state of inhibited rage. In this instance the muscles in opposition to those used in attack are sufficiently activated to prevent attack behavior. Under this circumstance, however, the central integrative aggression system would continue to be active and the human would continue to experience the subjective state of anger.

Humans, of course, learn better and faster than any other animal. It is therefore reasonable to expect that the internal impulses to aggressive behavior would be more subject to modification by experience in humans than in any other animal. In addition, because of the human's additional ability to manipulate symbols, and to substitute one symbol for another, one would expect to find a considerable diversity in the stimuli that elicit an inhibition of activity in the aggression system. One would also expect that the modes of expression of aggression would also be more varied, diverse, and less stereotyped in humans than in other animals.

# Chronic Behavior Tendencies

The interactions of all the preceding factors contribute to the determination of the aggressive tendencies of a given individual at a given time. One might be thought of as having a chronic behavior tendency to hostility if these factors function to produce activity in or a sensitivity of the neural systems for aggressive behavior over a prolonged period of time. The underlying factors that contribute to a chronic behavior tendency may vary considerably from one individual to another. The following are some examples.

A particular person may frequently react with anger to a wide variety of stimuli because his heredity has determined that the threshold for the activation of his neural substrates for hostility is relatively low.

The heredity of another individual may dictate that his neural substrates for aggression have a threshold well within the normal range. However, his environment may be such that he is subjected to constant frustration and stress, which may result in a hormone balance that sensitizes the neurons in the hostility system so that over time they become readily activated by a wide range of stimuli.

In another case, an individual may be born with a neural system for some positive affect with a particularly low threshold. Other things being equal, he may have a chronic behavior tendency to react to many stimuli with positive approach tendencies. If inhibitory neurons to the neural substrates for aggression are a part of that system, that individual will have less of a tendency to behave aggressively.

Chronic behavior tendencies may also be built up through a series of learning experiences. The individual may have been in a number of situations in which he was made angry. That anger becomes associated with a large number of stimuli that became cues. When those cues are encountered again, they cause the individual to remember the situation, the anger, and why the

36

anger occurred. These memories may elicit feelings of anger or hostility.

Chronic feelings of hostility may also occur in the absence of external cues. The individual may be angered because there is some evidence that his wife has been or is being unfaithful. As he thinks about this infidelity, he becomes progressively more angry. It does not matter whether his wife is really unfaithful. It matters only that he is convinced that she is. He may ruminate about these thoughts a great deal, increasing his feeling of anger until he is "driven" to an intense overt violent behavior. It may also be the case that his anger does not explode, but remains a constant source of feelings of irritability, which changes his reactions to many aspects of his life. His anger is constantly reinforced and exaggerated as he reconsiders the evidence that he has, or thinks he has.

If after either a short time of weeks, or a long time of months or even years, he takes positive action and either divorces his wife, or kills her, he may feel relieved, and relaxed because the all–encompassing thoughts of his wife have been dispelled.

It is also possible for an individual to have a chronic behavior tendency to hostility without having the neural systems for aggression particularly involved. He may simply have learned that aggressive behavior is what is expected of him if he is to receive the kinds of approbation that are rewarding to him. This is well-illustrated by Claude Brown in *Manchild in the Promised Land:*

> I was growing up now, and people were going to expect things from me. I would soon be expected to kill a nigger if he mistreated me, like Rock, Bubba Williams, and Dewdrop had. Everybody knew these cats were killers. Nobody messed with them. If anybody messed with them or their family or friends, they had to kill them. I knew now that I had to keep up with these cats; if I didn't I would lose my respect in the neighborhood. I had to keep my respect because I had to take care of Pimp and Carole and Margie. I was big brother in the family. I couldn't be running and getting somebody after some cat who messed with me (p. 121).[80]

Interactions of all the determining factors are, of course, the rule. The individual with an inherited low threshold for the activation of the neural system for hostility will be even more readily and intensely aroused to anger if he lives in a deprived, frustrating, and stressful environment. If, on the other hand, he is surrounded by love and protected from much of the harshness of the world and is exposed to relatively little provocation, his aggressive behavior will be limited.

# Neurological Set

Chronic behavior tendencies refer to the long-run probabilities of a particular kind of behavior. "Set," however, involves the proclivities toward a given kind of behavior at the moment. It should be emphasized here that the reaction to the environment is an interaction between what is going on in the environment and what is going on at the same time in the nervous system. It is obvious that what constitutes a provocation at time A is not necessarily a provocation at time B. If there is ongoing activity in the neural system for aggression, or if it is highly sensitized, the amount of provocation required by a relevant external stimulus to elicit an aggressive action will be less. The reason for the neural activity or hypersensitivity is irrelevant.

A teenage girl may have a highly sensitized neural system for irritable aggression because of the hormone balance characteristic of the third day before her menstrual period. At a different time, that neural system may be sensitive or active because she has been frustrated by the cutting and sarcastic remarks of a high school teacher. In either case she has an increased probability of responding aggressively to any appropriate external stimulus. Whether this increased probability of aggressive responses actually results in aggressive behavior in a given instance is determined in part by her previous experience with the eliciting stimuli. If she has been negatively reinforced for expressing hostility toward her parents, she will be less likely to make that response. However, if she stumbles over her dog, she may very well swear at it or kick it.

In the second instance, in which the girl's neural system is activated by the sarcasm of her teacher, her act of kicking the dog is referred to as displaced aggression. In the traditional psycho-analytic formulation the aggressive "energy" is transferred from one subject to another. In the analysis presented here, it will be seen that the two instances are not essentially different, except in the manner in which the neural system was initially activated or sensitized. In both instances the tendency to respond aggressively may be the same, and in both cases the particular stimulus responded to depends on the individual's reinforcement history.

It is also possible to have a neurological set in which the tendency to aggression is decreased. If the individual is in a "happy" frame of mind, it will take more provocation to elicit an aggressive response. As suggested, this is due in part to inhibitory neurons from the neural substrate in the "happy state of mind" that tend to block activity or reduce the sensitivity in the neural substrates for hostility.

# Summary

Aggression is defined and it is suggested that the concept of intent is essential to a useful definition of the term. An operational definition of intent is given and aggression-related terms are defined.

Aggression is not a unitary concept. There are different kinds of aggression. Some of the experimental evidence is examined to support the proposition that there are organized neural systems in the brain for the various kinds of aggression. When these systems are active in the presence of particular stimuli, the organism has an increased tendency to behave aggressively. Thus, aggressive behavior is stimulus-bound and dependent on the functional integrity of the relevant neural systems.

There are neural systems in the brain for complex behaviors other than aggression. The interactions among these systems are complex and activity in one system may inhibit or facilitate activity in another and the interactions between some systems may be reciprocal. For example, the neural substrates for irritable aggression and for euphoria may be mutually inhibiting.

Although the exact mechanism cannot yet be specified, the sensitivity of the neural systems for aggression may be raised or lowered by specific blood components, particularly from the endocrine system. If some hormonal influences occur early in the life of the organism, the effects on the neural systems may be permanent.

Learning has an important influence on aggressive behavior just as it does on any other behavior. Aggressive behavior that is rewarded tends to be repeated, and that which is punished tends to be inhibited. In certain circumstances the completion of an aggressive act is in itself rewarding.

The variables that influence the sensitivity of the neural system for aggression may function to increase the sensitivity of that system for aggression over a prolonged period of time. In that circumstance the individual may be said to have a chronic behavior tendency to hostility.

If the sensitivity of an aggressive system is relatively transient, the individual may be considered as having a neurological set for hostile behavior.

There are suppressor areas for aggressive behavior in the brains of humans, as there are in the brains of animals, and there is good reason to believe that those suppressor areas are associated with other motivational systems. The aggression-suppression effects of brain stimulation may also have a relatively prolonged effect. If the threshold for the activation of the neural systems for aggression is very high, it will take a great deal of provocation to activate them. There are other circumstances in which the threshold is very low and relatively little provocation will result in the activation of the neural systems with the result that the individual has an increased tendency to behave aggressively.

# CHAPTER

# IV

# Modulation of Thresholds for Aggression

It is a fortunate fact that in neither humans nor animals is aggression very frequent. It is relatively uncommon. Thus, in order to understand the physiology of aggression, we must understand what it is that turns these neural systems on and what it is that turns them off. The concept of threshold is most relevant here. In certain circumstances the threshold for the activation of the neural systems for aggression is very high. In that case it takes a great deal of provocation to activate them. There are other circumstances in which the threshold is very low and relatively little provocation will result in the activation of the neural systems with the result that the individual has an increased tendency to behave aggressively.

## Influences on Thresholds

As indicated in Figure 1, individual neurons have a variety of inputs to them. Impulses within the neural system of a particular aggression mechanism may be blocked if the neurons sending impulses to it are predominantly inhibitory.

There are a number of changes in the blood chemistry that result in the alteration of the brain mechanism, with a consequent change in tendencies to behave aggressively. In humans, as in animals, many of these changes are in the endocrine system.

41

However, this chapter also considers the role of hypoglycemia (low blood sugar), certain allergens, and some hostility-inducing drugs.

Because experimenters are unable to control all of the factors that may have an influence on the results, one is, at times, faced with the problem of making an educated guess about cause and effect. Manipulations of blood chemistry, either experimental or natural, do not occur in a vacuum. A large number of factors are, of course, constantly interacting to effect the changes in aggression potential that result from blood changes and there are wide individual differences in susceptibility to various drugs and hormones.

Changes in drug or hormone levels cause changes in subjective experience that may be interpreted differently by different individuals because of their prior learning. The individual's expectations may strongly influence their behavior, and the experience they have after a given manipulation will be influenced by their interpretations of the expectations of others about how he should be affected.

It is frequently difficult to interpret experiments or clinical observations on humans, but in spite of all the difficulties, it is possible to draw some tentative conclusions about the role of blood chemistry changes and aggressive behavior. Much of the evidence in this chapter is clinical and some of the studies have a small number of subjects and have fewer controls than one would find with comparable animal experiments. These findings must be interpreted with considerable caution. However, the results are frequently suggestive of hypotheses that should be followed up and tested more carefully in the future.

There is considerable experimental work in animals showing that prenatal sex hormones have an effect on later aggressive behavior. For obvious reasons, we must fall back on clinical data for humans. For example, there are a variety of reasons for therapeutic intervention during pregnancy. That intervention must frequently be the administration of sex hormones. Naturally occurring endocrine disorders during the prenatal period also provide relevant information. Heino, et al.[266] have summarized many of those data.

In general, the findings are closely related to what might be expected from the results of animal experimentation. However, as is frequently true with natural dysfunctions and those based on therapeutic interventions, the results are not as clean cut as would be desirable. Heino et al.[266] present a study that circumvents many of the problems. They studied fifteen girls and thirteen boys who had been exposed to medroxyprogesterone acetate (MPA) in utero, and twenty-eight closely matched controls. The subjects were followed up at ages nine to fourteen years. Questions and partially structured interviews were done with both the mother and the child separately. A battery of psychological tests with appropriate double-blind procedures were used.

It has been known for centuries, of course, that one can take the raging bull and convert it into a gentle steer by the operation of castration which reduces the level of testosterone in the blood stream. (Testosterone is the principal male hormone.) The formal work on this problem was done in 1947 by Elizabeth Beeman.[49] It has been repeatedly confirmed in many laboratories. Dr. Beeman worked with a strain of mice that would fight when put together. She castrated the animals of the experimental group prior to puberty. After maturity when those mice were put together they did not fight at all. The control group showed the usual amount of aggression characteristic of that strain. She then carried the experiment a step further and implanted pellets of testosterone subcutaneously in the castrated mice. When the testosterone became effective they fought at the same level as the control animals had. She then surgically removed the pellets of testosterone whereupon the mice once again became docile. It was possible to manipulate the aggressive behavior of these mice simply by changing the testosterone level.

## Testosterone Levels

Until recently, essentially no information has been available relating the endocrine function and affective response tendencies in humans. However, with improvement in assay techniques[243] such studies are beginning to appear. Persky et al.[448] studied two groups of men. The eighteen individuals in the younger age group ranged from seventeen to twenty-eight years of age, and the fifteen older men were between the ages of thirty and sixty-six years. The average testosterone production rate of the older men was about half that of the younger men. When all the subjects were considered as a group, a significant negative correlation ($r = -0.62$) was shown between age and testosterone production rate. This is an interesting finding in itself inasmuch as it has been shown that violent crime in the United States is most prevalent among males between the ages of fifteen and twenty-four. In order to measure the amount of hostility the subjects had, the authors used a paper and pencil test, the Buss-Durkee Hostility Inventory. The results showed that there was a relationship between the measure of hostility and the rate at which the subjects produced testosterone. When the testosterone production was high, the measure of hostility was high. However, among the older men, the results showed merely that the older they were, the lower their testosterone production was.

Another study gave somewhat conflicting results. Prisoners were selected on the basis of the number of times they had been placed in solitary confinement for rules infractions. Blood level of testosterone was used as a measure. The testosterone level in the blood stream was not related to their measure of aggression. However, the individuals who had committed violent and aggressive offenses during adolescence had a significantly higher testosterone level.[325]

A more recent study [165] investigated the levels of testosterone and cortisol, a steroid from the adrenal cortex, in male wrestlers after either a win or a loss. Winners of competitive matches showed greater increases in both cortisol and testosterone than losers. The author concludes, "These findings indicate that humans, like other social mammals, may undergo specific endocrine changes in response to victory or defeat. Not all studies show that there is a relationship between levels of testosterone and violent crime. Rada et al.[456] studied the levels of testosterone in the plasma in fifty-two individuals who had been convicted of rape. There was a control group of twelve not convicted of rape. Several instruments were used to measure the level of aggression. These included the Buss Durkee hostility scale and the Megargee overcontrolled hostility scale. The mean Buss Durkee score of the convicted rapists was significantly higher than the norm. However, there was no correlation between individual hostility scores and testosterone levels. Nor was there a correlation between testosterone levels and age, race, or length of incarceration. These results are difficult to interpret, and may be due, in part, to the limitations inherent in self report scales.

The findings on the role of testosterone in violent crime is certainly not determined as yet. Many more studies need to be done and replicated before we will find the answers.

## Castration*

A further understanding of the role of androgens [a term for all male hormones] in the aggressive behavior of humans can be

---

*It is obvious that the use of this operation as a control measure is fraught with problems. There are ethical, moral, and civil rights issues that must be considered. The discussion of castration as a deterrent for sex crimes does not imply advocacy.

gained from a study of the effects of castration. This operation has been carried out on man from ancient times for a variety of purposes. Eunuches were needed to guard the harems of sultans, and until the nineteenth century boy sopranos were castrated so that they would be able to retain their high, pure tones. In 1894 the first castration for the control of pervert sexual acts was performed by Dr. Pilcher of the State Training School of Winfield, Kansas. Denmark legalized the operation as a therapeutic measure for certain types of crimes in 1929 and other countries followed soon after—Nazi Germany in 1933, Norway in 1934, Finland in 1935, Iceland in 1938, and Sweden in 1944 .[74] Several authors have reviewed the results of these programs and concluded that castration, if it is combined with other therapeutic measures, is an effective method of dealing with sex crimes, particularly those of a violent nature.[91,252,321,336,560]

Bremer [74] did a follow-up study on 224 Norwegian cases and concluded that sex drive was drastically reduced by castration: "It can be stated at the beginning that in all cases without exception the amount of sexual activity has been altered. It has been reduced or abolished, irrespective of the direction or the form of sexual urge—heterosexuality, homosexuality, fetishism, zoophilic actions, masturbation, exhibitionism, or fetishistic actions—which are those represented in the material" (p. 67). In two-thirds of the cases sexual interest and activity essentially disappeared within the first year after the operation and in most cases the asexualization occurred immediately or shortly after the operation. However, the recidivism rate for noncastrated sex offenders was twenty-four percent. Hawke[252] reports that a sex crime has never been committed by a parolee or a castrate who escaped from the Kansas state training school institution.

About half of the cases considered by Bremer were dangerous. The others were considered to be merely asocial or troublesome, manifesting such offenses as exhibitionism, fetishism, and zoophilia. Castration was most effective in all respects when the sexual factor was the dominating cause of the criminal or disturbed behavior. Seventy-seven of the subjects were castrated in the hope of achieving a general pacifying effect to make the patients easier to control. Many of these individuals were feeble-minded and schizophrenics (a type of insanity involving hallucinations). Bremer reports that the operation was ineffective in controlling the disturbed mental cases and had no definite pacifying effect. This is an interesting and somewhat paradoxical finding in light of the animal literature, which seems to indicate that there is a reduction of inter-male and irritable aggression with a reduction of the androgen level in the blood.

Other investigators have found that castration [and androgen-

45

blocking by other means] does reduce hostility that is not directly associated with the individual's sexual behavior. Hawke[252] describes several cases in which a generally aggressive individual has had his sexual aggression curbed and has become less aggressive in other ways as a result of castration. He also reports on a series of observations in which relatively large doses of testosterone were given to large groups of castrates over a period of several weeks. In a number of cases it was necessary to terminate the injections because the patients became generally destructive. They "had reverted to all of their antisocial tendencies, were attacking small children, starting fights, breaking windows and destroying furniture" (p. 222). When the administration of the hormone was stopped, the individuals became tractable once again within a few days and no longer created disturbances on the ward. Many of the 330 individuals in the Kansas sample treated by castration were brutal homosexuals who were generally unstable and constantly created disturbances. After the operation they became stabilized and could be paroled or became useful citizens within the institution.

There are now a number of clinical studies indicating that female hormones may be used in the reduction of aggressive tendencies in men. Golla and Hodge[222] indicate that the estrogenic substances could be used as a form of chemical castration and would be more efficient than the operation itself because the estrogens would block the effects of adrenal androgens that are not controlled by castration. A number of authors have reported series of cases in which the aggressive tendencies of adolescents and young adults were blocked by the use of stilbestrol.[193,484,620] Stilbestrol is a synthetic drug that has been demonstrated to have the qualities of natural estrogens. It depresses anterior pituitary gonadotropic function. The pituitary gland located at the base of the brain secretes a number of hormones that activate the production of hormones from other tissues. The gonadotropic hormone, as the name suggests, causes the production of sex hormones.

A case is reported in some detail by Dunn[155] in which stilbestrol was used to control hyperirritable aggression and excessive libido. This patient was a twenty-seven-year-old male under maximum sentence for sexual offenses against female minors. He was a persistent troublemaker in prison and frequently placed in solitary confinement for insubordination. The prisoner had abnormal amounts of male hormone and gonadotropic hormone in the urine before therapy and was preoccupied with his sex life. After four weeks of daily treatment with stilbestrol, he reported that his sexual responses, both physical and mental, were reduced. He had also adapted much better to prison discipline and was no longer considered a troublemaker. He continued relatively symptom-free for more than three months after discontinuance of the therapy. Subsequently, however, he had a return of his symptoms and requested a resumption of therapy.

Two investigators have used subcutaneous (under the skin) or intramuscular (into the muscle) injections of long-acting estrogens [estradiol B.P.C. and oestrodiol valerianate] to avoid the necessity of daily oral therapy.[101,192] This approach permits the release of otherwise highly dangerous individuals and does not depend on their cooperation in taking the medication. Both reports indicate that the aggressive behavior and the sexual offending were essentially eliminated while the patients were under the estrogenic therapy.

There are now several substances available that have demonstrated antiandrogenic activity.[339] A-nonprogesterone,[340] chlormadinone acetate,[473] cyproterone acetate,[431] and medroxyprogesterone[515] have been shown to be potent antagonists of androgens. These synthetic hormones are steroids, as are the natural sex hormones. When administered to intact animals they produce, in some measure, chemical castration. Cyproterone acetate appears to block the use of naturally produced testosterone by competing with it at the receptor sites in the brain,[432] and medroxyprogesterone lowers the plasma level of testosterone from the testes.[400]

There appears to be evidence to show that cyproterone acetate helps an individual gain control over his sex-related behaviors. Many of these data have been obtained from individuals convicted of indecent assault, rape, and even sexual murders. (See Bowden, 1979, for a review of the available studies.)[68] However, there is a cost. Cyproterone acetate reduces the patient's interest in sexual matters, reduces sex drive, and in some individuals it may lead to impotence and depression. There are also physiological side effects including gynaecompastia (excessive development of the male breast, sometimes including milk secretion).[68,69]

It is interesting that cyproterone acetate does not block intermale aggression in either the gerbil[489] or the mouse,[70,156] but does appear to have some effect in the control of excessive libido and, apparently, sex-related aggression in man.[330,332] Seven individuals convicted of indecent assault and sexual murder have been successfully treated and at least one has been placed on probation with an order for continued therapy.[331] There is not as yet sufficient evidence to evaluate the effectiveness of cyproterone on aggression, particularly in humans. However, further work is certainly indicated.

Medroxyprogesterone [Provera, produced by Upjohn], which is chemically very close to natural progesterone, another female hormone, is highly effective in lowering testosterone level. There is some evidence that it may be effective in the control of excessive and impulsive sexual behavior and aggression in humans. Lloyd[351] indicates that sexually hyperactive and aggressive adolescent boys are made more tractable by Provera therapy. Although aggressiveness is not dealt with as such, Money[400] reports that Provera significantly and rapidly reduces a variety of illegal sexual behaviors in male offenders. In a preliminary study, Blumer and Migeon[62] found that a high level of Depo-Provera (300 mg. every ten days) successfully reduced sexual arousal and consequently sexual deviations, including one case of homosexual aggressiveness toward younger children. Perhaps even more interesting was the finding that one-third of the dose for sexual deviates was used successfully to control the episodic irritability and rage reactions of eleven temporal lobe epileptics. It should be emphasized that this is a preliminary study. The long-term side effects of Provera are not known and the risks involved are not yet clear.

## Summary of the Role of Androgens in Aggression in the Human Male

Unfortunately the data bearing on the relationship between the endocrines and aggressive behavior in humans seldom come wrapped in a neat package with a good experimental design complete with a statistical analysis. However, the preceding section seems clearly to implicate the androgens in some forms of aggressive behavior in humans. When the level or potency of androgens is reduced in certain populations of aggressive individuals, the tendency to aggressive behavior is also reduced. It is interesting that castration reduces the sex drive in essentially all individuals studied. It also essentially eliminated violent crimes and excessive aggressive or dangerous behavior in those subjects who were incarcerated for that reason. In the Bremer study, castration effectively reduced aggression related specifically to sexual behavior. Sex-related aggression also appears to be reduced by either estrogenic compounds or antiandrogenic substances. There also appears to be some evidence that a reduction in androgen level or potency reduces the probability of irritable aggression.

*This material is, at best, suggestive.* However, it certainly merits further controlled investigation. Now that improved hormone assay techniques and several androgen-blocking agents are available, we can expect an increase in the number of studies relating to the problem, which should provide us with more precise data.

## Aggression and the Premenstrual Syndrome

There is some evidence that during the period of ovulation, anxiety and feelings of hostility are at a relatively low level.[226] During the period just prior to menstruation, however, a significant number of women manifest a variety of symptoms that have been collectively called the premenstrual syndrome. This syndrome includes such physical changes as headache, edema, a collection of fluid in the tissue, particularly of the face, hands, and feet; and significant weight gain. Changes in appetite, a craving for sweets, and unusual bursts of energy may also be a part of the syndrome.[11,530] Emotional instability is a characteristic of a number of women during the premenstrual period. There is an increased tendency for women to seek psychiatric help during the premenstrual period[285] and a general increase in psychiatric symptomatology at that time.[215,585] Suicide attempts also increase.[122,215,372,466]

Of particular interest here is the increase in various manifestations of irritability and hostility. Shainess[518] describes it as defensive hostility. Ivey and Bardwick,[284] using Gottschalk's technique of analysis of verbal reports* found consistent themes of hostility during the premenstruum. In a more recent study of 1100 women who were the wives of graduate students in a large American university, fifty-two percent reported that they were markedly irritable in the premenstrual phase of some cycles and thirty percent reported marked irritability during their most recent cycle. The feeling of irritability was more marked than that of depression or tension.[242] Similar findings have been reported by other investigators.[115,407,562] Women in prison populations are more irritable during premenstrual and menstrual phases of the cycle.[169]

Irritable feelings are frequently acted out. In the Ellis and Austin[169] study significantly more aggressive acts occurred during the menstrual and premenstrual period. According to Dalton,[125] women prisoners themselves frequently recognize

---

*The Gottschalk-Gleser Content Analysis Scale is a method of determining from a verbal sample the individual's mood state. S. B. Sells summarized the work on this scale as follows: "In summary, the Gottschalk-Gleser Content Analysis Scales appear to be reasonably valid and reliable measures of the manifest psychological states evidence in verbal protocols. They thus provide a powerful psychometric tool in the diagnosis of psychological states of interest to clinical researchers and practitioners."[227]

that their behavior during this critical period is likely to get them into trouble and, as a result, request isolation. School girls show more infractions of the rules and receive more punishment during the critical period in the cycle, and older girls with legitimate disciplinary power tend to mete out more punishments during their own menstruation[123] The majority of women prisoners who are sufficiently violent so as to require removal to maximum security quarters menstruate during the few days of confinement.[517] Women prisoners are more frequently reported for "bad behavior" during the critical period.[124]

There is also evidence that more crimes are actually committed during the irritable period in the menstrual cycle. A study of prison records revealed that sixty-two percent of the crimes of violence were committed during the premenstrual week and only two percent at the end of the period.[409] However, the length of the "end of the period" was not indicated. A similar finding is reported by Dalton.[124] She found that forty-nine percent of all crimes were committed by women during menstruation or in the premenstruum. Thus, the association between menstruation and crime is highly significant. One would expect only twenty-nine percent of all crimes to be committed during the eight-day period if they were normally distributed. The probability of the obtained distribution occurring by chance is less than one in a thousand. The possibility of impulsive aggression and lawbreaking during the menstrual and premenstrual period is of sufficient magnitude that the criminal law in some countries recognized menstruation as an extenuating circumstance.[146] Severe premenstrual tension is placed in the category of temporary insanity in France.[450] In England, in 1980 and 1981, two women charged with murder were set free. The defense argued that the women had a reduced amount of responsibility for their actions because of the premenstrual syndrome. In both cases, the charge of murder was reduced to manslaughter and the women were given probation on condition that they seek therapy.[538]

Feelings of irritability, hostility and other manifestations of the premenstrual syndrome are not confined to a few asocial individuals who get into difficulties with the law. Moderate or severe degrees of the syndrome occur in about a quarter of all women.[115,244] Some authors estimate that as many as ninety percent of women undergo some irritability, hopelessness, depression, or other symptoms prior to or during menstruation.[286,446]

The underlying physiology of the tendencies to hostility associated with the menstrual-premenstrual syndrome is obscure. There seems to be rather general agreement that the symptoms are associated with a fall in the progesterone level and a relatively

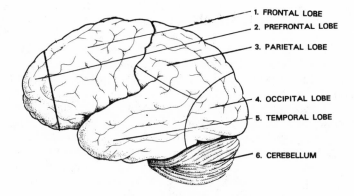

1. FRONTAL LOBE
2. PREFRONTAL LOBE
3. PARIETAL LOBE
4. OCCIPITAL LOBE
5. TEMPORAL LOBE
6. CEREBELLUM

FIGURE 2. *Lobes of the brain.*

greater amount of estrogen in the estrogen-progesterone ratio.[244,353,408] (Bardwick[37] maintains that the symptomatology is due to the absolute fall in estrogen.) Several studies have shown that the symptoms can be alleviated by the administration of progesterone.[125,233,350] Women who take oral contraceptives that contain progestogenic agents show significantly less irritability than do women who are not taking the pill.[37,244,442,632] It may be that the irritability-reducing effects of the progestagens are a function of their direct effect on the neural systems in the brain that relate to hostility. However, the explanation may be much less direct. Janowsky et al.[286] hypothesize that the irritability results from the cyclic increase in aldosterone, a hormone of the adrenals, inasmuch as weight changes, behavioral changes, and aldosterone changes seem to parallel each other. The resulting increase in sodium and water retention caused by aldosterone results in a secondary neuronal irritability and consequent psychic symptoms. It is not clear, however, why general neuronal irritability should affect the parts of the nervous system associated with irritable feelings and negative affect. The therapeutic effects of lithium[169] and diuretics[234,408,631] in treating premenstrual tension may then be due to their tendency to reverse the aldosterone effect on sodium metabolism.

Another physiological characteristic of the premenstrual syndrome is hypoglycemia, low blood sugar. Billig and Spaulding [54] found evidence of hypoglycemia during the period immediately prior to the onset of the menses, and Harris[248] noted an increase in the symptoms of hyperinsulinism in women at the same time in the cycle. Morton[408] suggests that the increased sugar tolerance is due to the action of the unopposed estrogen on carbohydrate metabolism and indicates that many of the psychic symptoms as well as weakness and fatigue can be largely ascribed to the hypoglycemia. He recommends diet changes including supplementary protein as an adjunct therapy. The hypoglycemic states may also contribute to feelings of irritability and hostility, as is discussed later.

Although the evidence certainly indicates an increase of feelings of irritability and hostility in some women during the premenstrual period, there is no good physiological explanation of the cause as yet. It must be recognized that the menstrual process is a phenomenon loaded with psychological meaning in most cultures. It therefore seems unlikely that the psychological changes associated with the period just prior to the onset of the menses are exclusively or even primarily of physiological origin.

As with most other manifestations of hostility, learning, culture, and the environment play an important role. However, the data do suggest the definite possibility that the particular endocrine balance characteristic of the premenstrual phase contributes to the feelings of irritability and hostility frequently found during that portion of the cycle. Further work on the physiology of this problem is clearly indicated.

## Aggressive Behavior as an Allergic Reaction

> You wouldn't believe it. Within twenty minutes of eating a banana this child would be in the worst temper tantrum (no seizures) you have ever seen. I tried this five times because I could not believe my own eyes. He reacted with behavior to all sugars except maple sugar. We went to California the Christmas of 1962 to be with my parents. Robbie's Christmas treats were all made from maple sugar. He was asking for some other candy. My mother wanted him to have it and I told her all right if she wanted to take care of the tantrum. Of course, she didn't believe me but predictably within thirty minutes she had her hands full with Robbie in a tantrum. It made a believer of her. These discussions did not take place in front of the child if you're wondering about the power of suggestion.
>
> If you go into this food reaction thing it will make you feel so sorry for people you can't stand it. After bad behavior from food, Robbie would cry and say he couldn't help it and feel so badly about it. You won't be able to read of a Crime of Violence without wondering if a chemical reaction controlled the aggressor—in fact, you'll be unable to condemn anyone for anything. . . .

The preceding case, quoted in a letter to me by Robbie's mother, was my introduction to the rather remarkable possibility that aggressive behavior could be the result of physiological changes brought about by a reaction to specific allergens. A search of the allergy literature reveals that aggression as an allergic response is a well-recognized phenomenon. As early as 1916, just ten years after the term *allergy* was coined by Pirquet in 1906, quoted in Speer,[545] Hoobler[283] described certain allergic children as "restless, fretful, and sleepless." Shannon[519] was one of the first to indicate that the behavior disorders were a primary allergic reaction and not simply a normal response to the discomfort caused by the other manifestations of the allergic reaction. The behavioral symptoms occurred without a history of preceding dermal skin discomfort and were out of proportion to the primary allergy. Also, they were not always caused by the same allergen.

The term *allergic tension-fatigue syndrome* was introduced in 1954 to describe the allergic behavior pattern.[543] It is important to note that behavior disturbances are only one of many possible allergic reactions and that most individuals with allergies do not show a behavioral alteration.

The most common descriptive term used in connection with this syndrome is *irritability*,[108,460] which is seldom defined behaviorally. However, the irritability syndrome (*irritable aggression* as used in this book) can be understood by the various synonyms used by different authors to describe the individuals so afflicted. Davison[130] has referred to irascibility and impulsiveness as behavioral allergic symptoms. Other descriptive terms have been uncooperative, "anti-social";[454] cross and irritable, resisting all handling . . . spells of intense temper and fury;[294] peevishness, unhappiness, unruliness, rebellious behavior;[119] incorrigible;[478] disobedient, perverse, cantankerous, antagonistic;[492] hot-tempered, hard to please, sulky, temperamental, hot-headed, wild, unrestrained;[546] aggressively irritable, ill-natured, resentful, domineering, slow to forgive;[543] combative, quarrelsome, delinquent;[195] snappish disposition, angry irritability, violent temper tantrums, negative, asocial, hostile, paranoid.[459] The descriptions are a veritable thesaurus of irritability.

> *Emotional Immaturity Reactions.* Included under this heading are temper tantrums, screaming episodes, whining, impatience, and excitability. Patients of this type are inclined to be erratic, impulsive, quarrelsome and irresponsible. Many admit having "childish" compulsions.
>
> *Antisocial Behavior.* These patients are inclined to be uncooperative, pugnacious, sulky, and perhaps cruel. Most have learned enough self-control to avoid serious aberrations of behavior (p. 31).[92]

The intensity of the symptoms may run from a mild irritable reaction in which the individual is a little more easily annoyed than usual to a psychotic aggressive reaction. Mandell[371] describes a ten-year-old girl with intractable asthma in whom an attack was brought on by an ethanol test. She was completely amnesic for the three hours during which the test lasted. She became infantile and did not know her name and address. Her mood ran from silliness and restlessness to withdrawal. Several times during the prolonged reaction, she became extremely belligerent and tried to bite her mother, whom she was unable to identify. In a case described by Speer,[544] a nine-year-old boy reacted to wheat by awakening in a nightmare completely disoriented, not knowing who he was, who his mother was, or where he was. He struck his head against the wall repeatedly and engaged in high-pitched, uncontrolled screaming. Numerous other case studies are available to demonstrate all variations in intensity from mild to severe. (See the papers of the investigators previously mentioned.)

Although there are a large number of case studies in the literature showing that individuals with allergic tension-fatigue syndrome lose that symptomatology under allergy management, the only reasonable way to determine whether the syndrome is an allergic one is to eliminate the allergen from the environment until the symptoms abate and then reproduce the symptoms by reintroducing the allergen into the environment, the so-called challenge technique. Crook et al.[119] report on fifty patients who had five signs and symptoms of allergy: fatigue, irritability and other mental and emotional symptoms, pallor, circles under the eyes, and nasal congestions. The majority of the patients in this study had their symptoms relieved and reproduced by the challenge technique. The fifty patients reviewed in this research were seen in the group pediatric practice during a four-year period. The authors conclude that allergy as a systemic or generalized illness is much more common than is usually recognized by most allergy textbooks.

Allergens that can produce the allergic tension-fatigue syndrome are highly varied. It can be produced by pollens;[294] a variety of inhalants;[460] drugs;[224,492] and many foods, of which milk, chocolate, cola, corn, and eggs are the most common.[119,547] The sensitivity of the individual varies idiosyncratically and according to the type of allergen. One patient showed such exquisite sensitivity to onions that she could tell when they were being cooked, not by the odor but because she had sudden and intense nervousness and irritability.[195] Other individuals can tolerate moderate amounts of some allergens. It is not uncommon for a child to be allergic to milk but manifest no reaction as long as the milk intake is limited to several times a week.

The basic physiological cause of the irritable allergic reaction is not yet clear. It has been suggested that allergens have a direct effect on the nervous system.[449,544] This is evident from the fact that some epileptic disorders have an allergic basis. In fact, early allergists hoped to demonstrate that all idiopathic epilepsy was due to an allergy.[545] Although that did not turn out to be the case, there is abundant evidence that in some individuals, convulsions and other epileptic phenomena can be produced at will by challenging the individual with the particular allergen to which he is sensitive. (An excellent review of the literature with several cases is given by Campbell.)[93]

Cerebral edema has been suggested as causing allergy-induced mental symptoms,[195,406] but generalized edema leaves much to be desired as an explanation of the specific symptomatology. Campbell[92] implies on the basis of the symptomatology that the limbic system is involved (as it must be), but gives no indication of what that involvement is. Perhaps the most reasonable hypothesis is suggested by Gottlieb,[225] who considers the possibility that the symptoms are due to allergically-caused, circumscribed angioedema (noninflammatory swelling) of the brain. There is some evidence that such localized edema occurs in the brain as a result of allergies just as localized edema occurs in the skin. Both types of edema are reversible. As with the skin, there is evidence that the edema may be localized in different parts of the brain. Thus, the number and kind of symptoms will be a function of the particular location of the resultant pressure in the brain.

The problem of detecting a transient localized edema in the central nervous system is obviously great. However, such edema has been detected in the optic nerve and in the retina of patients who were manifesting peripheral angioedema. The possibility that localized edema was also occurring in the brain seems to be indicated by the presence in these patients of cerebral manifestations that included unilateral paralysis, convulsions, sensory aphasia, motor aphasis, and partial loss of vision.[46,307] Other transitory CNS signs have been noted in some allergy patients. These have included transient palsies, radiculitis, and scotoma and were associated with allergic hives and transient edema of the optic nerve and retina.[308,309] Recurrent cerebral edema as a result of food allergies has also been described by Rowe.[479] These patients became somnolent and showed staggering gait, dizziness, and inability to focus the eyes.

It can be inferred from the preceding data that individuals with allergy-induced aggressive behavior may have angioedema in any one of several portions of the brain through which the neural system for irritable aggression courses. The pressure of the swelling may sensitize or activate those neural systems, or may deactivate some of the systems that have an inhibitory function, as appears to be the case with specific localized brain tumors.

## Hypoglycemia and Aggression

Hypoglycemia (low blood sugar) may be caused by hyperinsulinism resulting from tumors on the Islands of Langerhans in the pancreas or from a therapeutic overdose. It can also be caused by endocrine secretions that are inadequate to counter a normal insulin level, as found in Addison's disease (hypoadrenalcorticalism),[581,582] in hypothyroidism, and in several pituitary dysfunctions. It can occur during lactation, after starvation, and as a result of muscular exhaustion in certain predisposed subjects. Idiopathic blood sugar deficit, in which no cause can be determined, is also common.[293,310,622] Hypoglycemia is particularly prevalent in children whose glucose-regulating mechanisms are less stable.[623,624] In adulthood it occurs more frequently in middle age.[310] The physiological consequences of the hypoglycemic state are well-summarized in Bleicher[57] and need not be covered here. The important consideration for this section is the psychological symptoms that may accompany the disorder.

The symptoms of hypoglycemia are highly varied and are primarily psychological or neurological.[310,623] The individual may feel faint, dizzy, weak, disturbed, fatigued, and nervous. Patients frequently develop an exaggerated negativism during which they are inclined to reject any suggestions, even those obviously beneficial. The individual may refuse to take orange juice, for example, and hold his lips tightly closed even though his symptoms would be relieved by drinking it.[539] An intense loss of will also occasionally develops and the individual is unable to initiate any action, even that of taking candy he carries specifically to alleviate hypoglycemic attacks.* Other mental changes may include exhilaration, euphoria, and hilarity, but these are relatively uncommon. The negative emotions are more frequent and include anxiety, depression, and impulsivity. Aggressiveness and irritability in one form or another are quite common. The patient may be morose, asocial, sullen, and generally misanthropic. He is often rude and profane, and the aggressive reaction may develop into a full-blown rage in which the individual becomes violent and destructive, attacking both objects and people, at times with fatal results.[4,54,235,450,480,647] Wilder[625] has summarized a wide variety of crimes committed during a hypoglycemic state.

When the hypoglycemia is severe, the individual may become confused and disoriented and develop a fugue state in which he wanders aimlessly around the streets engaging in irrational and sometimes violent behavior. He may also show complete amnesia for the period of fugue. Several irrational murders have been committed and attempted by hypoglycemic patients and in some

---

*Candy or sugar will quickly reduce the hypoglycemia episode, but is not a useful therapy in general. The sugar consumption in some individuals will trigger an excess of insulin output with a subsequent hypoglycemia response. This type of patient needs a well-controlled diet of small high protein meals with an avoidance of sugars, alcohol, etc.

cases the subject has been judged not guilty by reason of temporary insanity.[12,105,310,500] The following case illustrates many of the symptoms of the hypoglycemia syndrome.

K., 51 years of age, a very sedate businessman, had been taking insulin for six years. After the usual injection of 30 units at 7:30 A.M. and breakfast, he went to his office one day and performed routine work. About 10:00 A.M. he took some fruit, and then made a few calls. At noon he went home for lunch by trolley. He had already had a "light dizzy feeling," and his companion told him the next day that he was amazed at the silliness and uncoordinated movements of the patient at that time. The patient felt the need for sugar which, incidentally, he always carried with him but he lacked the "power and will" to take it. What happened thereafter he could not recall. The conductor and the police officer agreed as to the following: K. entered the trolley behaving like a drunkard, opened his vest, set his hat on the side of his head, yelled and laughed. The perplexed conductor called the police officer who ordered K. to leave the trolley with him. K. was obviously confused, resisted stubbornly, and had to be overpowered by the policeman who dragged him by force to the police station, followed by a curious crowd. He was rabidly violent. Some time later, with decreasing disorientation and confusion, he begged the police to obtain some bread for him. This done, he was soon in complete possession of his senses, greatly surprised at his arrest and his preceding actions. The police surgeon examined him and found on him the marks of numerous injections, arousing vigorous protests on the part of the patient because of the accusation of morphinism. In court his personal physician testified that he had been treating K. for some time and that similar confusions had occurred previously, but to a milder degree, and that probably this episode was due to hypoglycemia with transitory psychotic manifestations. The case was dismissed when evidence of previous similar episodes was produced.

Several times, while on the trolley, the patient overlooked his point of destination, being slightly confused, was picked up at the end of the line, and brought to a police station where the officers already familiar with his behavior called his wife to take him home. A month before his arrest, while visiting relatives, he began to make stupid and silly remarks, a symptom very familiar to his family as indicative of a reaction. He fought off the attempts of his family to give him some food, and finally had to be overpowered by several people so that a few pieces of sugar could be forced between his teeth. A year prior to his arrest he had had a severe hypoglycemic reaction after erroneously taking a double dose of insulin (confusing U-20 with U-40 insulin, a mistake not noted then by his wife). At dinner he behaved normally at first, but then towards the end he became completely psychotic. He danced about the table and juggled oranges. Soon after, he lapsed into a coma from which he could not be aroused by the oral administration of sugar, but required hospitalization and intravenous glucose therapy. The reaction of the patient to these attacks was one of embarrassment and chagrin. He constantly proclaimed his innocence and insisted that the statements and stupidities uttered during hypoglycemia were beyond his control: that he could not even remember them. In fact, he was aware of them only through information gathered from his family. These accidents upset him greatly, for he was ordinarily very polite and correct, and could not understand how he could have been so rude and discourteous.[4]

Most of the work on hypoglycemia was done in the two decades following the description of the syndrome of hyperinsulinism by Harris in 1924. The many clinical studies appear to establish beyond a reasonable doubt that a relationship exists between a drop in blood sugar and some forms of aggressive behavior. There are a large number of studies showing that a drop in glucose level results in an aggressive episode that can be promptly terminated by sugar intake, and in some patients that sequence may recur repeatedly. For obvious reasons there has been relatively little experimental work on the problem. However, an anthropologist has recently confirmed the relationship in a field experiment with the Qolla Indians of Peruvian Andes.[64] Bolton hypothesized that the exceptionally high level of social conflict and hostility in the society could be explained, in part, by the tendency to hypoglycemia among the community residents. Approximately fifty-five percent of these villagers showed instability in glucose homeostasis. Peer ratings of aggressiveness (which had an acceptable reliability) were studied in relationship to blood sugar levels as determined by a glucose tolerance test. The aggression ratings were not known to the individual who read the glucose levels. An analysis of the data showed a statistically significant relationship between aggression ranking and the change in blood glucose levels during the four-hour glucose tolerance test. In view of all the other possible causes of aggressive behavior, this is a remarkable finding and indicates that the relationship must be powerful.

Dr. Bolton did a second study with the Qolla in which he asked a sample of thirty-six males to respond to a sentence completion test in which the individual's answer could be completely free. For example: The sentence to be completed is *A family* _____. One subject's answer was, "Yes, within a family people know how to fight with each other. They go around criticizing and

59

backbiting." The responses for each subject were scored for hostility.

A blood sample had been taken earlier and checked for sugar content and on the basis of that the population was divided into homoglycemics and non-hypoglycemics. Neither the individual administering the test nor the one doing the statistical analyses were aware of the hypoglycemic status of the subjects. As predicted by Professor Bolton, the hypoglycemic subjects showed significantly higher aggressiveness scores on the sentence completion task.

Bolton proposes the interesting hypothesis that fighting is both initiated and perpetuated in this society by hypoglycemic tendencies. He suggests that the individual gets into a social altercation because of the irritability associated with the low glucose level. However, as indicated earlier, a number of other uncomfortable symptoms, such as faintness, dizziness, and fatigue, accompany the hypoglycemic episode. When the person gets into a fight his metabolism is changed and the output of adrenalin and adrenal corticoids counter the insulin effects and cause liver glycogen to be converted to glucose with the result that the uncomfortable symptoms are reduced. He is thus rewarded for engaging in fighting behavior and is thus more inclined to be aggressive when he again experiences the physiological cues associated with the hypoglycemic reaction. Related to this hypothesis is a case report by Duncan[153] describing the antidotal effects of anger on a diabetic during hypoglycemia produced by an insulin injection.

The reasons for increased aggressive tendencies during hypoglycemia are not yet clear, although some of the effects of low blood glucose on the central nervous system give some indications. According to Ervin,[172] hypoglycemia is a well-known provocation for epileptic foci, and the limbic system appears to be particularly sensitive to it. Thus patients with minimal deep temporal lobe damage may only have episodes of aggressive dyscontrol under conditions of hypoglycemia. There is considerable evidence that low blood glucose levels are associated with disruptions in the EEG pattern. (See a summary of this evidence in Fabrykant & Pacella.)[180] The hypoglycemic murderer studied by Hill and Sargant[275] showed an abnormal EEG pattern only during periods of low blood sugar.

The brain, although it has stores of glycogen, is unable to convert glycogen to glucose when the need arises as other organs can. It is therefore dependent on the glucose in the bloodstream. If there is a deficiency of glucose, the brain loses its fuel supply and is less able to extract oxygen from the blood. One result is a loss of function of some of the neural systems. If, as in the case of alcohol, the systems first affected are the ones related to neural

60

inhibition, the hyperaggressiveness associated with hypoglycemia might be expected to occur.

It is difficult to determine whether the tendency to hostility produced by low blood sugar is a problem of practical significance. Greenwood in 1935[235] reported that routine estimates of blood glucose level showed that 2.8 percent of patients in general hospital wards and 4.35 percent of patients in psychopathic wards had levels of 70 mg. per 100 cm$^3$ of blood (normal levels begin 90 to 110 mg. per 100 cm$^3$). It has been estimated that 0.5 percent of patients in general practice show hypoglycemic tendencies.[622] If one assumes the validity of these estimates, the absolute numbers of individuals is large indeed. Abramson and Pezet[2] estimate the number of hypoglycemic patients at a minimum of ten million in the United States and perhaps as many as thirty million. Although it is true that all hypoglycemic patients do not manifest overt aggression, and very few become violent, it would seem that the irritability resulting from this disorder would at least contribute to the unhappiness of many patients and their close associates and, at worst, would account for some irrational crimes of brutality. There are, of course, adequate therapies for this disorder.

# Drug–Induced Aggression

The ingestion of drugs is another method of changing the blood chemistry that in certain instances, and in certain individuals, results in an increase in the potential for aggressive behavior. This section will deal with drugs that have a facilitating effect on hostile behavior. Those that function to produce aggression inhibition will be covered in Chapter IX.

The amphetamines, including amphetamine sulfate, amphetamine phosphate, dextroamphetamine sulfate, and methamphetamine, are widely used central nervous system stimulants that have come under strict federal controls because of their considerable potential for abuse. Therapeutically, the amphetamines (generally dextroamphetamine) are used in the treatment of obesity, narcolepsy, Parkinsonism, depressive syndrome, and some behavior disorders.[223]

When taken in therapeutic doses the individual may feel slightly more restless and have a moderate lift in mood. Larger amounts result in increased restlessness, dizziness, tremor, insomnia, hyperactive reflexes, tenseness, anxiety, and irritability. There is general agreement that moderate use and occasional abuse of amphetamines does not result in violence.[59,580] In fact, Blum goes so far as to say that there is no research to support linking amphetamines and violence. That appears to be true for

61

moderate abuse, particularly if the drug is taken orally. However, long-term users of high doses are potentially dangerous. During acute intoxication individuals suffer from hyper-irritability, aggressiveness, and loss of judgment.[296] Their actions tend to be impulsive and may be violent.[110] Tinklenberg and Stillman[580] report having observed a progressive deterioration of the ability of amphetamine abusers to control their behavior. Such users may recognize their impulsive destructive acts as being inappropriate but are unable to inhibit them. These investigators conclude that there is a "cumulative amphetamine effect that predisposes the user toward assaultive behavior" (p. 334).

The abuse potential and the severity of the assaultive tendencies are increased when the drug is taken intravenously. On intravenous injection the subject experiences a "rush," which is a generalized, intense, pleasurable feeling. After the rush, the euphoric state gradually dissipates and in a matter of several hours the pleasant feelings are replaced by a general state of irritability, vague uneasiness, anxiety, and body aches. The user is then likely to administer another intravenous dose of the drug to avoid the discomfort and to reestablish the feeling of the rush. The pattern of self-administration of methamphetamine may continue every two hours for days or for more than a week. This prolonged administration is referred to as a "run." During the run the subject is constantly awake, eats very little or nothing, and frequently engages in repetitive purposeless activities. When the run is finally terminated, the discomforts associated with the down period after a single dose of amphetamine are magnified many times and it is at this point that the individual is most likely to be destructive and assaultive.[322,324,580] Paranoid symptoms begin to appear the second or third day of a run and become increasingly severe. Paranoia is characteristic of prolonged amphetamine intoxication and is the major feature of amphetamine psychosis when it develops. Some investigators[71,246] maintain that the paranoid tendencies associated with amphetamine abuse are little more than an exaggeration of a premorbid paranoid personality. Connell[113] rejects that as a necessary factor.

There is little doubt that the subculture of the methamphetamine abuser (speed freak) is dominated by suspiciousness and feelings of persecution, and it seems likely that the physiological effects of the drug are reinforced by the attributes of the culture. The subculture of the speed freak is also violence-ridden. Individuals who have or believe that they have been cheated in a drug transaction are expected by their peers to gain revenge and retribution. The probability of violence is further enhanced by the general tendency of the members of this particular subculture to carry concealed weapons.

Some amphetamine abusers develop an acute psychosis that may last for days or years after the withdrawal from the drug. The major feature is paranoid delusions. The delusions may be disorganized as in paranoid schizophrenia or they may be well organized and internally consistent as in true paranoia. In the latter type of psychosis the individual's thinking is intact except for a set of circumscribed delusions. They may, for example, believe that the Mafia or the communists are plotting to kill them.[110,113,167] Connell[113] reports on forty-two cases on amphetamine psychosis and indicates that eighty-one percent of the individuals had paranoid delusions and twenty-two percent were hostile and aggressive.

The paranoid panic accompanying acute amphetamine intoxication, which occurs during the down period after a run, may result in aggressive action. Ellinwood[168] reports on thirteen cases of homicide related to amphetamine abuse. In one case a twenty-seven-year-old truck driver shot and killed his boss because he believed that the boss was attempting to kill him by releasing poison gas into the back seat of the car in which he was riding. This subject had taken 80 mg. of amphetamine in a twenty-hour period in an attempt to complete a 1600-mile trip nonstop. He had not slept for forty-eight hours and had begun to have persecutory ideas six to eight hours before the murder. Masaki (quoted in Kalant)[296] reported that thirty-one of sixty convicted murderers in Japan in May and June of 1954 had some connection with amphetamine abuse. Rylander,[482] reporting on 146 central stimulant addicts,* indicated that the aggressive crimes perpetrated by these individuals included murder, manslaughter, robbery, assault and battery, and destruction of property.

As Ellinwood[168] is careful to point out, the precise role of the amphetamines in cases of murder and assault is difficult to assess because other factors such as specific environmental conditions, predisposing personality characteristics, and the use of other drugs are frequently involved.

## Alcohol and Aggression Facilitation

There can be no doubt that alcohol and violence are related. In a study of homicides in Philadelphia between 1948 and 1952, it was shown that either the victim or the offender had been drinking just prior to the crime in sixty-four percent of the cases.[634]

---

*A number of these persons were abusing the drug phenmetrazine (Preludin), a CNS stimulant related to amphetamine.

In a study of rape, the results indicate that alcohol was present in one-third of the rapes, and in most instances both the victim and the offender had been drinking.[59] Aggravated assaults are also significantly associated with alcohol. A 1966 study by the President's Commission on Crime in the District of Columbia found that thirty-five percent of the offenders in 124 cases of assault had been drinking prior to the attack, as had forty-six percent of 131 victims. Drinking delinquents commit more crimes of assault than do those who do not drink.[399]

That alcohol and aggression are associated is a fact. What that fact means is not immediately clear. Obviously, all individuals who consume alcoholic beverages do not become homicidal, assaultive, or even have an increase in feelings of hostility. In fact, self-reports of mood changes during alcohol consumption have included increases in cheerfulness, lovingness, and friendliness;[200] increase in happiness;[303] less irritability, more relaxation, and more self-satisfaction.[428] (See Wallgren & Barry[610] for further studies.) No doubt many readers can substantiate these data with their own subjective impressions. In this section we briefly examine the evidence relating alcohol and aggression and attempt to resolve the apparent paradox above.

A number of studies have shown that alcohol, even in moderate doses, results in a statistically significant increase in evidence of hostile feelings. Aggressive fantasy as measured by the Thematic Apperception Test (TAT)* increased significantly among college men after three to four drinks containing 1.5 oz. of an eighty-six-proof alcoholic beverage. The TAT protocols did not change during a comparable period in similar situations (living room discussion groups or stag cocktail party) when nonalcoholic beverages were served. Aggression themes decreased between four and six drinks and were replaced by thoughts of physical sex. After six drinks the story themes showed a decrease in inhibitory thoughts regarding aggression restraint, fear anxiety, and time concern. Thoughts of physical aggression recurred with high frequency in subjects who drank very heavily (more than ten drinks).[299] Similar increases in themes relating to aggression and self-assertion, among other things, were found by Takala et al.[564] when they compared the TAT protocols of young men in a social drinking situation (0.09 to 0.17 percent blood alcohol) with the protocols of control subjects. The same subjects also showed increases in overtly aggressive themes on the Rosenzweig

---

*The TAT is a test used to assess the various mood states of an individual. The individual is shown a series of ambiguous pictures and asked to tell a story about them.

Picture Frustration Test.* The later finding, however, was not substantiated in a well-controlled study by Nash[428] who found a decrease in extrapunitive or overt aggression themes among subjects with 0.065 percent of blood alcohol.

In another study by Taylor et al.,[568] forty male college students were provoked after they had consumed either high or low doses of alcohol (1.5 oz. or 0.5 oz. of one hundred-proof ethanol, or ginger ale for the control subjects). The expression of physical aggression (shock administered to another subject in the experiment) was directly related to the amount of alcohol consumed.

Young men under the influences of moderate amounts of alcohol rate cartoons as funnier than do those consuming a placebo, and the difference is greater for cartoons portraying hostile humor as opposed to those dealing with nonsense humor.[271] Nathan et al.[429] studied skid-row alcoholics over a prolonged period during drinking and nondrinking sessions and found that most subjects became more sociable at the start of drinking but as drinking continued, anxiety, depression, and hostility as measured by a Mood Adjective Checklist increased significantly. Loomis and West[357] reported that all of their subjects became more talkative and less inhibited with an alcohol blood level of 0.03 to 0.09 percent. However, about half of them also became argumentative. Tiredness and tendencies to withdraw from the group predominated when the blood levels reached 0.10 to 0.17 percent alcohol.

It is important to note in all the preceding studies that although statistically significant increases occurred in various measures of hostile tendencies, there was also considerable variability and all subjects did not react to alcohol consumption with increases in aggressiveness. Further, as indicated earlier, a number of studies report an increase in positive affect with no indication of hostility increases, and some such as Fregly et al.[200] reported increases in positive affect in some subjects but increases in irritability, aggressiveness, and nervousness in others.

There are relatively few studies that provide an opportunity for actual overt aggression in the laboratory situation. However, Shuntich and Taylor[524] and Taylor and Gammon[567] have shown that college students involved in a competitive reaction-time situation tend to set significantly higher shock levels after having ingested alcohol. The expression of physical aggression is related to the quantity of alcohol ingested. Low doses of alcohol (0.5 oz. of one hundred-proof bourbon or vodka) appear to inhibit

---

*This test is also designed to assess reactions to frustrating situations.

aggressive responding, whereas high doses (1.5 oz.) facilitate aggressive responding when compared with placebo controls. The subject's judgment of his opponent was also influenced by the level of alcohol consumption. Those individuals receiving high doses of vodka rated their opponents as being bloodthirsty, aggressive, cruel, and revengeful. The authors point out that this negative affect appears to be exaggerated and inappropriate since, from the subjects' point of view, the opponent did not initiate the aggressive interaction.

In another experiment by Bennett et al.[51] there was no evidence of a change in aggressive tendencies (level of shock set for an experimenter confederate) related to alcohol consumption. The mean blood alcohol concentrations of 0.030, 0.058, and 0.086 percent were observed at the three doses used. The discrepancy between the Taylor studies and the Bennett et al. study seems to be due to the nature of the experiment. In the other case, however, the subjects were engaged in a competitive situation in which the individuals' opponents could retaliate.

The relationship between alcohol and homicide has been extensively reviewed by Wolfgang,[634] Wolfgang and Ferracuti,[635] and Blum[58,59] and will therefore be dealt with only briefly here. As indicated earlier, alcohol is involved in sixty-five percent of homicides. The method of killing is more likely to be violent and brutal when alcohol is involved. When the method of killing is stabbing, seventy-two percent of the cases involve the use of alcohol. When the method is beating, alcohol involvement occurs in sixty-nine percent of the cases. For shooting it is fifty-five percent, and for miscellaneous methods, only forty-five percent. Among whites, alcohol is present in the majority of killings only when the method used is that of beating.[634] Several more recent studies have confirmed the essential findings of Wolfgang's earlier work.[213,239,606]

Alcohol is also associated with the more violent types of crime among women. A study of feminine felons in California showed that drinking was associated with fifty-five percent of the homicides, sixty-two percent of the assaults, and forty-three percent of the robberies. On the other hand, alcohol usage was related to only twenty-nine percent of the offenses against property (Ward, quoted in Mulvihill et al.[417]

Although the studies cited here have all been conducted in the American culture, similar results have been obtained in other countries. This material is succinctly summarized by Blum.[59]

A Mexican appraisal[134] indicates that alcohol compared to marijuana and other narcotics is most often implicated in male criminality. A study in France[416] shows involvement in fifty percent of the acts of homicide, seventy-eight percent of robberies as derived by a random sample of arrested offenders. A German review[597] reports a rising rate of juvenile offenses in which the offender had been drinking and in Argentina [269] alcohol, and in particular alcoholism, have been identified as major contributing factors in several crimes of violence, those of vengeance and passion, as in response to adultery, and those involving insult to self-esteem, that is, a challenge to manliness arising out of social drinking among male companions (p. 1475).

There are many social, cultural, and learning factors involved in the tendency for an individual under the influence of alcohol to become aggressive. In some subcultures an individual is not considered responsible for his behavior when he is inebriated, with the result that the drinker's behavior is less restrained by his perception of social pressure. Because of past experience, particular social groups expect certain individuals to become hostile after alcohol consumption, and some of the resulting aggressive behavior may be attributed to the fulfillment of the expectations of the group. The particular social situation in which the drinker finds himself may also precipitate aggressive behavior. A drinking companion is often a provocateur of violence. Although it may help, it is certainly not necessary to be drunk to respond aggressively toward an obnoxious intoxicated companion. Homicide and assault victims are frequently involved in drinking at the time of the assault.[634] Alcohol may be only one element in a subculture where physical aggression is common, and in that sense alcohol may not be a causal factor.

The alcohol-aggression-crime relationship is obviously a complex one having many contributing factors. Any or all of the preceding variables may contribute to a given alcohol-aggression incident.

In addition to the psychocultural factors mentioned, there is good evidence that, for some individuals, physiological factors resulting from alcohol consumption interact with nonphysiological variables to increase the probability of aggression in the drinker. There appears to be a selective suppression of the neural mechanisms for inhibition in the central nervous system by alcohol. In the patellar tendon reflex, for example, ethanol enhances the response and reduces reflex latency, which implies a reduction in inhibitory influences from higher centers.[587,595] (See Wallgren and Barry[610] for a review of inhibition suppression by alcohol.) They conclude that both excitatory and inhibitory functions are suppressed by the ingestion of alcohol, but the inhibitory functions are suppressed somewhat more. It is common knowledge that social inhibitions are also reduced by alcohol consumption.[417] If the stimulus situation contains factors increasing the probability that the neural systems for hostility will be activated, the likelihood is increased that the individual will both feel and act aggressively.

With alcohol, as with any other drug, there are wide individual differences in its effect. Some of these differences in physiological reaction relate to whether or not a threshold for aggressive action is lowered by the drug. In one study personality inventories were given to a population of subjects who were then divided into two groups on the basis of plethysmographic* recording under conditions of alcohol or placebo dosage. The results showed that individuals who reacted to alcohol (0.23 ml. per pound body weight in tomato juice heavily spiced with Tabasco sauce) with constriction of the blood vessels were significantly more hostile than those who reacted with peripheral dilation.[474] It is not clear how these findings relate to the effect of alcohol on the central nervous system, and there is no evidence that the hostility of these subjects was increased by the alcohol. However, there is evidence that a small percentage do respond to ethanol consumption with pathological aggressive reactions.

Pathological intoxication has been a recognized clinical entity and it was initially described by Krafft-Ebing [323] in 1892 (quoted in Banay).[30] The state is characterized by its dramatic and sudden onset. Although the duration is relatively short, a few moments to an hour or so, the reaction may continue for a day or more. Consciousness is frequently impaired and the perception of the environment is distorted by delusions that are always of a persecutory nature and hallucinations that have a hostile content. Maniacal outbursts occur and include fits of rage and an irresistible desire for destruction. Movements are not well coordinated, but they are vigorous. The attack occurs early in intoxication and is not related to the quantity of alcohol consumed. The reaction is usually terminated by deep sleep and amnesia for the entire incident.[30,528]

There is evidence that some cases of pathological intoxication result from the action of the alcohol on the *temporal lobe* (2-5), which can be verified by electroencephalic records that show temporal lobe spiking. (See the section on epilepsy and aggression in Chapter V.) In one study EEG records were taken on 402 patients because they had been involved in incidents of confusion, abnormal behavior, destructive rage, and other mental

---

*The plethysmograph is a device for measuring the volume of a given part of the body.

dysfunctions as a consequence of alcohol consumption. They were given alcohol in the form of beer, whiskey, or gin, depending on the type of beverage that had precipitated the incident for that individual. The results showed no diagnostic abnormality in 347 cases (eighty-six percent). In fifty-five cases, however, specific anterior temporal lobe spikes were recorded. Forty-two of the cases showed unilateral spikes and thirteen had bilateral temporal lobe spikes. Spiking appeared from twenty-five seconds to thirty-five minutes after the first doses of alcohol. Eighteen patients had definite psychomotor episodes.[374]

In another study of ten patients who showed the clinical symptoms of pathological intoxication, EEG spiking was, after alcohol administration, found only in two patients, and in them only when the recordings were made from electrodes implanted in the *temporal lobe* (2-5) in the region of the *amygdala* (4-5 & 6-3). Thus it would appear that alcoholic activation of temporal lobe spikes cannot be ruled out even though they do not appear on a surface recording.[25] A particularly interesting aspect of this study was the fact that alcohol was given intravenously and the subjects were not told when or if they would be given the drug. All of the patients showed signs of drunkenness, nystagmus, slurred speech, and grossly impaired gait, but only one of them recognized that he was drunk. None of the patients became violent during the study. The authors suggest that these apparently paradoxical results may be explained by the complexity of alcohol, aggression, brain dysfunction, and environmental interactions. In the experimental situation, conducted in a sterile hospital environment in which the welfare of the patient was of prime concern, there were no stimuli capable of eliciting an aggressive response. They suggest further that the experimental situation was supportive and nonstressful and that stress of some kind may be necessary to bring about the temporal lobe dysfunction during the application of alcohol. A number of case reports of pathological intoxication are on record.[30,348,374,528] The following case is typical.

A 27-year-old male had been perfectly normal until the age of twenty-three years, when a craniocerebral injury resulted in a right temporal skull fracture and an associated period of unconsciousness. Subsequently, following the ingestion of even a minor amount of alcohol he became belligerent, confused, and destructive. On one occasion, the patient had two cocktails five minutes before he walked into a liquor store to purchase additional liquor. On being refused the sale of the liquor he went into a rage, and the salesman attempted to subdue him. The patient picked up a knife from the counter

69

and stabbed the salesman several times. He was overcome by several bystanders before police arrived. The salesman was dead on arrival of the ambulance. An alcohol-activation electro-encephalogram was requested by the public defender. The routine study showed generalized instability and isolated short spikes in the right anterior temporal area (region of the skull fracture). Following alcohol-activation, profuse spikes were recorded in the right anterior temporal area with spreading to the right parietal and temporal areas (p. 246).[374]

## Other Drugs and Aggression Facilitation

Increase in irritability, feelings of hostility, and overt aggressive behavior are side effects in some patients for several drugs. However, except in the case of the benzodiazepines, librium, valium, etc. this phenomenon has generally not been systematically studied. In the subculture of drug-users, abuse of the barbiturates is considered likely to result in the sudden onset of aggressive incidents.[78] Ban[29] indicates that the euphoria found with barbiturate drug abuse is occasionally replaced by irritability, quarrelsomeness, and a generally hostile attitude with paranoid ideation. These same drugs may also increase the activity of, irritability of, and difficulty in managing hyperactive children.[464]

One of the first symptoms of overdosage with L-dopa is an increase in irritability along with agitation, helplessness and insomnia. If the dose is further increased, anger, hostility, and overt violence with paranoid delusions may occur. Barbeau[36] described one patient who concealed a knife under his pillow and had plans to use it on his roommate because of a paranoid delusion that the roommate was going with the patient's sister. Barbeau tentatively concludes that Dopamine and Cyclic AMP play a role in mania and aggressivity in humans.

## Benzodiazepine-Induced Aggression

One of the most interesting features of early animal studies on the benzodiazepines (chlordiazepoxide, diazepam, and oxazepam)* was their profound taming effect.[267,458,494] They also had a significant anti-aggression effect in humans (discussed later). However, early in the clinical use of this class of drugs it was noted that in some individuals an acute "rage" reaction resulted from the administration of high doses.[583] Also

---

*These are all minor tranquilizers, Librium, Valium, Serex.

70

see more recent studies by Rickles,[468] and Lion et al.)[345] Because the reaction appeared in a limited number of individuals and was contrary to the usual effect it was labeled paradoxical rage. Since the early reports there have been a number of clinical and experimental reports on benzodiazepine-induced hostility in humans. Feldman[186] reported that many patients receiving diazepam showed a progressive development of dislikes and hates. These patients were aware that their hateful feelings were irrational, but were nevertheless, unable to control them. In some instances the hostile feelings were acted on, resulting in overt violence, such as throwing trays of food or attacking other patients.

In experimental studies designed to determine the effectiveness of Librium and Serex in the control of anxiety, DiMascio and Barrett[43,149] found an indication that the two drugs had different effects on hostility. Librium tended to increase aggressive tendencies, whereas Serex had no effect on them. The data on hostility were not reported in those publications but were followed up in a carefully controlled double-blind study. High, medium, and low-anxious subjects (on the Taylor Manifest Anxiety Test) were given daily doses of 45 mg. of oxazepam, 30 mg. of Librium, or a placebo. The subjects were tested prior to any drug ingestion and again two hours after taking the final dose one week later on the Buss-Durkee Hostility Inventory[88] and on the Gottschalk-Gleser Hostility Scales.[277] The placebo had essentially no effect on the level of hostility in any of the three groups. Serex also produced no consistent changes in the hostility scores on the Buss-Durkee inventory. Librium, however, produced a significant increase in the hostility measures for the high-anxiety group and a trend in the same direction for the medium-anxiety group. The scores on the subscales indicated that the increase was greatest for indirect hostility, irritability, and verbal hostility. Librium also significantly increased the ambivalent hostility scores on the Gottschalk-Gleser scale for the high-anxious subjects. The authors suggest that Serex should be used for anxious patients who have inadequate impulse control and a history of aggressive or destructive behavior, and that chlordiazepoxide be used with anxious subjects who are inhibited and would benefit therapeutically from an ability to express aggression.[207]

There are currently no physiological data that help to explain these results.

## Summary

In spite of the many problems in interpreting studies on humans, it appears clearly justified to conclude that there are a variety of blood chemistry manipulations that affect the threshold of aggressive reactivity in humans. The blood chemistry variables always interact with social and environmental and learning factors, but the evidence indicates that in many instances the physiological variables make an important and significant contribution to the overall aggressive potential.

Androgens are related to aggressive behavior in the male but there is still much to be learned about the exact nature of that relationship. Other things being equal, a higher level of androgen is associated with increased hostile behavior of some kind, and a reduction or blockage of androgenic compounds tends to reduce some kinds of hostile behavior in aggressive individuals. It is clear that the androgens are important in sex-related aggression and there is some indication that they may play a role in generalized irritable aggression. However, much more work needs to be done to establish that relationship unequivocally.

Endocrine factors also seem to be involved in the production of the irritability and feelings of hostility that accompany the premenstrual syndrome. Although there is no doubt that social, cultural, and experiential factors are important variables in this syndrome, it is possible to reduce the feelings of irritability by physiological manipulations including changes in the progesterone-estrogen ratio.

Although relatively little hard evidence exists on the underlying physiological mechanisms, there is good reason to believe that aggressive behavior may be a reaction to allergens just as Urticaria can be an allergic reaction. The allergic aggressive reaction can be eliminated by removing the allergens from the individual's environment and reinstated by once again challenging the patient with the offending substance.

A precipitous drop in blood sugar may produce a pathological proclivity for aggressive behavior in some individuals which can be dramatically and immediately alleviated by restoring the blood sugar level to normal. Because the tendency to hypoglycemia affects a small but significant number of individuals in the total population, this dysfunction may be of some practical importance.

There is unequivocal evidence that a large number of drugs can profoundly influence the tendency to hostility. The threshold for aggressive behavior tendencies can be reduced in some individuals by alcohol, the amphetamines, and paradoxically by Librium and Valium. Although no drug is a completely specific antiaggression agent, there are now quite a few that have an antiaggression component in their therapeutic spectrum. These drugs include the phenothiazines, diphenyl-hydantonin, haloperidol, lithium, and in many individuals, chlordiazepoxide and diazepam as well as the other benzodiazepines and will be covered later.

# CHAPTER
# V

# Disorders Producing
# Aggression Facilitation

There are a large number of disorders of the human brain that result in hostility malfunctions, from chronic irritability to pathological homicidal rage. There are a variety of disorders that involve generalized damage to the central nervous system, including cerebral arteriosclerosis, senile dementia, Korsakoff's Syndrome,* and Huntington's chorea.** These dysfunctions frequently present a common symptomatology referred to as chronic brain syndrome, which is characterized by memory deficit, orientation loss, and affective disturbances. There are wide fluctuations of mood and a general emotional instability, but the affective pattern is dominated by anger, rage, and increased irritability.[365]

Diffuse brain lesions may produce personality changes that include loss of impulse control with increases in irritability. In some instances it is possible to specify the area damaged; in

---

*This is a disorder characterized by hallucinations, loss of memory, and imaginary reminiscences. It frequently involves marked agitation. This syndrome is frequently found in chronic alcoholics.
**Huntington's Chorea is an hereditary disorder of a chronic nature that usually occurs between the ages of 30 and 50 years. It is characterized by irregular, spasmodic movements of the limbs and facial muscles. It is accompanied by a gradual loss of mental capacity, and a generalized hyper-irritability.

others the trauma may be diffuse. Head injuries caused by falls or automobile accidents frequently result in loss of consciousness. As the individual regains consciousness he goes through a period of uncontrolled violence and aggression towards those around him.[377] The behavior of children is particularly affected by injury to the brain. The child's personality may show a complete reversal; the child may change from a lovable youngster to one that is antisocial and unmanageable. Such children show emotional instability with a characteristic unrestrained aggressiveness and a lack of impulse control They may be cruel and show such asocial behaviors as lying and stealing.[56,302,559]

The cry "mad dog" has always meant that a dog is loose that will attack anyone or anything that crosses its path. The dog has no restraint on its aggressive behavior and its selection of victims is indiscriminate. If the animal bites and infects a human and the disease process is not blocked by rabies vaccine, the sequels may involve bizarre behavior changes, which may include excesses in sexuality, alcoholism, and violent rages involving irrational assaults. During the terminal stages of the disease the patient manifests extreme irritability and is subject to pronounced spasms of the throat muscles, which cause excruciating pain. The spasms are precipitated by any attempt to drink water, with the result that the patient refuses all fluids in spite of severe thirst, thus the name hydrophobia. Death occurs within three to five days from exhaustion, general paralysis or asphyxia.

Rabies (derived from the Latin word meaning "rage") is caused by a filterable virus transmitted to the victim in the saliva of the infected animal. Being neurotrophic, it travels up the peripheral nerves to the spinal cord and then to the brain. The entire brain is affected to some extent in that nerve cells are damaged and there is a generalized fluid build-up in the brain and particularly in the mengies, the membrane around the brain, with multiple minute hemorrhages. As might be suspected from the behavioral symptoms, there is a particular involvement of the limbic system* with damage most extensive in the *temporal lobe* (2-5).

The evidence from the victims of rabies implies that there are neural systems for rage behavior and that the virus provides an irritative focus that produces the activation of those neuron complexes with the resultant hyper-aggressivity. It seems remarkable that the rabies virus not only has an affinity for the

---

*The limbic system consists of a series of brain structures including the amygdala (4-5 & 6-3), hippocampus (6-4), and portions of the hypothalamus as well as other parts of the brain. It has been proposed that the limbic system underlies emotional feelings and thus influences emotional behavior.

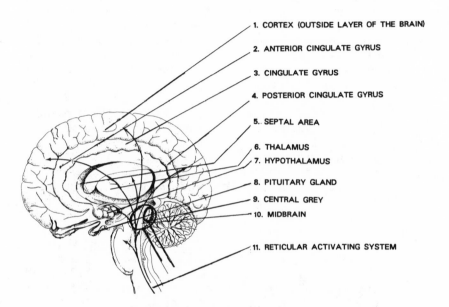

1. CORTEX (OUTSIDE LAYER OF THE BRAIN)

2. ANTERIOR CINGULATE GYRUS

3. CINGULATE GYRUS

4. POSTERIOR CINGULATE GYRUS

5. SEPTAL AREA

6. THALAMUS

7. HYPOTHALAMUS

8. PITUITARY GLAND

9. CENTRAL GREY

10. MIDBRAIN

11. RETICULAR ACTIVATING SYSTEM

FIGURE 3. *Section through the middle of the brain from front to rear.*

nervous system, but has a particular tendency to infect that specific part of the nervous system that is related to aggressiveness. Although the specificity is far from perfect, it is sufficient to suggest that there is considerable potential for the development of pharmacological agents that may be used in the precise manipulation of certain types of hostile behavior in humans.

In Romania in 1915 a few cases of encephalitis lethargica, or sleeping sickness, began to appear. The disease rapidly spread to other countries and became a worldwide epidemic by 1924. A part of the symptomalogy of this disorder frequently included a radical change in personality characterized by a loss of impulse control, including violent displays of temper. After the acute phase of the disease process, about fifty-four percent of the patients who showed mental symptoms continued to manifest them, frequently for prolonged periods.[630] The behavior disorder was most common in children between the ages of three and ten. Not uncommonly, the personality change occurred prior to the onset of identifiable neurological symptoms. The conduct disorder sometimes occurred immediately after the acute infection but was at times delayed for a period of months or even years. Brill[77] gives a good description of the characteristics of these children.

> They showed a marked destructiveness and impulsiveness, with a tendency to carry primitive impulses into headlong action. Children who had previously been normally behaved would lie, steal, destroy property, set fires, and commit various sexual offenses, without thought of punishment. The motivation was less comprehensible and less subject to immediate control than in the so-called psychopathies, but the capacity for real remorse was strikingly well retained. There was marked instability of emotion which, coupled with disinhibition of action, led to serious aggression, usually against others, but occasionally against the patient himself, resulting in gruesome self-mutilation (p. 1167).

The following case study is illustrative of this syndrome:

Roy was admitted to the Child Guidance Home in February 1927, at the age of 13 years. It was stated that the boy had been a behavior problem for two and one-half years. . . . There were 4 siblings, 3 boys and 1 girl, all in good health and all doing well at school. They presented no behavior problems. The developmental history showed that Roy's birth and early development had been normal. He had had chickenpox, measles, and whooping cough. The ages at which he contracted these were not

76

stated. The boy had an attack of acute epidemic encephalitis at 9 years of age.

At the Child Guidance Home the physical examination disclosed no significant abnormality, but there were positive neurologic findings in the form of Pyramidal tract changes. The boy had an intelligence quotient of 122. From the moment he entered the Child Guidance Home it was noted that he was extremely difficult to control. He was impulsive, egocentric, depressed and suspicious. He exhibited violent temper tantrums during which he was unmanageable. His emotional instability was pronounced. The children obviously annoyed him and he did not hesitate to bite pieces out of their arms and legs when he became angry. There was no one with whom he could get along. He was extremely irritable and had a serious sex problem. He ran away five and six times a day. There was no way of appealing to him or obtaining his cooperation. He did as he pleased and did not hesitate to destroy or injure anything or anyone in his path. He had unusual physical strength and on one occasion tore a tie off of one of the children. In forcibly removing the tie he almost choked the boy. On the other hand, there were times when Roy appeared to be tractable and affectionate. At such times he would put his arms around anyone at the Home and act in a tender and loving manner, but a moment later his mood would change and he would try to injure the object of his former affection. Such bizarre behavior as plucking hair from a child's head or sticking another with pins was of frequent occurrence. He could not be left alone with the other children, and because of his unusual physical strength no adult person at the Home was able to handle him alone. The children were in mortal terror of him. In psychiatric interviews, contacts were on an extremely superficial level because of the boy's apprehensiveness, antagonism and unwillingness or inability to respond. Attempts to reassure him and to get him into a more responsive frame of mind were unsuccessful. In most of the interviews he refused to answer at all and would sit with his head in his lap. Occasionally he spoke about his family. He was bothered about the poor economic conditions in his home. He felt that his mother did not have enough money to take care of the family properly. He showed many fears, particularly of the laboratory tests. There was no evidence of delusions or hallucinations.

It was felt that the boy had had an attack of lethargic encephalitis with resultant psychiatric disturbances, principally in the sphere of volition. It was recommended that he be institutionalized. The parents were both ununderstanding and uncooperative, and made no attempt to carry out the recommendation. A year later the mother reported that the boy had been committed to the boys' industrial school (a state correctional institution) as a result of conviction on a charge of assault and battery. The boy's record at the industrial school was bad. He did not adjust in any way. He was paroled in March 1929 and returned to his home. A short time later he was arrested and sent to a state hospital for the mentally ill, where the same diagnosis as that given at the Child Guidance Home was made. Later in that year, another report from the hospital stated that he had become much more difficult, was quarreling with the other patients, attacking them and threatening every one with assault. In October 1931, the state hospital reported that Roy was home on trial visit. He was attending classes in high school However, after being home for eight months, he had to be returned to the hospital because the family could not control him. Each year Roy's behavior has become more difficult. In January 1946, at the age of 32, he was still in the state hospital; here it was reported that his behavior was both bizarre and unpredictable. His intelligence quotient was still 122.[231]

Similar behavior problems appeared in adults who contracted the disease but the symptoms were not as intense. The impulsive-aggressive behavior has a peculiar compulsive quality to it, as though the individual is *driven* to his hostile action. The patient's conduct is particularly distressing to him because, as with the children, the adult retains his capacity for remorse and is capable of adequate and insightful self-criticism.

When the neurological signs do appear, they are most characteristically of the Parkinsonian type, including tremor, rigidity, and masklike face. The onset of symptoms is slow and insidious and once started tend to progress in an irregular fashion. Brill[77] suggests that the syndrome characteristic of chronic encephalitis lethargica differs from that brought about by the residual damage caused by other encephalitic disorders in that the symptoms are more diffuse and are relatively fixed. With chronic encephalitis lethargica, there are clinical and pathological indications of a chronic and progressive inflammation.

The neural damage from encephalitis lethargica, although more localized and specific than that found in other encephalitic disorders, is still rather diffuse and it has not been possible to relate particular behavioral symptoms to the brain area damaged. The *hypothalamus* (3-7 & Fig. 5), *midbrain* (3-10), and brain stem (particularly in the area of the *central gray matter* (3-9) generally sustain neuron loss.[77] The *temporal lobes* (2-5) are also frequently involved.[277] The *basal ganglia* (Fig. 4) and the substantia nigra are also damaged, which accounts for the Parkinsonian symptoms.[77]

Such a diffuse pattern of neuron necrosis tells us little about the specific neural mechanisms that underlie aggression in humans. It should be noted, however, that the *temporal lobe* (2-5), the *hypothalamus* (Fig. 5 & 3-7), and the *midbrain* (3-10) are involved and have been shown to be important in the neural circuitry of aggression in lower animals. The characteristic behavior patterns could result from the activation of the hostility systems by the inflammatory process or the loss of neurons in the neural systems that function to suppress activity in the aggression systems once it is started. The impulsive, compulsive aspects of the behavior appear to make the latter interpretation plausible.

An interesting side note is that individuals with encephalitic syndrome are frequently misdiagnosed as having functional psychiatric disorders. Such was the case in seven of eight cases reported by Himmelhoch et al.[277]

Epilepsy is a disorder involving abnormal spontaneous activations of various neural systems in the brain. It is not a disease entity but a symptom of nervous system dysfunction. The etiology of epilepsy is highly varied and may be the result of brain trauma, cerebral circulation defects, various poisons, birth injury, metabolic disorders, or brain tumors. In about two-thirds of the cases, no specific cause can be determined and it is therefore referred to as idiopathic. The classification usually used for epileptic disorders includes *grand mal, petit mal,* and *psychomotor* or *temporal lobe epilepsy.*[388] Grand mal involves the characteristic convulsion in which the patient falls to the floor in a fit of generalized muscular contractions and loss of consciousness. The seizure is usually followed by a period of confusion, drowsiness and amnesia for the seizure period. Petit mal is characterized by a temporary loss of consciousness in which the individual may stare straight ahead and automatically repeat the acts in which he was engaged at the time of the attack. There is no major muscle involvement. Psychomotor epilepsy, which is the most common form in adults,[611] usually includes more subjective experiences, dream states, depressive seizures, and paroxysmal behavior disorders. One reason for the higher incidence of psychomotor epilepsy is the higher probability of brain damage in automobile accidents in which the brain is banged against the temporal portion of the skull.

Since epilepsy is an indication of some brain damage it is not surprising that one finds a higher percentage of behavior disorders in some types of epilepsy. There is now considerable literature on this topic that has been reviewed by others.[55,99,131,292,401] Although there are some studies that take exception,[532,553] it has generally been concluded that individuals manifesting temporal lobe epilepsy show a higher percentage of personality disorders than do persons with other types.

The behavior of the temporal lobe epileptic may vary from periodic irritability to catastrophic rage. An example of the latter is given below.

CASE. At about age 2 this girl had two or three generalized "spasms" followed by sleep. At age 4 she was thrown against a wall by her alcoholic father, suffering a bruise to the right side of her head. Father left the family one year later. At age 6 she began to suffer from very sporadic generalized seizures. In spite of bad family situation she had maintained a good disposition. It was only after the onset of the epilepsy that she changed: for the slightest reasons, she would become mean, foul-mouthed and assaultive. She threw things at her mother, would bite her, attacked her sisters with scissors, beat up peers with a baseball bat and lead pipe. Initially, she had been apologetic for her outbursts (which she recalled), but by age 9, when there were almost daily rages, she didn't seem to care. She was also hyperkinetic. Because of the finding of an atrophic lesion in the right temporal lobe with adjoining spike focus, a right temporal lobectomy was performed at age 10, in spite of the rarity of her seizures. The rage ceased promptly, and no further seizures occurred (p. 211).[368]

One might expect a variety of dysfunctions, depending on where the damage is in the temporal lobe and which neural systems in the brain are activated by the epileptic process. Although our concern is with the deviations in aggressive behavior, it should be noted that other problems also occur, although much less frequently, in the sexual sphere. Epstein[171] summarized some of the literature on disordered sexual behavior associated with temporal lobe dysfunction. Case reports are available on patients who experience sexual activity and sexual sensations in association with seizures.[121] Hyposexuality is most commonly reported as being associated with temporal lobe epilepsy. It can be alleviated, if not converted into hypersexuality, by temporal lobe surgery.[61,609]

It is certainly true that temporal lobe epilepsy is not necessarily accompanied by an increased tendency to impulsiveness and hostility or any other disorder.

It has to be emphasized that many patients become not aggressive but merely impatient, easily angered and contrary on certain days, some time after onset of the temporal lobe attacks. Others show not the slightest trace of irritability. If temporal lobe patients are approached with patience and consideration, they will almost invariably respond good-naturedly and will be very cooperative.

There are a number of reports that disclaim any relationships between epilepsy and aggression or crime.[132,349] However, most of the evidence on the subject supports the contention that there is a significantly greater probability that disorders of impulse control and aggressiveness will be found in the population of temporal lobe epileptics than in a normal population.

Ictal rage* does occur but it is less common than either fear or depression.[614,626] Rage is most likely to occur as an ictal emotion when the recorded EEG discharges are from the anterior temporal regions.[627] It is, however, relatively rare for ictal rage to be converted into effective aggressive behavior. During the seizure state and the period of confusion that usually follows it, the individual is sufficiently disorganized that attack behavior usually occurs only if the patient is restrained and in his confusional state misinterprets these attempts at restraint.[132,401] Monroe[401] describes a case in which a father attempted to loosen the belt of a patient during a seizure. The boy jumped up and began to beat the father and indiscriminately break up the furniture.

It occasionally happens that the seizure is relatively prolonged and the patient engages in what has been described as "automatic behavior." During this period the individual may engage in a variety of actions in a mechanical, unmotivated, or driven manner and generally shows amnesia for the period. The patient may then awaken in a portion of the city strange to him and have no memory for how he got there or what actions he may have been involved in during the forgotten period. In some cases that ictal behavior may involve considerable aggression or even homicide. Although a number of cases have now been reported and reasonably well verified,[75,151,187,238,366,608] ictal homicide actually appears to be quite rare. Gunn and Fenton[238] concluded that "automatic behavior is a rare explanation for the crimes of epileptic patients."

Although well-directed ictal aggression is a relatively rare phenomenon, there is abundant evidence that uncontrolled, impulsive, assaultive behavior is not uncommon as an interictal behavior pattern, particularly among temporal lobe epileptics. Gastaut[208] concludes that the "psychomotor epileptic behaves, in the interval between his fits, like an animal presenting a state

---

*Ictal emotion or behavior is that which accompanies an actual seizure or massive discharges recordable with scalp electrodes.

of continuous rhinencephalic* excitation, and during his fits, like an animal presenting a paroxysmal rhinencephalic discharge." In describing the behavior difficulties that psychomotor epileptics display during the interval between fits, Gastaut says, "Subjects become impulsive, aggressive and inclined to angry violent reactions, sometimes dangerous. Sometimes perverse character traits associated with sensitiveness and hypocrisy render them unsupportable in their social milieu and even in their family".[209]

Falconer et al.,[183] reporting on fifty patients, indicated that thirty-eight percent of them showed spontaneous outbursts of aggression. Psychomotor epilepsy is the most difficult to control with medication and seizure control is ineffective in about thirty percent of the cases. About half of those patients develop destructive behavior and paroxysmal bursts of anger as a part of a behavior disorder.[499] Glaser et al.,[214] also indicate that impulsive, aggressive, and unstable states characterize some of their psychomotor patients. The aggressiveness noted in patients afflicted with temporal lobe epilepsy has a peculiar aspect to it. Outbursts of anger, abusiveness, and assaultiveness occur with little or no provocation and contrast with the patient's usual good-natured behavior. The change is abrupt and striking [609]. Serafetinides[514] indicates that aggressive behavior was the most common interictal behavior pattern in temporal lobe epilepsy and among one hundred consecutive temporal lobe epileptics selected for temporal lobe surgery, thirty-six displayed overt physical aggression.[513] He also concludes that aggression is more common among younger patients whereas depression is more common among older patients.

Among children showing temporal lobe epilepsy, there is a high incidence of aggressive behavior.[305,437] Ounsted[440] reported that thirty-six of one hundred children with psychomotor epilepsy that had been followed for a decade showed outbursts of catastrophic rage.

It is important to emphasize that the subjects in the preceding studies were from a highly selected population of individuals with epilepsy. They were, in general, persons who had been committed to an institution or were candidates for surgery. There are, of course, thousands of epileptics who are making an adequate adjustment in the real world and do not suffer from personality disturbances, impulsiveness, or uncontrolled aggressive tendencies. The individuals with very serious antisocial tendencies are removed from society and institutionalized. It is

---

*Refers to the lower brain.

thus possible for studies that involve those patients remaining in society to show no more criminal or antisocial behaviors than are found in the rest of the population.[132,349] Whether a patient manifests a lack of hostility control may depend on whether or not the spontaneous neural activity resulting from the lesion involves the neural systems for aggression. Another possibility, as suggested previously in another connection, is that there is damage to those neural systems that are important in the inhibition or suppression of the neural systems for aggression. In addition, there is necessarily an interaction between the dysfunction in the central nervous system, the learning experiences, and the rest of the environmental input. Except in extreme cases that involve massive output from the hostility systems, the individual is subject to the same kinds of socialization and inhibitory training as is the rest of the population. However, because of the lower thresholds or increased spontaneous activity of those brain mechanisms that bring on irritability or rage, socialization training is less effective. This may be another way of stating the thesis of Taylor,[566] who suggests that the important variable involved in the hyper-aggressiveness of epileptic patients is the damage to the structures necessary to learn adequate controls, and Keating's position[305] that behavior disorders of epileptic children result largely from their reaction to environment and handling.

## Brain Tumors

As tumors of the brain grow, they may produce the intermittent activation of braincells in the immediate area. Ultimately, of course, the normal cells in the area of the tumor are destroyed. The symptomatology of brain tumors varies widely. Headache, nausea, and vomiting generally result from an increase in intracranial pressure. In many, the symptoms are apathy and somnolence. However, there are also a wide variety of psychological symptoms, ranging from hallucinations to an impairment of mental faculties and psychotic episodes. When various portions of the limbic lobe are involved, changes in personality and in affect frequently occur, and may result in disorders of emotional expression and fundamental motivational states. The patient may have inappropriate bouts of laughter, euphoria, or depression. He or she may become hyperphagic (excessive eating) or anorexic (self-starving) and manifest hypo- or hypersexual behaviors. Of interest here is the well-documented evidence that a frequent behavioral result of limbic system tumors is an increase in irritability, temper outbursts, and even homicidal attacks of rage.[316] The resulting personality changes are frequently completely out of keeping with the individual's behavior patterns prior to the onset of the pathological state.

Malamud [369] describes nine cases of confirmed tumors in the *temporal lobe* (2-5) that showed psychiatric symptoms. Three of these patients showed increased tension and aggressive behavior, ranging from intense sibling rivalry to unpredictable assaultive tendencies. Two violent patients with tumors of the temporal lobe are described by Sweet et al.[563] One man, a powerful individual, attempted to kill his wife and daughter with a butcher knife. When brought to the hospital, he was in a full-blown rage reaction, during which he snarled, showed his teeth, and attempted to hit or kick anyone who came close enough. History-taking revealed that over a period of six months, his personality had gradually changed and that he had complained of blurred vision and intense headaches. When the tumor that was pressing on the *anterior temporal lobe* (2-5) was removed, his symptoms rapidly abated. Another patient who had shown hyperirritability for years began to show destructive rages. He drove his car recklessly and began to direct his outbursts of rage against his wife and son. Although intellectually capable as a chemist, he was unable to hold a position for longer than a few months because of his volatile and irritable behavior patterns. After the removal of a slow-growing tumor that had evidently invaded the *temporal lobe* (2-5) over a period of several years, his symptoms disappeared. He became stable, more placid, and functioned adequately as a chemist during the nineteen-month follow-up. Vonderahe[605] describes the onset of sudden outbursts of aggression in a female patient who, upon autopsy, was found to have a tumor the size of a cherry on the anterior and inner aspect of the left (2-5) *temporal lobe* encroaching on the *amygdala* (4-5).

Temporal lobe lesions, including tumors, may also result in paroxysmal symptoms that include various affective disturbances and automatisms in which the patient carries out "automatic" activities in a state of impaired consciousness. During this period he is apparently able to make decisions and is not amenable to reason. The individual may continue to drive his car and engage in other activities at an automatic level and yet show amnesia for his behavior during the period of the fuguelike state. During the period of the automatisms the patient may engage in highly destructive behavior, breaking furniture and assaulting others.[415]

One of the most celebrated cases of extreme hostility that may have resulted from temporal lobe pathology was that of Charles Whitman. It is particularly instructive because he recognized his impulses to violence, was concerned about them, and sought help from a psychiatrist. He was also an introspective young man who kept extensive notes in an attempt to understand his own obviously pathological motivations. He was also concerned that others understand his behavior so that individuals with problems similar to his could get help before it was too late. One letter, which was started before he killed his wife and his mother and finished after the double murder, provides some insight into the thought processes of an individual whose mental world is governed in part by what appears to be excessive activation of the neural systems for hostility.

I don't quite understand what it is that compels me to type this letter. Perhaps it is to leave some vague reason for the actions I have recently performed.

I don't really understand myself these days. I am supposed to be an average, reasonable and intelligent young man. However, lately (I can't recall when it started) I have been a victim of many unusual and irrational thoughts. These thoughts constantly recur, and it requires a tremendous mental effort to concentrate on useful and progressive tasks. In March when my parents made a physical break I noticed a great deal of stress. I consulted a Dr. Cochrum at the University Health Center and asked him to recommend someone that I could consult with about some psychiatric disorders I felt I had. I talked with a doctor once for about two hours and tried to convey to him my fears that I felt overcome [sic] by overwhelming violent impulses. After one session I never saw the doctor again and since then I have been fighting my mental turmoil alone, and seemingly to no avail. After my death I wish that an autopsy would be performed on me to see if there is any visible physical disorder. I have had some tremendous headaches in the past and have consumed two large bottles of Excedrin in the past three months.

It was after much thought that I decided to kill my wife Kathy, tonight after I pick her up from work . . . I love her dearly, and she has been a fine wife to me as any man could ever hope to have. I cannot rationally pinpoint any specific reason for doing this. I don't know whether it is selfishness or if I don't want her to have to face the embarrassment my actions would surely cause her. At this time, though, the prominent reason in my mind is that I truly do not consider this world worth living in, and am prepared to die, and I do not want to leave her to suffer alone in it. I intend to kill her as painlessly as possible . . .

Later in the night he killed both his mother and his wife, and then wrote;

I imagine it appears that I brutally killed both of my loved ones. I was only trying to do a good and thorough job.

If my life insurance policy is valid please see that all the worthless checks I wrote this weekend are made good. Please pay off all my debts. I am 25 years old and have never been financially independent. Donate the rest anonymously to a mental health foundation. Maybe research can prevent further tragedies of this type (p. 79).[291]

During his consultation with the psychiatrist several months earlier, Whitman had revealed that he sometimes became so angry that he would like to go to the top of the university tower and start shooting people. The morning after having written the preceding letter, he did just that. He took a high-powered rifle with a telescopic sight and several hundred rounds of ammunition to the tower. He killed the receptionist, barricaded the door, and spent ninety minutes shooting anyone he could bring into his powerful sight. He was a good marksman. When he was finally killed by the police he had wounded twenty-four and killed fourteen innocent people. Autopsy revealed that Whitman had a malignant infiltrating tumor (glioblastoma multiforme). Because there was extensive damage to the brain from gun shot wounds, the neuropathologist was not certain of the precise location of the tumor, but it was probably in the medial part of one *temporal lobe* (2-5).

It is not possible to determine after the fact whether the temporal lobe malignancy actually caused the extreme aggression displayed by Whitman. Valenstein[601] concludes that it is unlikely because Whitman's actions were planned and not typical of a burst of impulsive rage characteristic of the dyscontrol syndrome. That is, of course, true, but it is beside the point. The Whitman case is, in fact, more typical of the progressive effects of expanding tumors. As indicated in other parts of this section, the change in the individual's personality may occur over a period of years. In some instances the only symptom is an increase in irritability. As the tumor growth progresses, the patient may become more and more irritable and ultimately homicidal. There are now a significant number of cases in which progressive irrational aggression of several years duration has been alleviated by the removal of a limbic tumor.

Tumors in other areas of the limbic system also result in excessive irritable behavior and rage responses that are not characteristic of the patient's normal personality and that he does not understand. Tension, ambivalence, negativism, and hostility characterized one patient with a tumor that involved primarily the white matter of the *cingulate gyrus* (3-3). Another with tumor damage in the *cingulate gyrus* (3-3) and left *frontal lobe* (2-1) was described as having had attacks of assaultiveness and convulsions. Between attacks, as the tumor progressed, he became increasingly irritable and abusive.[369]

Zeman and King[643] report a number of cases in which tumors of the septal region (3-5) result in restlessness and irritability with some maniacal outbursts. These patients showed an excessive startle reaction, temper "flare-ups," and irrational assaultiveness. One became homicidal, attempted to stab her husband with a paring knife, and threatened to poison him. *Frontal lobe tumors* (2-1) also result in pathological affect. Over half of one series of eighty-five patients with frontal lobe tumors had affective disturbances and the most frequent change was in the direction of increased irritability. In many cases it was the first and in some it was the only mental symptom during the course of the disease. Some of the patients reported to being "raging."[557,558]

Finally, as might be expected from our knowledge of the neural systems involved in aggressive behavior in animals, tumors in the *hypothalamus* (Fig. 5 & 3–7) result in a facilitation of hostile impulses. Alpers[9] reports a case of tumor in the third ventricle area around the hypothalamus that resulted in damage to the *anterior hypothalamus* (5-6); in this case the patient's character changed radically and became very aggressive. About a year prior to the other tumor symptoms he became irritable, aggressive, argumentative, and unreasonable. He frequently flew into rages over trivial matters. Reeves and Blum[462] have recently reported a case in which the *ventromedial hypothalamus* (5-7) was destroyed by a rapidly growing tumor, which resulted in manifestations of many of the symptoms found when similar lesions are made in animals. The patient developed overeating, became obese, and had a very low threshold for aggression. At times she would become uncooperative and hostile without apparent reason and would hit, scratch, and attempt to bite the examiner. Subsequently, she would sometimes express regret for her unprovoked hostility. A similar case is reported by Killeffer and Stern[311,552] Sano[485] has reported on 1800 cases of brain tumor of which 297 were in the limbic region. He concluded that increased irritability and rage attacks characterized patients with tumor involvements in the *anterior hypothalamus* (5-6).

The evidence from brain tumors demonstrates again that the neural systems for aggression in humans can be activated by internal physiological processes that result in the individual feeling and behaving in an inappropriate, hostile manner. As with other neurological dysfunctions, the behavior could result from the neurological mechanisms for aggression, or it could result from the destruction of inhibitory mechanisms. It is not yet possible in any given case to separate these two mechanisms.

## Aggression and the Abnormal EEG

The nerve cells of the brain, when they are functioning, generate electrical impulses. These shifts in voltage can be recorded by the electroencephalograph. When a normal individual is sitting quietly, thinking about nothing in particular, the brain waves occur at a rate of about eight to thirteen times per second. These are called alpha waves. When the subject begins to concentrate on something, the alpha waves disappear and are replaced by beta waves which occur at a rate of about fourteen to thirty-two cycles per second and have a smaller amplitude. A number of other brain waves have been identified, including the delta wave, associated with deep sleep, the theta wave that relates to pleasure and displeasure, particularly in children. The kappa wave has been found in about thirty percent of the population and is related to thinking.

There is considerable variability between the brain waves of individuals, and in the same individual when the records are made at different times. In spite of this variability, it is possible to discern some pathological characteristics in the EEG, but it must be remembered that EEG records may differentiate between groups of individuals and yet, some of the subjects in the control group may have records similar to the pathological group, and vice versa.

Many studies have now been published which purport to show that individuals manifesting a variety of behavior disorders, particularly aggression are significantly more likely to have an abnormal EEG than does the general population.[166] Abnormal tracings can take the form of spikes, i.e., sudden, brief, large amplitude tracings, particularly in the temporal lobe, and in the areas below the cortex. Normal alpha or beta waves may be beyond the normal range in terms of cycles per second and in terms of amplitude. Although there is considerable disagreement on the details and the interpretation of the findings, it can be concluded that individuals manifesting a variety of behavior disorders, particularly aggression, are significantly more likely to have an abnormal EEG than does the general population.[166] (Also see the review by Bonkalo.)[65]

88

# Abnormal EEG and Behavior Disorders in Children

A number of studies show that children with behavior disorders are more likely to have an abnormal EEG that may reflect a diffuse brain pathology. From five to fifteen percent of normal children show a variety of EEG abnormalities, but fifty to sixty percent of those with behavior disorders have abnormal records.[401] In a study of two hundred problem children, Bayrakal[48] found one hundred with normal EEG tracings. Among the disturbed behaviors that correlated with the abnormal EEGs were poor impulse control, inadequate social adaptation, and hostility. The overwhelming majority of the abnormal records were found in the *temporal lobe* (2-5) and the subcortical regions. One hundred disturbed children whose principal symptoms were hyperactivity, temper tantrums, destructive behavior, aggressiveness, and antisocial behavior were studied by Aird and Yamamoto.[3] Forty-nine percent had abnormal EEG records and sixty-seven percent of those abnormalities had a temporal lobe focus.

Gross and Wilson[237] suggest that an EEG should be taken routinely on all children who manifest behavior disorders and learning problems. They found over half of the children referred to a suburban psychiatric clinic had abnormal EEGs. Forty-five of the children, although they showed no tendency to seizures, were given anticonvulsants as their only treatment; half of them showed significant improvement, and ten of the cases showed dramatic improvement.

Although temporal and subcortical foci are most frequently reported to be associated with the aggressive-behavior disorders, Cohn and Nardini[111] describe an abnormality of the occipital focus. The abnormal waves were bilateral, slow, and synchronous and were found in young adults who were hostile, hypercritical, irritable, nonconforming, and lacking in adequate impulse control. Treffert[588] found that psychiatric patients with EEG abnormalities in the temporal lobe but without overt epilepsy tended to be combative with rage episodes and paroxysmal symptoms in the form of blackouts and hallucinations. Control subjects with a matched diagnosis, however, tended to have disorders of thought.

The diagnosis "psychopath" tends to be a catchall category and is sufficiently ambiguous that some investigators tend to avoid it.[628] However, several studies have shown that individuals given that diagnosis are far more inclined to show EEG abnormalities.[211,272,273,276,418,527] Whereas only fifteen percent of normals have abnormal EEGs, forty-eight percent of the psychopathic group had abnormalities. When the aggressive psychopaths were differentiated from those classed as inadequate, sixty-five percent of the aggressives showed abnormalities but only thirty-two percent of the inadequate subjects did.[276]

Most of the psychopaths studied either were prisoners or had criminal records, and there is general agreement that prisoners, in general, show more EEG abnormalities than the rest of the population.[319] Studies of juvenile delinquents in Japan have shown that EEG abnormalities are markedly higher in them than in the general population.[16,641] The abnormal patterns showing theta waves in the delinquents were directly correlated with tendencies to habitual violence.[641] Jenkins and Pacella[288] concluded that delinquency per se was not related to EEG abnormalities but that habitual aggressiveness was. Abnormal tracings were more frequently found in delinquents with assaultive tendencies showing emotional instability, irritability, and poor impulse control.

In one study of sixty-four English murderers, it was found that only one of eleven who killed in self-defense, or incidentally in the commission of another crime, had an abnormal EEG. However, seventy-three percent of those individuals who committed murder without apparent motive showed electroencephalographic abnormalities.[548] In another study of thirty-two insane murderers, the EEG records were read "blind" and compared with control subjects who were not patients. The incidence of abnormal records in the murderers was four times that of the control group.[642]

An extensive study of the EEGs of criminals in the London area was carried out by Dennis Williams.[628] He selected a sample of 333 subjects at random from his total population of 1250 criminally aggressive subjects who had been referred to him by prison officials during the past twenty years. He then compared the records of those individuals who were habitually aggressive with those who had committed a single major violent crime. Sixty-five percent of the records of the habitual aggressives were abnormal, but abnormalities were found in twenty-four percent of the second group. Williams places the percentage of abnormalities in the general population at twelve percent. When the records of individuals who were mentally retarded, or had had a major head injury, or were epileptic, were removed, the percentage of abnormalities among those subjects who had committed a solitary violent crime of major proportions was the same as that of the general population. However, the *habitual* aggressives still showed fifty-seven percent abnormalities. In sixty-four percent of the habitually aggressive subjects the abnormalities were bilateral. The *temporal lobes* (2-5) were affected in all the hyperaggressives, and over eighty percent manifested rhythms known to be associated with temporal lobe dysfunction.

## Interpretation of Data on Abnormal EEG and Aggression

Although the preceding evidence is, in general, mutually support-ive, it should be mentioned that some investigators have not found the relationship between abnormalities in the electroen-cephalographic record and aggressive tendencies.[20,320] This probably reflects, at least in some measure, difficulties in defini-tion of both aggression and EEG abnormalities. However, at best the EEG has very little prognostic value in regard to aggressive behavior. As the preceding statistics indicate, there are far too many false negatives and false positives for the EEG to have much predictive value. The various types of behaviors manifested by juvenile delinquents cannot be discriminated on the basis of the EEG record.[531] Gibbens et al.[211] found that the abnormal EEG in criminal psychopaths did not, in general, give any indication of the prognosis for recidivism. However, as indicated previously, the EEG may be useful in predicting which individuals might benefit from some type of anticonvulsant medication.[237]

The relationship between abnormalities in the EEG, and ag-gressiveness and crime in general, is open to various interpreta-tions. It might be hypothesized that the abnormalities reflect brain damage that directly affects the neural systems for aggres-sion so that spontaneous activation occurs in the system with the resultant acting out of hostile impulses. Or there may be damage to the brain mechanisms for aggression, so that the aggressive behavior threshold is functionally lowered. The abnormalities may also indicate a generally lowered level of neurological competence, with the result that the individual is unable to cope with the usual demands of society and resorts to criminal behavior as an adjustive mode.

The mechanisms may be even more indirect. The brain dam-age implied by the irregularities in the EEG may result in a very low tolerance for frustration that makes the individual more prone to hostile action and subsequent incarceration. Further-more, there is no reason to believe that the several interpretations offered above are mutually exclusive either across individuals or for any given individual. Finally, it should be recognized that any of the preceding dysfunctions interact with the individual's environment and the type of inhibitory training he has received. The possible neurological limitations previously indicated are neither a necessary nor a sufficient cause for criminal behavior. In most studies approximately half of the deviant populations investigated show no indication of abnormal EEG tracings. Obviously, anyone with a normal, adequately functioning brain can acquire any of these behavior deviations through learning. Moreover, a nonstressful, supportive, sheltered environment can protect the brain-damaged individual from environmental situations that are likely to provoke criminal activity. Thus, any interpretation must take into account the many possible interactions among the various etiological agents.

## Episodic Dyscontrol

There are also significant numbers of individuals who for a variety of reasons have episodic loss of control over their impulses to aggression and destructiveness. The etiology of many of the cases of episodic hostile behavior has been discussed above and include such factors as epilepsy, various other brain dysfunctions, endocrine disturbances, allergies, hypoglycemia, and some pathological reactions to drugs. In many cases, however, there are no obvious physiological pathologies.[344,401] Charles Whitman, whose case has been discussed in some detail earlier, may have behaved aggressively because of a brain tumor. However, Whitman has counterparts in many universities and, of course, in the rest of society. These are globally hostile individuals who have homicidal impulses and the means to carry out their threats with firearms. This behavioral pattern is now being referred to as the Whitman syndrome. Kuehn and Burton[326] provide three cases with this syndrome and recommendations on how they should be handled. These three individuals were globally hostile ("pissed off at the world"; hated all people, particularly those in authority; fantasized shooting people from the university carillon tower, "just for the hell of it"). They were also paranoid, in the process of losing their control, and had the means (access to firearms) to act on their homicidal impulses. Fortunately, they had come to the counseling service (as had Charles Whitman) for help because of their fears of loss of impulse controls. These three students were seen in a relatively short time at a university of 16,000 full-time students and led the authors to conclude that there are "numerous severely disturbed and potentially dangerous people in a large university setting," as well as those in the non-university.

A significant number of people in the non–university setting also have violent, sometimes homicidal impulses. They have sufficient concern about their impulsive behavior to seek help. Frequently they are unable to get help from their physicians or from the hospital emergency room. This type of patient is discussed in detail in John Lion's book *Evaluation and Manage-*

*ment of the Violent Patient* (1972), and in a series of papers by Lion and his colleagues.[346,347]

Ervin provides a case study of an individual who might be classed as having episodic dyscontrol.

> . . . he would eventually come in one day and say something like, "Well, this is one of those weeks when it blew and I'm in trouble." "(What happened?)" "Well, I got up in the morning and I had that feeling I always have when things are going to go bad." "(Oh, really, why don't you tell us about that feeling you always have.)" "Vague, though in the general area . . . butterflies in my stomach, a tight band around my head, flashing lights in the left visual field—" A wife might chime in: "Yah, he always looks kinda funny. I think his mouth droops a little bit on days like that. I always know when he's going to do it." "(What do you do when you feel like that?)" Usually he mentions one of two things: eiher he does nothing—he goes on about his business—or he tries to self-medicate. In general he uses alcohol for self-medication. However, the drinking of alcohol does not improve the situation. Indeed, it usually makes the dysphoric internal state worse and contributes, I think, to a greater loss of control when the trigger comes along. Such a dysphoric state might last as long as two or three days.

> During the course of the next hours or days, some trigger of face validity would occur—that is to say, a provocation would arise, perhaps some small event which, looked at from the outside, is barely understandable as a provocation. A classic example is provided by a fellow who finally got to me because his mistress brought him in while his wife was in the hospital as a result of the following sequence of events: Morning scene at the breakfast table. He says, "Do we have to have burnt toast for breakfast every morning?" She says, "If you don't like the way the toast is fixed, why don't you make your own goddamned toast?" Shortly after that, an ambulance was called to take her to the hospital with a fractured mandible, a fractured clavicle, three fractured ribs, and a ruptured spleen that had to be surgically removed. He came in led by someone else, full of remorse, depressed; he was weeping, and pointed out that he had done this several times in the preceding two years, once nearly killing his child; he seemed very upset about his behavior, reporting, as nearly half of this group did, previous suicidal gestures while in the depths of despair over their behavior and the consequences to the world around them (p. 127).[377]

Finally, there are many people, manifestly normal and in good contact with reality, who experience a chronic, relatively low level of hostility and who have a low threshold for the expression of angry feelings. These are the thousands of men and women, husbands and wives, who shout at each other, who, in moments of loss of impulse control, scream at their children and slap them, or worse, only to regret it a moment later, feel guilty, and fervently wish that they did not feel so "mean." Many of these individuals have a strong desire for better control over their hostile feelings and aggressive behavior.

# CHAPTER
# VI
# Theoretical Issues

## The Importance of Theory

There are now a number of different theories of aggressive behavior and they vary widely in their explanations and predictions of different aspects of aggression. Konrad Lorenz,[360] for example does not consider predatory behavior as a form of aggression, while Robert Ardrey[19] on the basis of work done by Raymond Dart sees predation as the basis of human violence. Niko Tinbergen[579] believes that "aggressive urges" are a primary source of energy that enables humans to engage in constructive projects. (The Dutch have such a fine complex of dikes because they were able to redirect their "aggressive energy.") J. Paul Scott[506] on the other hand does not accept the idea that there is such an entity as "aggressive energy." Many more theoretical issues will be discussed in this chapter. Theories, of course, are important because in some measure, they govern our behavior. We react to others and to our environment on the basis of what our theoretical understanding is. Our behavior is influenced even though we are unable to make an explicit statement about theoretical position. We do occasionally encounter a well-reasoned, well-stated interpretation of relationships among a variety of factors which may contribute to a theory. More frequently, however, our position is much less

95

well-defined. The influences on our behavior are governed by an implicit rather than explicit understanding of those influences.

We react on the basis of partially formed constructs that we derive from our general reading, television, conversations with friends, and the all-pervasive impact of the media. Over the past thirty or forty years the concepts associated with psychoanalysis have invaded all of our communication networks. It is taken as a given, for example, that it is maladaptive (leading to neurosis) to permit feelings of hostility to remain unexpressed. (It is not necessarily so.)

Although we operate on the basis of half-formed and half-understood theories, there is no other way. No one has the time, the energy, or the inclination to investigate the variety of complex interactions that various theories attempt to explain. For many of us our understanding of nutrition comes from the printed matter on cereal boxes with an occasional column by Dr. Jean Mayer and Jeanne Goldberg, tied together with misinformation from a high-school course on foods. Sexual knowledge may be based on an amalgam of ideas from Freud, Ann Landers, and Penthouse magazine. How we feel about exercise may depend on one of many books on running, television commentaries by Richard Simmons, and a weekly afternoon with the National Football League.

There are certainly well-thought-out theoretical positions in each of these complex areas. The interpretation of the evidence by each may be quite different and incompatible. It is important when a new theoretical position is presented to show how that theory relates to other theories.

As indicated in Chapter III, a theory or model, to be useful, must make predictions that facilitate our understanding of related phenomena. Those must differ from the ones indicated by other theories.

Different models purporting to explain violence and aggression have quite different implications for the management of *"nonadaptive hostile behavior."**

In this chapter an attempt will be made to indicate the important issues about which there are major disagreements

---

*What is considered to be *non-adaptive hostile behavior* depends, of course, on whose definition of non-adaptive is used. Violence during rebellion may be considered adaptive by the rebels and non-adaptive by the Establishment. However, there are obviously some kinds of violence that are rejected by all civilized peoples. These would include among others: sadistic murders in sexual attacks, brutalization of children for any reason, and torture for religious, political or any other reason.

among the different theoretical positions. The implications for aggression inhibition will be discussed in Chapters VII and VIII.

## Internal Versus External Stimulation to Aggression

J. P. Scott[504,505] has reviewed an extensive series of experimental studies on aggressive behavior and has done a great deal of research himself on the role of training on aggressive behavior in mice and has come to the conclusion that, "All of our present data indicate that fighting behavior among higher mammals, including man, originates in external stimulation and that there is no evidence of spontaneous internal stimulation" (p. 173).[505] In 1965 Scott[505] said, "All that we know, (and this comprises a considerable body of information in certain species) indicates that the physiological mechanisms associated with fighting are very different from those underlying sexual behavior and eating. There is no known physiological mechanism by which spontaneous internal stimulation for fighting arises."

Another group of individuals studying this problem has arrived at exactly the opposite conclusion. Lorenz,[360] on the basis of ethological studies, Lagerspetz[328] on the basis of behavioral studies with mice, and Feshbach[189] on the basis of experiments with humans, have all concluded that there are, indeed, internal mechanisms that operate to activate aggression. These investigators refer to the relevant mechanisms as a *drive*.

There are many problems with the term "drive." The concept means very different things to different people. The term is generally used without reference to what is going on inside the organism. However, Ethel Tobach and others have expressed the view that the term "drive," to be useful, must be given a sound physiological basis. However, the more one investigates physiological mechanisms, the less need there is for this term. Eibl-Eibesfeldt[162] agrees that a drive must have a physiological basis. "Drive" is a purely descriptive term, acknowledging the fact of internal causation. The situation is not that we are faced with mechanisms according to a single pattern—far from it. Internally, sensory stimuli, hormones, and factors from the central nervous system interact in a highly complex fashion to bring about readiness for a specific action.[162]

The study of the physiology of aggression shows that there is abundant evidence that the activation of a variety of physical processes result in aggression. (See Chapter V.) It also seems clear that these neural and hormonal mechanisms are spontaneously active just as are other systems that regulate eating or sexual behavior.

It is important to note that the potential for spontaneous activation of the neural systems for hostility does not mean that hostile behavior is inevitable or that it cannot be controlled. Nor does it mean that man is "innately depraved" or "evil," as suggested by Montague.[403,404] Humans are as they are, and their physiological mechanisms are beyond good and evil.

The "instinct" theorists,[360,556,579] who accept the idea that the urge to aggression may arise spontaneously, are pessimistic about the possibility of controlling these innate tendencies in humans by educational means or by reducing or eliminating the various social instigations to hostility such as the frustrations and deprivations endured by significant portions of the world population.

Berkowitz,[52] in reacting to Freud's idea of an innate aggressive tendency, criticizes it by saying that if the position of the innate theorist is valid, "Civilization and moral order ultimately must be based on force, not love and charity" (p. 4). Megargee responding to the same idea says:

> If the notion that aggressive instigation is innate and that it must be expressed periodically is correct, a number of implications for the control of violence result. It would follow that it is fruitless to seek to remove environmental conditions that seem to cause aggressive instigation, such as poverty, slums, and the like, for man will have aggressive instigation no matter what environmental manipulations are performed.[392]

Although that conclusion may be drawn from some theories that recognize a spontaneous internal activation of aggression potential, it is clearly not an implication from the model proposed in this volume. There are two considerations that invalidate such an interpretation. First, although feelings of hostility do sometimes arise spontaneously, they are also readily evoked by frustration or aversive external stimulation. Secondly, aggressive behavior is amenable to learned inhibition just as any other behavior is. However, the amount and type of inhibitory training necessary for hostility reduction may be much different for different people. Some individuals may need much more intensive inhibitory training than others.

The concept of aggressive energy is interwoven with the concepts of the aggressive drive, and internal impulses to aggressive behavior. However, the influence of the term aggressive energy is widespread, both in the scientific literature and in common parlance. That requires that it be given separate consideration.

A number of authors have claimed, on the basis of an aggressive energy model, that aggression is valuable. Anger is presumed to serve constructive ends because it energizes behavior. Thus, it is said that the scientist who becomes angry at his apparatus works hard to fix it,[190] or that the Dutch have successfully directed their "aggressive urge" against the sea and now have valuable land.[579] These arguments are based on the faulty assumption that the only source of energy available to man is an "aggressive energy." It is implied that unless the scientist were angry at his broken apparatus, he would sit quietly and look at it, which is obviously not the case. Many people work hard and enthusiastically with no hint of anger; the fact that an angry person may also work hard is irrelevant. Further, the internal turbulence of anger may very well function as a distractor that provides a less-than-optimal environment for problem solving. Thus, there is no physiological basis for the concept that the source of man's energy is a reserve of hostility.

According to some theorists of psychoanalytic persuasion[196,556] the drive results from some innate but as yet undefined mechanism. Ethologists[360,579] hold a similar position. Many psychologists also accept the drive concept,[152,189] maintaining that the aggressive drive is produced by frustration that results when goal-directed behavior is blocked. These investigators agree that, regardless of the origin of the drive state, the result is a build-up of an aggressive force, or "energy," which continues to accumulate until reduced by the expression of some hostile act, or by some behavior which may serve as a substitute for hostility.

Scott deals with the inadequate physiological basis for an "aggressive energy" when he says:

> There is no known physiological mechanism by which any large amount of energy can be accumulated in the nervous system. Therefore, hydraulic models of motivation are chiefly valid only in that they may represent subjective interpretations of motivations; in short, how it feels to be motivated. The entire organism is, of course, a mechanism by which energy can be accumulated and stored. However, such energy is not specific to any particular kind of behavior and does not represent motivation (p. 27).[506]

Scott is, of course, correct when he suggests that energy can be accumulated and stored. He is also correct in indicating that available energy is not specific to any particular kind of behavior. However, there are mechanisms that direct the available energy into particular channels, with the result that there can be an accumulating potential for hostile expression. One of the major functions of the nervous system is to give direction to the utilization of energy resources. There is abundant evidence that there are specific neural systems for different types of aggressive behavior, and that those neural systems can be progressively sensitized by a number of factors, such as blood chemistry changes. (See Chapters VIII and IX for a more complete exposition of this point.) Thus, there are indeed physiological mechanisms that permit the gradual increase in the potential for aggressive behavior, or, in other words, the energy available to the organism has a greater probability of being expressed in a hostile manner. The end result is essentially what one might expect if there were an accumulation of *aggressive energy*. Eibl-Eibesfeldt has used the above argument to insist that there is now good physiological evidence for aggressive energy. Unfortunately, Professor Eibl-Eibesfeldt did not consider the rest of the argument. As explained below, this is *not* support for the concept of aggressive energy. These physiological mechanisms can provide for either a relatively transient increase in the tendency to hostility or a prolonged or chronic behavior tendency. For example, a precipitous drop in blood sugar level may, in some patients, result in a rapidly mounting level of irritability.[217] The tendency to inter-male aggression is gradually increased with increasing titers of Testosterone in the bloodstream during puberty and lasts for a prolonged period.

However, although the gradual physiological changes in the thresholds for the activation of the neural systems for aggression result in the *appearance* of a build-up of aggresive energy, an hydraulic model is not an appropriate representation. The apparent energy is no more than a lowering of the response threshold which may change as a function of alterations in the individual's physiological status. There is no aggressive energy which continues to accumulate, and there is no *necessity* for the expression of hostility. The hypoglycemic patient described above may have intense, irrational, and progressively mounting feelings of hostility. However, if, because of early inhibitory training or a lack of an appropriate external target, he does not behave aggressively, a glass of orange juice will return him to the ranks of the rational and his internal tendencies to hostility will be eliminated without ever having been expressed. The so-called *energy* has dissolved. A woman who has intense feelings of irritability during her premenstrual period because of her particular hormone balance may very well be able to keep her behavior under control and not display hostilty. As the endocrine cycle continues and her hormone balance returns to normal, the neural system for irritability is desensitized and she loses her aggressive tendencies, whether she has expressed her hostility or not.

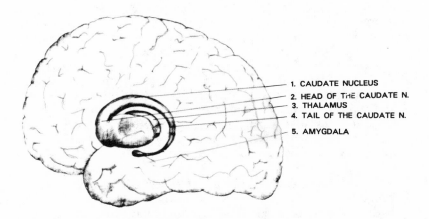

1. CAUDATE NUCLEUS
2. HEAD OF THE CAUDATE N.
3. THALAMUS
4. TAIL OF THE CAUDATE N.
5. AMYGDALA

FIGURE 4. *Basal ganglia.*

# Catharsis

Catharsis is another principle which can be derived from the hydraulic model of aggression. Dollard et al.[152] had catharsis as a major principle: "The expression of any act of aggression is a catharsis that reduces the instigation to all other acts of aggression" (p. 33). Since the pressure of mounting aggressive energy is supposedly inevitable, hostile tendencies can only be reduced by the draining of some of that energy. Thus, the angry man becomes less angry when he strikes out. Striking out is frequently not an adjustive response. In order to reduce aggressive feelings in a more socially acceptable manner, it is suggested that the individual engage in aggressive competition as a participant in sports, for example, or vicariously as an observer of competitive sports. In some situations hostile behavior may generate more hostility. A description of public behavior during the 1968 Democratic Convention in Chicago offers another example.

> The ones who actually got arrested seemed to have gotten caught up among the police, like a kind of human medicine ball, being shoved and knocked back and forth from one cop to the next with what was obviously *mounting* fury. And this was a phenomenon somewhat unexpected, which we were to observe consistently throughout the days of violence—that rage seemed to engender rage; the bloodier and more brutal the cops were, the more their fury increased.[644]

Another example comes from a Vietnam veteran.

> First you strike to get mad, then you strike because you are mad, and in the end you strike because of the sheer pleasure of it. This is the gruesome aspect of it which has haunted me ever since I came back from Vietnam (*Toronto Star*, November 24, 1967).

The evidence indicates that the principle of catharsis is not necessarily so. The tendency to behave in a hostile manner is a function of the sensitivity of particular neural systems as they interact with the environment. If those systems are not firing spontaneously, there is no "aggressive energy" to be drained off. However, if those neural systems are sensitized, hostile feelings and behaviors may very well be increased rather than decreased by competitive sports. In competition there is a winner and a loser, and losing is frustrating. Winning also involves frustrations on the way to the goal. Frustration tends to activate the sensitized neural system for irritable aggression, and the competitive activity provides the opponent as a convenient target for the expression of that generated hostility. The competition also generates a high level of arousal that tends to amplify the activity in the neural system for aggression once it is started. Unless the individuals involved have well-learned inhibitory tendencies, the result may be, and frequently is, violence.

There is also little reason to believe that the spectator of competitive sports has aggressive tendencies reduced as a result of the observation. In May, 1964, a riot, precipitated by a referee's decision, erupted at a soccer match in Lima, Peru, with the result that a number of spectators were killed. Goldstein and Arms[220] did an interesting study in which they showed that an observer's hostility increased significantly after watching a competitive sport [football] and, further, that the increase in hostility did not interact with the individual's preferred outcome of the game. It made no difference whether their side won or lost. No such increase in hostility was found for observers of a gymnastics meet.[220] Competitive sports may have many values, but it seems likely that the general reduction of aggressive tendencies is not one of them.

There are also instances in which aggressive action does block, limit, or inhibit further aggressive action. The question is why does it work, and how does that fit into our general theoretical structure. There have been countless experiments on catharsis, each subject to its own interpretation. We will cover only one set of experiments here, the work of Hokanson.[279,280,281,282]

As a dependent variable, he used a variety of measures of arousal, in particular the blood pressure changes. Preliminary experiments showed that these states of arousal reflected the individual's perception of his own level of anger. The initial experiments demonstrated clearly that within the experimental design, the subjects showed a reduction in arousal level after they were given an opportunity to shock the individual who had angered them. However, their reaction was not inevitable.

In Hokanson's most frequent experimental procedure, the subject was given painful electric shock that caused his blood pressure to rise. The shocked individual was then permitted to shock the person who had administered the shocks to him. Or, he could, if he chose, make a friendly response. It was expected, of course, that those subjects who expressed their anger would show a significant drop in blood pressure level. That was exactly what happened in men. On the other hand, that result was not manifest when the subjects were women.

Men, in our culture, Hokanson hypothesized, have learned that threatening behavior can best be terminated by counteraggression. Since this counteraggression is successful, their arousal level is reduced. Women, however, have had just the opposite training by the culture. They have learned that aggression can most easily be terminated by a friendly response.

Hokanson reasoned further, that if threat reduction was the important variable influencing tension or arousal level, it should be possible to change the response of the subjects with a learning procedure. Results showed that when a friendly response was rewarded and an unfriendly one punished, the men not only learned to give friendly responses, they also showed the same blood pressure reduction that they once showed after showing counteraggression. As expected, the women showed quite the opposite response pattern.

These experiments show that tendencies to aggression can be reduced by counteraggression, but that aggression is neither necessary nor inevitable. An individual will respond as a function of his past experience., These results are encouraging because they show that it is quite possible to change the probability that people can respond in friendly rather than hostile ways.*

Experiments with children also shed some light on the catharsis controversy. In an experiment done by Lovaas,[262] one group of children was encouraged to make hostile and aggressive remarks to a doll. A second group of children was encouraged to make remarks to the doll that were not hostile. The principle of catharsis would predict that the first group would manifest significantly less aggressive behavior because their aggressive tendencies had an opportunity to dissipate. Such was not the case. The group encouraged to be aggressive showed a greater tendency to behave in aggressive play by getting toys that stressed aggressive modes of play whereas the second group did not.[362]

Everyone recognizes that frustration produces aggression. One needs no experimental confirmation because introspection alone provides positive proof. The relation between frustration and aggression was, of course, well-recognized long before the classic studies at Yale in 1939.[152] The basic concept of the relationship between frustration and aggression was developed by Freud.[201] However, it was the Yale group that organized the material in terms of specific hypotheses that could be tested. A recognition of that relationship, however, does not require that all of the propositions of the Yale group be accepted. Does aggression always follow frustration? And is aggression only derived from frustration? The evidence indicates clearly that neither of these propositions is supported. Just a few examples are cited here. One of the initial authors of the frustration-aggression hypothesis revised his thinking and limited the generality of the theory.[396]

---

*See an excellent discussion of these experiments in Megargee (1969).

It is also obvious that frustration need not precede all aggressive responses. Instrumental aggression, that is, aggressive behavior that has been rewarded in the past, may occur in the absence of any emotion, including that produced by frustration. Some obvious examples include the aggression of a *Mr. Speleni* of Chapter I and the behavior of the Nazis in the concentration camps in the 1940s.

It is clear, as already indicated, that aggression is not a unitary phenomenon. There are, in fact, a number of different kinds of aggression. Frustration tends, under many circumstances, to precede increases in irritable aggression. The effects of frustration on other types of aggressive behavior is not at all clear.

## Arousal and Aggression

Some authors argue against a specific physiological substrate for feelings of anger and hostility because visceral arousal during emotional states is relatively diffuse. (See in particular, Bandura p. 55.)[33] It is possible to determine from physiological records of autonomic nervous system activity whether an individual is experiencing fear or anger. Some experimenters have found differences in autonomic patterns during emotional arousal,[22,490] but it is clear that these differences are minimal. Further, Schachter and Singer,[491] in a classic experiment, have shown that subjects excited and aroused by adrenalin injections tend to define the emotional experience from that arousal on the basis of the environmental cues available to them. Thus, even though the autonomic arousal pattern was the same for all subjects, those interacting with an angry stooge felt more angry than controls and those interacting with a stooge behaving in a euphoric manner felt happier than controls. This experiment shows that when subjects are viscerally aroused and they do not have a reasonable explanation for that arousal, they label the state in terms of the thinking processes available to them.

This experiment does not prove, as Schachter and Singer are careful to point out, that there are no physiological differences among the various emotional states. However, this experiment has been badly misinterpreted many times to support the position that since it is difficult to differentiate among emotions on the basis of feelings in the gut, the *only* way in which emotions can be differentiated is on the basis of thought processes. In a much quoted *Science* article by Lennard et al.,[337] the Schachter-Singer experiment is cited to prove that psychotropic drugs can have no specific emotion-altering effect. Drug effects, according to Lennard et al., can only produce diffuse physiological reactions, which are then interpreted on the basis of the patient's thoughts.

The fallacy in these misinterpretations of the Schachter-Singer experiment is the assumption that the *only* determinant of emotion is the individual's interpretation of how his viscera feels. Within limits, the emotions experienced are a function of which neural systems in the brain are active. When certain patterns of nerve cells in the brain are functioning, the individual has an emotional experience. In general, that experience is not confused with other emotions. The external environment may have some impact, but it is seldom powerful enough to alter or directly activate internal experiences.

One of the ways to demonstrate the preponderant importance of the brain in emotional experience is to directly stimulate the brain of a conscious human through an implanted electrode. In the case reported by King (see Chapter III for detail), the woman had an electrode implanted in the amygdaloid region. Although she was in the relatively sterile environment of the hospital, among friendly people whom she knew were interested in her welfare, when the electrode was activated, she had an intense feeling of rage that lasted through duration of the stimulation. She also attempted to behave in a hostile manner. When the current was turned off, she again became calm. She did not depend on the external environment to tell her what her emotional responses should be. Her feelings changed even though her environment remained essentially the same. Many other examples of specific emotions activated by direct brain stimulation can be found in Chapter III. This argument is not to deny the importance of environmental or cognitive determination of affective states. In the normal course of events the neural systems which control the various emotional experiences are heavily influenced by environmental input. It is a common experience for one to be tired, frustrated, and highly irritable after a bad day at the office, yet achieve a state nearing euphoria at a social function with good friends a few hours later. In summary, the model that best fits the available data is an interactive one. Feeling states and the correlated behaviors are most frequently the result of an interaction between the activity (or reactivity) of complex neural systems in the brain and the individual's cognitive reactions to external events. There is always some interaction involved but in any particular situation either the internal or the external conditions may have a predominant influence.

Lorenz has suggested that because there is an inextricable link between hostility and affiliation, attempts to control aggressive behavior may not be in the best interest of humans. "Thus, intraspecific aggression can certainly exist without its counterpart, love, but conversely there is no love without aggression" (p. 217).[360] This argument and others leads Lorenz to the conclusion that the elimination of aggressive tendencies would be a disastrous step, eliminating or severely limiting ambition, artistic and scientific endeavors, and "countless other equally indispensable behavior patterns," including laughter. Lorenz [359] has cited the evidence that, in the course of evolution, tendencies to intraspecific aggression and social bonding have developed together. However, it is an unwarranted extrapolation from that argument to take the position that social bonding or "love" is necessarily dependent on a viable system for hostility.

There is no physiological support for such a model. It is quite possible to activate a variety of positive non-aggressive responses without initiating tendencies to hostility. In fact, the evidence seems to indicate that the activation of some of the neural systems for what Lorenz calls "indispensable behavior patterns," including love and laughter, tends to inhibit aggression. Lesions in the neural substrates for aggression may, in fact, release from inhibition a variety of positive social tendencies. Vicious rhesus monkeys that showed violent attacks on the experimenters were operated on by Kluver and Bucy.[318] They removed the *temporal lobes* (2-5) of the brain. That drastic operation changed the animals in many ways. They not only lost their excessive hostility toward their handlers, but became overtly friendly and initiated attempts to play with the experimenters.* A patient who showed uncontrollable aggressiveness received a brain operation that included the destruction of a portion of the brain mechanism related to the expression of hostility. After the operation, his violent tendencies were controlled and he was seen to laugh for the first time in his life.**

## Innate Aggression

Cruelty and compassion come with the chromosomes:

All men are merciful and all are murderers. Doting
on dogs, they build their Dachaus; Fire whole cities

---

*It should be noted that the temporal lobe of the brain is a large and complex structure. It contains within it neural systems for both the facilitation and the inhibition of aggressive behavior. Thus, lesions or stimulation within it may produce either more or less tendency to aggression depending on what particular portion of the lobe is involved.

**There is concern among neurosurgeons, scientists in several fields, ethicists, and many others about the very real problem of the patient's rights during what is now called psychosurgery. The answers are neither obvious nor clear cut. This problem will be considered in Chapter IX.

and fondle the orphans; Are loud against lynching, but
all for Oakridge; Full of future philanthropy, but
today the NKVD. Whom shall we persecute, for whom feel
pity? It is all a matter of the moments mores, Of words
on wood pulp, of radios roaring. Of communist kindergartens or
first communions. Only in the knowledge of his own Essence
Has any man ceased to be many monkeys.

Aldous Huxley<br>
Ape and Essence<br>
Harper and Row, 1948.

Permission given by L. Rogers, Permissions Department, Harper & Row.

Is aggressive behavior innate, and if it is, what are the implications? It has been suggested by some[162,360] that the tendency to aggression is inherited.

This theory states that aggressive behavior is a relatively fixed series of behavior patterns that are in the germ plasm and cannot be escaped. Because these aggressive tendencies are innate, they are forever present and inevitable. Some go so far as to suggest that war is unavoidable.[579] Baron[41] presents a similar view.

> While various instinct theories of aggression differ sharply in terms of specific detail, all encompass similar implications. In particular, the suggestion—central to each—that aggression arises largely from instinctive, innate factors leads logically to the conclusion that it is probably impossible to eliminate such reactions entirely. Neither the satisfaction of all material needs, the elimination of all social injustice, nor other positive changes in the structure of human society will succeed in preventing the generation and expression of aggressive impulses. The most that can be attained is the temporary prevention of such behavior or a reduction in its intensity when it occurs. According to such theories, then, aggression—in one form or another—will always be with us. Indeed, it is an integral part of our basic human nature.[41]

On the other hand, the possibility that aggression may be inherited is elsewhere rejected in the strongest terms. "All of man's natural inclinations are toward the development of goodness." Also, "There is not a shred of evidence that man is born with hostile or evil impulses which must be watched or disciplined."[403]

That human beings inherit genes which influence human behavior is a fact. It is also a fact that genes for basic forms of human behavior such as aggression, love, and altruism are the products of a long evolutionary history, and that in any serious examination of the nature of such forms of human behavior the evolutionary history of the species and its relations must be taken into account. In the development of human behavior evolutionary pressures have been at work over a long period of time, but they are evolutionary pressures that have been influenced by a unique social environment, a wholly new zone of adaptation, namely that of culture.

As a consequence of cultural selective pressures humanity has greatly influenced the genetic substrates of its own behavioral development. This does not mean that humans have been altogether freed from the influences of genes which similarly affect the behavior of other animals, but it does mean that in humans, behavior is far less under the direction of genes than is that of other animals. Furthermore, that the educability, lack of fixity and remarkable flexibility of the human genetic constitution is such that humans are able as a consequence of their socialization to canalize the behavioral expression of genetic influence in many creative as well as destructive ways.[405]

The complete literature on the role of heredity in animal and human aggression is too vast to be covered in detail in this book. However, a brief review is here presented.

There is reasonable evidence that some of the factors that contribute to the sensitivity of the neural substrates for aggressive behavior have an inherited component. (An excellent review of this material can be found in McClearn.)[387] There can be no doubt that animals can be bred specifically for particular kinds of aggression; for example, fighting cocks, fighting bulls, and pit dogs have been selectively bred for fighting behavior. There are clear-cut strain differences in the probability of predatory attack. Seventy percent of Norway rats kill mice, whereas only twelve percent of the domesticated Norways kill mice.[301] A significantly higher percentage of Long-Evans hooded rats kill chickens than do Sprague-Dawley albinos.[31]

There are also strain differences in inter-male fighting.[501,542] A number of experimenters have shown that it is possible through selective breeding, to develop aggressive and non-aggressive strains of animals. In these cases the behavior studied was also inter-male aggression.[241,328,555,640] The most extensive study of the genetics of aggression had been done on mice selectively bred for high and low aggressiveness according to a seven-point scale of behavior during a period in which formerly isolated mice were paired. It is interesting to note that the selection process was carried out only on males, since the females did not show enough aggression to score. Table 1[328] shows the mean aggression score for each successive generation.

109

## TABLE 1
## THE SELECTIVE BREEDING EXPERIMENTS

| Generation | Number of selected males | | Range of test Age at selection (months) | Scores of selected animals | |
|---|---|---|---|---|---|
| | A | N | | A | N |
| P | 3 | 3 | 3–6 | 5.3–7.0 | 1.8–2.1 |
| $S_1$ | 4 | 4 | 4½ | 4.1–5.9 | 1.5–1.9 |
| $S_2$ | 6 | 4 | 4½ | 4.1–6.6 | 1.3–2.4 |
| $S_3$ | 6 | 6 | 4½ | 5.0–6.2 | 1.1–1.9 |
| $S_4$ | 7 | 7 | 4½ | 6.1–7.0 | 1.0–1.7 |
| $S_5$ | 7 | 8 | 4½ | 5.9–6.9 | 1.4–1.7 |
| $S_6$ | 9 | 9 | 4½ | 6.4–6.9 | 1.0–1.6 |

Adapted from K. Lagerspetz, Studies on the aggressive behavior of mice, Annalis Academiae Scientiarum Fennicae, 1964, Series B, 131, p. 51, Table 4.
A = Aggressive
N = Nonaggressive

As McClearn[387] points out, "In combination with the differences among inbred strains in aggressiveness, this success in selective breeding for aggressive behavior constitutes unassailable evidence of the importance of hereditary factors in determining individual differences in mouse aggressiveness."

There is, of course, no comparable data on humans. However, the model presented here would predict that there would be hereditary factors contributing to the determination of individual differences of some kinds of aggression in humans. Certainly there are vast inherited differences in the human nervous and endocrine systems. If, as suggested in this model, there are specific neural systems that are responsible for particular types of aggression, one would expect genetic variability in the sensitivity of those systems. If, as appears to be the case, the sensitivity of these sytems varies as a function of level of certain circulating hormones (see Chapter IX), one would also expect genetic variability in the factors that contribute to the determination of the hormone levels in the bloodstream. This is not to imply that these genetically determined factors cannot be modified or that they are uninfluenced by interactions with the environment. It does indicate, however, that other things being equal, some individuals are more likely to behave aggressively in a given situation than are others.

Although the information on the relationship between hereditary factors and aggressive behavior in humans is not conclusive, it is certainly suggestive. However, one group of studies must be discussed because there has been a great deal of misinformation about them. Generally, men have forty-six chromosomes. Two of them together determine the individual's sex. These chromosomes are an X and a Y. (Women also have 46 chromosomes, but the two sex-determining chromosomes are both X.) It is clear then that the Y chromosome determines maleness, including presumably, one of the differentiating characteristics between the sexes, aggressive behavior.

There is a relatively rare chromosomal abnormality in which the individual has an extra Y chromosome in XYY. It was reasoned by some that the extra Y would give the individual a double dose of maleness including an extra amount of violent tendencies. Thus, there should be a greater number of these individuals in jail. A number of studies did show that there was a larger number of XYY men in jail than could be expected by chance alone. However, these XYY people were generally incarcerated for non-violent crimes such as stealing. Finally, better controlled studies were done using large samples[633] demonstrated conclusively that XYY individuals were no more violent than the others. (For a detailed review, see Shah).[517] It has been known for many years that criminal fathers tend to have criminal sons. One of the best predictors of whether a young man was going to be a criminal was whether his father had a criminal record.[471] However, this tells us little or nothing about the genetics of aggression or violence. Obviously genetic and environmental variables are inextricably mixed.

There have been studies on the criminality of fraternal and identical twins. The latter develop from a single egg [monozygotic], and fraternal twins develop from two eggs [dizygotic]. Thus, the identical twins, as the name implies, have the same hereditary determinants while the fraternal twins are no more closely related than brother and sister. (For a review of twin studies; see Mednick and Christiansen).[391]

When the twins are alike on any given variable, in this case criminality, one can say that they are concordant. In the largest twin study carried out by the late Dr. Christiansen[104] and continued by Mednick and Christiansen,[391] 3,586 twin pairs were studied. The results showed thirty-five percent concordance for male identical twins and thirteen percent concordance for the nonidentical male twins. The rate for identical twins is 2.7 times the rate for the nonidentical twins.

Mednick and Christiansen[391] conclude that the results suggest that the monozygotic twins (identical) show some genetically-controlled biological characteristics, or set of characteristics which in some unknown way increases their common risk of being registered for criminal behavior. This is not some mysterious force, as implied by the title of the first twin study "Crime as destiny."[329]

The study of the possible inheritance of criminal behavior does not necessarily speak to the problem of proclivities to aggressive reactions or violent behavior. The relevant studies have not been done.

One does not inherit behaviors, or tendencies to behaviors; one inherits only structures. More specifically, one inherits a complex of DNA which interacting with the environment directs innate structure. However, aggressive behaviors are based on underlying neural and endocrine mechanisms. The structures underlying those mechanisms are, of course, inherited.

# CHAPTER

# VII

# Potential for the Inhibition of Aggression: Learning and Direct Neurological Interventions

The methods for producing aggression inhibition that one considers as possible (although not necessarily desirable) depend on the kind of model one has of human behavior. Much aggressive behavior is, of course, learned. Some authors, when they deal with the problem of aggression inhibition, offer solutions to that problem based entirely on the premise that the behavior is *only* subject to control by techniques involving learning .[33,278,505] Others, although accepting the basic idea that there are internal impulses to aggression, conceive of it in terms of an energy construct and consider measures related to the draining off of the "aggressive energies."[360,556] No theoretical group considers the possibility of the manipulation of the individual's internal environment. Scott, whose emphasis is on the learned aspects of aggression, concludes that drugs cannot be effective in aggression reduction because "we still have no drug that will selectively erase the effects of training (p. 38)."[506]

It is obvious from earlier chapters that a variety of physiological manipulations result in the reduction of one or another kind of aggression. The model developed in this book has a number of implications for the inhibition of aggression. This chapter considers some of those implications. The potential effectiveness, the possible side effects, the probable problems, the potential for abuse, and the potential for further development are discussed. Further, whenever one individual directs behavior and the affective states of another person (for good or ill), ethical problems are involved. The problems arise whether the controlling manipulations are the result of educational measures, the manipulation of the contingencies of positive reinforcement, the application of psychological or physical punishment, or direct changes in the physiological substrates of the individual's behavior. However, since control by physiological manipulation is relatively new, and also relatively powerful, there is currently considerable, justifiable concern about these methods. It is therefore necessary to devote some space to ethical considerations.

More space will be devoted to the physiological mechanisms for aggression inhibition than for the techniques based on the principles of learning. This is certainly not to imply that techniques based on learning (in the broadest sense) are less valuable. If civilization is to be saved (and wise individuals around the world have some doubts that it will), it must depend upon the learned and culturally determined inhibitions to hostile behaviors.

Some physiological mechanisms are useful and useable, but relatively little is known about them. These techniques do not turn patients into zombies, and each technique is subject to limitations and side effects. As Svengali is presumed to have abused hypnosis, there is also a presumption that the physiological techniques may also be abused. Although these techniques are quite useful for the mitigation of human misery they are not very powerful beyond the individual patient.

If all of the procedures for the physiological manipulation of behavior were concentrated in the hands of a single vicious dictator, he would not rule the world. In fact, his push for power using these procedures might be his downfall.

There is an increasing incidence of violence and violent crime in the world today and the potential for the further escalation of violence with the acceleration of population increase seems a distinct possibility. If civilization is to be preserved, means must be found to mute the expressions of hostility in large segments of the population in general, and in world leaders in particular. This

114

general problem merits the consideration of specialists in many fields and the solutions will require the expertise of individuals in many disciplines. However, the emphasis in this chapter is on methods of limiting aggression in individuals.

The ability to deal with feelings of hostility and the tendency to overt aggressive action varies greatly from one individual to another. Some persons are pathologically violent and are unable to exercise any constraints on their tendency to injure either themselves or others. Fortunately, they are uncommon. If they and those around them are to survive, their aggression must be reduced. Many of these individuals, although not all, are mentally retarded, and their behavior requires institutionalization. Many of them have readily diagnosed brain pathology. The extremely hyperactive, brain-injured child, for example,* "is indiscriminately aggressive and impulsively violent. He may keep in constant and socially disruptive motion—running, shouting, and destroying any object that he gets his hands on (p. 57)."[377] Andy and Jurko[14] describe a "hyperresponsive syndrome," the main characteristics of which are hyperkinesia, aggression, and pathological affect. The following excerpt from one of their cases is illustrative.

> D. D., 7-year old. This mentally retarded child said single words at 2–3 years of age, and stopped talking at 5 years of age. At about 1 year of age, the patient began to have tantrums and fits with loud screaming which lasted 20 minutes or 2 hours. At 3 years of age, she developed spells of aggression consisting of biting, scratching, and kicking her mother and others in the family. Her mother's arms and hands were scratched so badly that they bled. The child also bit and scratched herself. The attacks began by whining. Following one of these attacks, she sometimes slept for 3–4 hours. She frequently plugged her ears with her fingers, particularly for some sounds that were unpleasant. Her "temper tantrums" became more frequent and severe. She had one such episode the night prior to admission characterized by biting, scratching, turning over furniture, kicking the wall, etc.[14]

Heimburger et al.[265] report a case of a retarded fifteen-year-old boy who had been institutionalized for years in a locked room without furniture because of his uncontrollable destructiveness

---

*This complex of symptoms should not be confused with the so-called "hyperactive child" found in the average classes. The children described here are pathologically hostile.

and hostility toward attendants. Another sample of a hyperaggressive patient was described as follows:

> In this overly aggressive and hyperactive group the aides were almost continuously confronted with such behavioral problems as hostile aggressiveness [fighting, biting, scratching, kicking, pulling hair, slapping], passive aggressiveness [hollering, screaming, singing loudly, cursing, talking vulgarly, tantrums, denudation], destructiveness [pulling down curtains, breaking windows, throwing furniture, rending clothing, filthy habits, excretory soiling, smearing of feces, coprophagy, eating rags, plaster, etc.] and restlessness [excessive walking or running, insomnia, rapid ingestion of food].[570]

There are no reliable estimates of the number of these unfortunate individuals in institutions, but the number must run into the thousands.

## Nonphysiological Methods for the Prevention of Aggression

Much aggressive behavior is learned and is subject to the same types of influence as any other learned response. In its purest form, aggression based on learning may be completely unrelated to the physiological substrates for aggression discussed in earlier chapters. It has no underlying biological basis except in the sense that all behavior and all learned behavior has such a basis. Pure instrumental aggression will not be altered by physiological measures. It can only be controlled through therapeutic techniques based on an understanding of the basic principles underlying learned behavior.

Internal impulses to hostility are also, in some measure, subject to learned inhibition, as are all internal impulses. Therefore therapeutic measures based on learning theory will be useful in helping all types of individuals to inhibit maladaptive hostile tendencies. Thus, a number of investigators recommend the use of multiple approaches to aggression inhibition[26,197,344] Many, although not all, individuals whose neural systems for aggression are easily activated may still learn to inhibit overt behavior even though they feel extreme anger.

One technique for teaching aggressive impulse control uses the "Law of Effect." If a subject is rewarded for engaging in aggressive behavior that individual will have a greater tendency to engage in aggression in the same or a similar situation. As Arnold Buss put it a number of years ago, "Aggression pays off." The opposite is, of course, true. If the individual is rewarded for non-aggressive behavior, that type of behavior will predominate.

The general therapy using the above approach is called contingency management. It is well illustrated by the following example from a therapeutic session. The professional is interviewing the mother of an aggressive child for the first time:

*Professional*: Tell me about Jim's aggressive behavior.

*Mother*: Well, uh . . . I don't know. It's just his nature. He's a mean boy. None of my other kids act like him.

*Professional*: I see. I wonder though if he's always acting up? Are there any times during the day when he's not fighting?

*Mother*: Oh yes, most of the time. It's just that when he blows, he really gets mean.

*Professional*: What you're saying is very interesting. It sounds like he's capable of being not aggressive but that some things really get to him. When is it that he "blows"? When is it that he's at his worst?

*Mother*: Oh it's mostly with his sister over the TV. When he wants to watch a program, he's got to have his way. When she won't give in, he uses such foul language and he sometimes hits her! I can't believe the way he acts!

*Professional*: What happens after he hits his sister? Does he get to watch his program?

*Mother*: Yes. It's the only way we can get them to stop. We can't stand all the shouting and crying.

*Professional*: Do you think he knows that if he hits his sister, he'll get his way?

*Mother*: Oh he knows alright. He even says it. He tells her that he's stronger than her and he'll watch any program he likes.

*Professional*: From what you're saying, his aggression sounds like it really pays off.

*Mother*: That's for sure.

*Professional*: Is it possible that Jim keeps hitting his sister because he keeps getting his way every time he does it?

*Mother*: Oh, I see. I suppose so.

*Professional*: Maybe it's not his "nature" to be aggressive.

117

After all, he is good most of the time. Maybe he sometimes swears and fights because it pays off so much.

*Mother*: I hadn't really thought about it that way before.

*Discussion*. This interaction is a common one at the beginning of training. The parent (or other adult) attributes the child's aggressiveness to some global factor such as bad genes, maliciousness, or emotional conflicts, and ignores the fact that the child's aggression is usually specific to situations in which the aggression produces benefits (i.e., reinforcers) for the child. The professional's role is to guide the parent away from conceptualizing in terms of vague factors and towards seeing aggressive behavior as a function of its reinforcing consequences (pp. 24–25).[221]

Punishment is one of the oldest methods of reducing aggression known to the human race. It does, of course, work in certain circumscribed circumstances but obviously many problems result from its use.[529] It is frequently ineffective and may under some circumstances facilitate the learning of the responses against which it is directed. The punishing parent may serve as a role model for the child. Aggressive parents do produce aggressive children[389] and the factor most strongly related to the development of aggressiveness in children is the use of physical punishment.[190] (For general reviews of the use, effectiveness, and limitations of punishment, see Skinner,[529] Bandura[33] and Buss.)[87]

Aversion therapy is a fairly recent technique that is closely related to the age-old method of punishment. It differs only in that the aversive consequences of aggressive behavior are systematically manipulated and the parameters of that manipulation are derived from a significant body of experimental work. This technique is the subject of the violent novel and motion picture *A Clockwork Orange*.[85] Aversion therapy has been used most frequently in cases of pathological hostility in which other methods have been unsuccessful. The procedure consists of assuring that physically painful consequences, usually electric shock, follow a clearly defined aggressive act. Chronic assaultive and violent behavior in a thirty-one-year-old female schizophrenic was brought under control by the administration of shock after any of the following three types of behavior: (1) aggressive acts, (2) verbal threats, and (3) accusations of being persecuted and abused. Her general level of adjustment improved and she began to substitute more positive relationships for her previously combative responses.[364] Aversion therapy has also been used successfully to reduce dangerous self-mutilating behavior in children. Children kept in restraints at all times to prevent them from doing serious permanent injury to themselves by head-banging, self-hitting, or self-biting can be released if each self-destructive act is systematically followed by painful shocks.[82]

A less drastic form of treatment of aversion therapy consists of a brief time-out from social reinforcement for clearly defined deviant behaviors. These behaviors have included aggression, tantrums, self-destruction, sibling aggression, continuous screaming, biting, and destruction of property. When the patients engage in any of the designated behaviors, they are placed in isolation in a "time-out room" for a relatively short period, which, in different studies, varies from five to thirty minutes. The procedure has been used successfully with both children and adults and in some cases is remarkably effective in the control of severe, long-standing behavior problems.[8,67,194,621] (See Smolev[534] for a review of several studies of this type.)

The systematic use of reward can also be useful in limiting destructive hostile behavior. Responses that are desirable and incompatible with the deviant behavior to be eliminated are specified, and when they occur the individual is given a positive reinforcement. The reward may consist of attention in the form of hugs and smiles, candy, or tokens that may be exchanged for money or other desirables at a later time. Vukelich and Hake[607] describe a case of an eighteen-year-old severely retarded female whose dangerously aggressive behavior was rapidly reduced to a manageable level through the use of this procedure. Under a time-out contingency alone, the patient attempted to choke others within minutes of being released. When positive reinforcement in the form of attention and candy was provided continuously as long as there were no aggressive responses and the rewards were contingent on incompatible responses, her dangerous behavior was essentially eliminated.[394,534,550]

Since aggressive behaviors are frequently maladaptive, it is not surprising that a variety of psychotherapeutic techniques have been used in attempts to systematically reduce it. Milieu therapy, in which the entire social environment is controlled, has been successfully used to deal with the aggressiveness of hyperaggressive boys.[388] In several cases psychodrama has been useful in reducing the aggression of students.[188,355] Maladaptive anger responses have been brought under control by systematic desensitization and reciprocal inhibition.[178,179,230,469] Finally, group therapy has been useful in helping violent outpatients to deal with their excessive aggressive tendenices.[346]

One need not accept all the propositions of the frustration-aggression theorists to recognize that frustration plays a role in the generation and perpetuation of aggressive behavior. It has been proposed earlier that frustration and stress, particularly if prolonged, may activate the endocrine system to produce particular hormone patterns that, in turn, sensitize the neural system for hostility. There is no doubt that a large proportion of our population lives in conditions under which frustration, deprivation, and stress are dominant aspects of the lifestyle. One would expect that a reduction of those factors would mitigate some of the hostile tendencies of the people involved. These conditions for the ghetto residents in the United States have been well described and recommendations for their alleviation have been detailed in the Kerner report (Report of the National Advisory Commission on Civil Disorders, 1968).

Any method that contributes to an increase in empathy among individuals should decrease aggressive behavior because greater identification with the aggressee is then possible and the aggression is thus inhibited.[189,190,191]

Cognitive restructuring may also reduce aggressive tendencies if the individual learns a more realistic, less threatening perception of certain aspects of his environment. This may be accomplished in individuals through role-playing, for example,[436,584] or through more conventional therapeutic or educational approaches.[190]

Any shifts in the culture that reduce the number of violent role models after whom children may pattern their behavior may serve to reduce the general level of expressed aggression in the society.[616,618]

Finally, the expression of aggression can be reduced by removing some of the cues that instigate aggressive behaviors. Berkowitz[53] summarizes an outstanding series of studies demonstrating that individuals react with greater hostility in the presence of objects, such as guns, that have previously been associated with aggressive incidents.

# The Role of the Culture

The inhibition of the expression of aggressiveness is, in a number of instances, a result of the input of a particular culture. Paddock[441] has referred to those societies as *antiviolent*. On the other hand, some cultures are proviolent and hostility is woven into the fabric of their culture. Perhaps one of the best-studied of the proviolent is the Yanomamo in the jungles of Venezuela. These people are in a constant state of war with their neighbors and their entire lives from birth to death are under the constant pressure of war or the preparation for war.

These vicious Yanomamo do not confine their brutality to the battlefield. The following quote from Chagnon's book illustrates the interactions of husband and wife.

Women must respond quickly to the demands of their husbands. In fact, they must respond without waiting for a command. It is interesting to watch the behavior of women when their husbands return from a hunting trip or visit. The men march slowly across the village and retire silently to their hammocks. The woman, no matter what she is doing, hurries home and quietly but rapidly prepares a meal for the husband. Should the wife be slow in doing this, the husband is within his rights to beat her. Most reprimands meted out by irate husbands take the form of blows with the hand or with a piece of firewood, but a good many husbands are even more brutal. Some of them chop their wives with the sharp edge of a machete or axe, or shoot them with a barbed arrow in some nonvital area, such as the buttocks or leg. Many men are given over to punishing their wives by holding the hot end of a glowing stick against them, resulting in serious burns. The punishment is usually, however, adjusted to the seriousness of the wife's shortcomings, more drastic measures being reserved for infidelity or suspicion of infidelity. Many men, however, show their ferocity by meting out serious punishment to their wives for even minor offenses. It is not uncommon for a man to injure his errant wife seriously; and some men have even killed wives.

Women expect this kind of treament and many of them measure their husband's concern in terms of the frequency of minor beatings they sustain. I overheard two young women discussing each other's scalp scars. One of them commented that the other's husband must really care for her since he has beaten her on the head so frequently![100]

Anthropologists have studied a number of other societies whose records of war, cruelty, and violence are major portions of their culture. These include the Zulu of southern Africa, the Dani of the highlands of New Guinea, and the Plains Indians of western United States, as well as others. As noted in Chapter II, we can note a significant amount of violence in our own lives. Culture has a powerful impact and that impact may be either pro- or antiviolent.

Abundant material will be presented to show that there is an inborn physiological basis for aggressive behavior. These data have forced some theorists to conclude that war and violence are therefore inevitable and that war and violence, like taxes and the poor will be forever with us. *Not so.* The ability to learn is the most human of characteristics, and that learning frequently includes the possibility of the control of powerful basic physiological needs. As indicated earlier, one would expect no less of other types of behavior. The pervading influence of the culture can teach the acceptance or rejection of the values of violence.

It is of considerable interest to compare violent and nonviolent cultures to gain some insight into how they differ in an attempt to understand the origins of their differences. It is generally the case that compared cultures are different on so many variables that it is difficult to find meaningful patterns. However, in the valley of Oaxaca in Mexico, there are violent and antiviolent communities living close together and having remarkably similar cultures. Those that eschew hostile solutions to their problems are able to control interpersonal violence. They accomplish this remarkable feat without a formal police force, and without the judicial system generally found in the industrialized societies. These communities are surrounded by others showing the more common violence levels.

There are many similarities between proviolent and antiviolent groups. They share the same biological inheritance. Their general cultures are similar. They speak the same language (Zapotec and Spanish). Both are subject to the same climate, poverty, ecology, and both use considerable amounts of alcohol. Thus, those variables cannot be used to differentiate between them as determinants of their violent or nonviolent tendencies.

There are differences between these two communities. The antiviolent show an essential absence of *machismo*. This is remarkable in a country that has that characteristic as an important part of the male pattern. The nonviolent tend to have a much stronger social role for women. The child-rearing practices also show differences. Before the age of three, the handling of the children is essentially the same. After that, the antiviolent show firm but consistent discipline. *Good behavior* is expected as much as possible; misbehavior is ignored. Competitive behavior is not encouraged.

In the violent societies, discipline tends to be arbitrary and subject to the whims of the adults. The parents threaten the child but do not follow through with the result that the children have little faith in the threats. The children are also made highly competitive. These are remarkable findings. The data available on these Oaxaca communities are at this time limited. Fortunately Dr. Paddock is continuing the studies.[441] The anthropologists have provided considerable insight on the origins of aggressive behavior.

Studies of the Utku and the Qipi also show the importance of learning and cultural impact in the control of aggressive behavior. Young children are told, among other things, that they can injure themselves and others through their uncontrolled behavior. They are also told that thunderstorms and darkness and all other fearful things are the result of their hostility: "It got dark because you were angry."[76]

The Semai of Malaysia inculcate their children into a nonviolent way of life without any recognition that they do. Although the Semai live in a culture based on a nonviolent way of life, they are quite capable of showing considerable violence against outsiders. When the Malaysian government recruited these people into their counterinsurgency forces in the 1950s they fought with fierce intensity. It was said that they were "drunk on blood." Although the Semai are in general nonviolent in many ways, it is an error to consider them totally without aggressiveness.[145]

Sorenson[540] studied the New Guinea South Fore people who were an essentially peaceful group with few constraints and no hierarchical system or order. However, the same basic population began to fight and develop a rigid social structure with a significant increase in population density. These findings show once again that the impact of the culture can have a profound effect on individuals' expressions of hostility. However, that effect may be either an increase or a decrease depending in part on environmental conditions.[540]

# Neurological Methods of Dealing with Excessive Aggression

Because there are physiological substrates for aggressive behavior, it is possible to alter hostile tendencies by altering the physiology of the individual. Four basic methods can be used to accomplish this: (1) a portion of the neural substrate for aggression may be lesioned in order to limit or reduce activity in that system; (2) the neural systems inhibiting the neural substrates for aggression can be activated by direct electrical stimulation; (3) since particular hormone patterns sensitize the neural systems for aggression, and others tend to reduce that sensitivity, it is possible to reduce particular kinds of aggressive behavior by the direct manipulation of the hormonal status; (4) finally, a number of drugs that are reasonably specific in their antihostility action can be used to help an individual gain control over unwanted hostile feelings and actions.

# Brain Lesions

There can be no doubt that a large number of different brain lesions in both animals and humans can reduce the tendency to aggressive behavior. In humans, feelings of hostility may also be reduced. This is a finding of considerable theoretical importance in that it shows the relationship between the brains of animals and humans. There is a remarkable congruence between the two. From a surgical standpoint the risk is relatively low and the results can be highly dramatic. However, the side effects of a number of the techniques are so great that no surgeon would suggest that they be used. The patient with a bilateral temporal lobectomy who shows all of the Kluver and Bucy Syndrome,[22]* including loss of immediate memory, hypersexuality, and overeating, has been little helped by the operation even though his impulsive pathological aggression has been significantly reduced.[572] The results of the prefrontal lobotomy in reducing aggression are so variable and the side effects so unpredictable that is is now used relatively infrequently, and should not be used at all for the reduction of aggression.

The use of brain surgery for behavior control is one of the most controversial medical procedures today. Except in relatively rare cases this procedure is not appropriate. There is no surgery or any other procedure that will generally solve the problem of the violence-prone individuals in prisons much less the violence-prone of the population at large. As with any innovation in medicine, the techniques have been used inappropriately and by some individuals who are inadequately trained. As a result, there have been a number of malpractice suits around the country. Two state legislatures, in California and Oregon, have essentially banned most forms of psychosurgery.

In this section, two brain operations will be considered in some detail. These include lesions in the *temporal lobe* (2-5) and in the *amygdala* (4-5 and 6-3). However, it should be noted that there are a number of places in the brain where damage will inhibit the tendencies of the patient for aggression. This is to be expected because we are dealing with a system and not a center. There are, then, a variety of brain areas where the system can be disrupted by lesions. These include the *prefrontal areas* (2-2) of the brain, the *anterior cingulate gyrus* (3-2) and the *posterior cingulate gyrus* (3-4), the *thalamus* (3-6), the *ventral hypothalamus* (5-7) and the *posterior hypothalamus* (5-4). All of these surgical procedures involve side effects and multiple problems.

---

*This syndrome was first observed in monkeys by Kluver and Bucy in 1938.

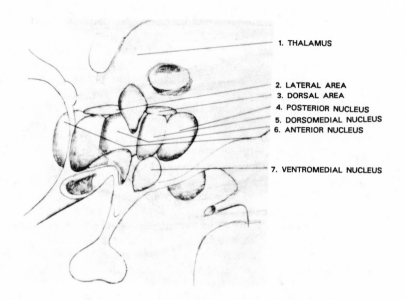

1. THALAMUS

2. LATERAL AREA
3. DORSAL AREA
4. POSTERIOR NUCLEUS
5. DORSOMEDIAL NUCLEUS
6. ANTERIOR NUCLEUS

7. VENTROMEDIAL NUCLEUS

FIGURE 5. *Three-dimensional view of the hypothalamus.*

For example, Sano[485,486,487] has done what he calls sedative surgery. The operation involves making a lesion in the *posterior hypothalamus* (5-4). This is a most complex portion of the brain including some of the neural networks for temperature regulation, sleep, food consumption, sexual behavior, and the tendency to respond aggressively. With a knowledge of the functions of the posterior hypothalamus, it would seem to be madness to attempt such an operation.

There are a variety of therapeutic reasons for making brain lesions, and much can be learned about the neural mechanisms underlying aggressive behavior through the brain-lesion technique. Lesions in a variety of loci in the brain result in the reduction of aggressive behavior. Wild cats, wild monkeys, and a variety of other animals have been surgically tamed by the ablation of precise brain areas that apparently interfere with the function of the underlying neural systems for hostility.

There have now been at least several hundred cases reported in which aggressive behavior in humans has been reduced, in many instances dramatically, by specific brain lesions. Although these operations provide us with some general insight into the types of neural mechanisms involved in what is probably irritable aggression in humans, there are many problems in interpreting the various studies. It is possible to determine the general areas of the limbic system that are involved, but an understanding of the precise brain areas included in the neurological substrates of aggression must await many more and far-better-controlled studies than have as yet been done on humans. The neurological and behavioral evidence is very difficult to interpret.

The lesions produced in almost all the following descriptions of surgery are relatively large and undoubtedly involve a number of mechanisms underlying aggressive behavior and other basic motivational systems. *Amygdalotomy* lesions are made in a most complex structure. As will be indicated later some portions of the *amygdala* (4-5 and 6-3) involve the facilitation of different kinds of aggression and others involve their inhibition. Other portions are a part of the neural substrate of fear-motivated behavior, and consummatory behavior. Lesions in the amygdala also have a significant effect on the endocrine system, which is also important in the regulation of some kinds of aggression.

For many reasons, including the fact that most of the patients are still alive when the studies are reported, good histology is not available, so it is not possible to determine with precision the location of even the relatively large lesions.

On the behavioral side, as Valenstein[601] points out, it is frequently difficult to make an independent judgment about the results of a given study because the clinical reports are generally

126

written in a subjective style and objective test data are seldom included. In any given study there are relatively few subjects, and pre- and postoperative objective evaluations often are not made. Further, the individuals making the evaluations of the behavior frequently know the nature of the lesions and the expected results, and the behaviors reported on are not precisely defined behaviorally.

Of course the clinic is not a laboratory and surgeons are not generally trained in experimental procedures. They seldom have either the time for or the interest in rigorous scientific procedures. It is therefore important to interpret clinical material with caution. However, the clinical material is a valuable source for the generation of specific hypotheses and anyone working in this area must have a knowledge of what has been done. Consequently, it is critical to survey this now extensive literature. It is also important that future studies utilize good experimental designs and scientific procedures within the constraints of comfort for the patient and medical ethics.

The experimental work of Kluver and Bucy, which involved bilateral temporal lobe ablation and resulted in surgicallyinduced docility, inspired some surgeons to attempt the same operation on humans in an attempt to modify aggressive behavior and agitation in schizophrenic patients.[572] As might be suspected from the results of Kluver and Bucy, this radical operation resulted in a variety of dysfunctions. In one case report presented in detail by Terzian and Ore,[572] bilateral removal of the *temporal lobes* (1-5), including most of the *uncus* and *hippocampus* (6-4), exactly reproduced the Kluver and Bucy syndrome. Rage and fear were reduced, ability to recognize people decreased, and there were increased sex activity, bulimia, (overeating), and serious memory deficiencies. Prior to the operation the patient had frequent attacks of aggressive and violent behavior during which he had attempted to strangle his mother and to crush his younger brother under his feet. After unilateral temporal lobectomy, he attacked the nurses and doctors and threatened some with death. After the second temporal lobe was removed, he became extremely meek with everyone and was "absolutely resistant to any attempt to arouse aggressiveness and violent reactions in him."

Temporal lobe lesions, both unilateral and bilateral, have been extensively used in humans to control epilepsy that is not susceptible to drug therapy. A frequent side effect of the operation, in addition to seizure control, has been a general reduction in hostility compared to the individual's reactions prior to the operation.[60,181,182,184,198,232,274,452,509,571,592] Although cases have been reported in which aggressive behavior has been increased by the operation,[488,638] the increase is generally temporary. Some authors report no change in psychiatric symptoms.[212] Bailey[27] indicates that temporal lesions do not generally reduce the psychiatric problems of the patient, except that in certain subjects the attacks of aggressive behavior were reduced or completely eliminated. He believes that the aggressive attacks were, in fact, psychomotor seizures. Falconer et al.[183] report definite personality changes for the better after temporal lobe lesions and conclude that the most striking way in which they improved was in the reduction of aggressiveness. "Whereas, previously, the relatives of the patient might be very careful as to what they said to the patient for fear of provoking an aggressive outbreak, they can now talk freely and joke with him."[183]

Vallardares and Corbalan[600] removed the tip of the temporal lobe, including the uncus, specifically in order to modify their patients' aggressive impulses. Their sample included sixteen feebleminded, seven psychopaths, and thirteen individuals with psychopathic personalities. They indicate that the patients were examined from the medical, neurological, psychiatric, psychological, EEG, and pneumoencephalographical point of view, but they do not report the results of those examinations. In terms of the degree of reduction of aggressiveness and impulsiveness, they report great improvement in thirteen of the thirty-six patients, no change in nine, and no information on fourteen. Although they do not report the criteria for change, they indicate that only one patient showed an intellectual impairment. They imply that memory improved as aggressiveness was reduced.

Of all the brain lesion techniques that have been used to block excessive aggressive behavior, the amygdalectomy seems to have been the most used. Precise lesions of 8 to 10 mm. in diameter are made with the aid of a stereotaxic instrument. (See fig. 9.) The procedure generally produces less trauma than other techniques, and the side effects reported have been minimal but can be serious. The side effects reported have included two cases of visual field defects,[499] one case of hemiparesis (a paralysis that affects only one side of the body),[199] and one case of diabetes insipidus[265]* Sawa et al.[488] have also reported two cases with severe vomiting and abdominal pain, and one case of transient palsy was reported by Narabayashi et al.[427] Only Sawa et al.[488] have reported defects in memory as a result of this procedure and then only in three cases who exhibited agnosia (memory loss) for persons and objects.

---

*A pituitary gland deficiency that has some symptoms similar to the more common type of diabetes.

128

In general, intellectual functions have not been impaired by the stereotaxic amygdalectomy. Heimburger et al.[265] have concluded that the surgical procedure has no effect on mental retardation, but Narabayashi et al.[427] have reported a gain in intellectual capacity in five of nine retarded children in one series. They found no evidence for memory difficulties and no deterioration of psychic function.

In a study of sixteen patients with temporal lobe epilepsy who had received coagulation of the amygdala, no intellectual deficit was found. Eight of the patients were lesioned in the right amygdala, six in the left, and two bilaterally. Four subtests on the Wechsler Intelligence Scale were used as well as various continuous performance tasks and the Stroop Colour Word Test, a test for word fluency, and tests for learning and memory. The subjects were tested pre- and postoperatively. Although there was no indication of general intellectual loss, selective differences were found in relation to the response to the novel situation at the beginning of the learning process. No other information is given on those differences.[13]

In addition to the reported side effects, it is quite possible that the individual has been drastically changed (for better or for worse) in many aspects of his total being. There may be many subtle changes in intellectual functions, and there may be long-run limitations on the individual's adaptability, flexibility, and social awareness. Only well-designed pre- and postoperative evaluations will permit judgments on the total effects of these various psychosurgical procedures.

In the real world many of the preceding questions, although important, are academic. If the patient is, like Heimburger's individual described earlier, retarded and locked in a room without furniture for years because of his uncontrollable hostility and destructiveness, it makes very little difference whether a brain lesion will produce subtle intellectual or motivational changes. If a patient's reaction to the testing situation is to destroy the test materials and attack the psychometrist, the evaluation will obviously not have much meaning. An amygdalectomy, however, may enable the patient to be released from a solitary and completely sterile environment or even be released into the outside world. To argue that this patient is made "less of a person" by the operation is essentially meaningless.[72]

Psychosurgery is used for a number of dysfunctions other than the cotnrol of violent behavior. It has been used to reduce intractable pain as well as self-induced starvation. Individuals suffering from depression and pathological anxiety have also been treated with surgical procedures.

Some individuals oppose all psychosurgical procedures regardless of possible benefits. Included in that ban is the use of psychosurgical procedures to control the not infrequent excruciating pain that comes with terminal cancer [73].

## PROBLEMS WITH BRAIN LESIONS

There are obvious problems in using lesions for the inhibition of aggression. The most serious one is that they are not reversible. Once the lesion is made, nothing can be done to restore the individual to the preoperative state. When the operation is not successful the patient is brain-damaged to no avail. It therefore appears clear that surgery should be a last-resort therapy and should be used only after all other procedures, both psychological and physiological, have been tried.

If the various psychotherapeutic methods discussed earlier have been given an adequate trial, a variety of physiological methods should be attempted before psychosurgery of any kind is performed. As indicated later, there are now a number of drugs and hormone preparations that, in some patients, produce a clear reduction of hostility. However, since the state of the art is not yet refined, it is seldom clear at the outset which drug will be the most effective. Therefore a casual trial with a couple of the major tranquilizers in no way exhausts the possibilities for the less drastic physiological control techniques and does not justify attempts to control the behavior by brain surgery. There is evidence that in some of the hospitals around the world in which aggression blocking operations are performed, relatively little care is taken to ensure that brain surgery is, indeed, the "last-resort therapy" that it should be. (See Valenstein[601] for a further exposition of this point). Some of the physiological methods are more effective than others, and some have more side effects. Some are much more experimental than others and clearly need more work before they can be put into general use. These are, in general, powerful techniques and therefore need careful consideration. Some of the methods are more subject to abuse than others.

## NEED FOR FURTHER WORK

None of the operations described above is one hundred percent successful, but as of now there are no good criteria for deciding which patients will be helped by which operation. Detailed behavioral analyses and psychological evaluations of all psychosurgical candidates may ultimately permit a more precise identification of the individuals most likely to have their symptoms alleviated. It has recently been suggested, for example, that

130

the tendency to violence toward persons may have a different neurological substrate than the tendency to self-mutiliation or the destruction of objects. In a series of eighteen patients, seven of nine who showed interpersonal hostility were benefited by amygdalectomy, whereas none of nine patients who were either destructive or self-mutilating showed persistent improvement after the operation.[312] Heimburger [265] has also suggested that more detailed analyses need to be made of the electro-encephalographic records. Some patients whose EEGs have improved, that is, displayed fewer epileptogenic discharges, have not shown a behavioral improvement, whereas others who have improved behaviorally have shown no changes in their EEG record. Well-controlled sleep records, with temporal and sphenoidal leads and depth recordings during surgery, may also be useful in finding the type of patient for whom the oepration is potentially successful.

It is a far cry from the first crude prefrontal lobotomies, with their massive damage, to the relatively precise amygdalotomy done with the stereotaxic instrument. By comparison, current techniques are highly refined, but they are in need of further refinement. The amygdala is a complex entity that has an influence on a number of behaviors. In animals there is evidence that it is involved in at least three different kinds of aggressive behaviors. and that the different nuclei may be involved in either the facilitation or the inhibition of one or more kinds of aggression. Some of the failures to minimize antisocial behavior through operative techniques may very well be due to the imprecision in electrode location. Thus, a great deal more research is needed to gain this relevant information.

## POTENTIAL FOR ABUSE

As with any other therapeutic technique, there is a potential for abuse. The operation may be used prematurely, when it is unwarranted, or by individuals who have the legal right but not the competence to undertake this type of surgery. It is also conceivable that surgery to prevent aggression might be used as a political tool to minimize hostile actions of dissidents or as a threat to contribute to the management of particularly disruptive prisoners. Psychosurgery for aggression reduction would not be a particularly effective political tool. There is no reason to believe, and no evidence to suggest, that the precise lesions currently available for the mitigation of uncontrollable violence would have any effect in reducing the aggressive behavior of an individual who has decided to resist oppression on the basis of intellectual processes rather than anger. Thus, that kind of abuse would be the result of ignorance on the part of the user. It is, of course, true that brain operations are possible that could restrict an individual's political activity by reducing his general reactions to all stimuli and putting him into a coma or semicoma, by destroying portions of the arousal system, for example. That type of surgery, however, has no more relationship to therapeutic psychosurgery than does simple murder. This important point is developed later in the section on the limitations of physiological methods of aggression control.

## Brain Stimulation and Aggression Reduction

Direct brain stimulation is a therapeutic procedure that provides us with some insight into the neurological basis of aggressive behavior in the human. There are a number of different kinds of patients for whom there is good reason to believe that some kind of brain stimulation would be beneficial. When temporal lesions are being considered for the control of epilepsy, it is necessary to identify precisely the focal areas of abnormal electrical activity. This can be accomplished by recording from implanted depth electrodes and by stimulating in an attempt to replicate the details of the epileptic process.[377] Some patients with intractable pain resulting from terminal carcinoma can get relief (sometimes dramatic) from direct brain stimulation.[174] Small brain lesions are useful in the control of tremor caused by Parkinson's disease and the exact lesion location is determined by stimulation.[510] The procedure has also been used in patients with anxiety neurosis, involuntary movement[137] and chronic schizophrenia.[261]

With the development of the stereotaxic chronic implantation of electrodes in 1952,[133] it was possible to take brain stimulation out of the operating room and test the patient in relatively natural conditions, without anesthesia or sedation. The electrodes are well-tolerated by the brain and there are relatively few side effects. Heath[256] reports on one patient with 125 implanted electrodes that remained accurately fixed in position for a period of two years. It is not possible to say how many patients have now experienced direct brain stimulation, but the procedure is no longer rare. Just one investigator reported in 1966 on eighty-two patients in whom 3,632 electrodes had been implanted.[510]

There is now considerable evidence indicating the presence, in the brains of animals and humans, of suppressor areas that, when activated, function to block ongoing aggressive behavior. This has been accomplished repeatedly in both animals and humans and thus provides another possible method for the therapeutic intervention of intractably aggressive individuals. The evidence indicates clearly that the reaction to stimulation is not a general arrest phenomenon. In humans, depending on the site of stimulation, the patient's mood may change from a generalized feeling of hostility to one of euphoria, superrelaxation, or a sexual motive state.

Although there can be little doubt that suppressor systems exist and can function to block aggression, little is known about the details for the effects of the repeated stimulation of those systems. A great deal more work needs to be done before this technique can be demonstrated as safe and practical. Most of the technical hardware problems have been solved and will be discussed later; however, there is a real lack of knowledge of the potential physiological and psychological problems.

The surgical risk of mortality through electrode implants is even lower than that for stereotaxic brain lesions and can be considered negligible. There are, however, other serious side effects that merit a great deal more research before electrical stimulation of the brain of humans can be considered risk-free.

Although there are no data on humans, it has been shown in mice, rats, cats, and monkeys that repeated brief, subthreshold stimulation of the *amygdala* (4-5 and 6-3) results in a progressive lowering of seizure threshold and ultimately in behavioral convulsions. This increase in seizure potential resulting from brain stimulation has been referred to as the "kindling effect." (See Goddard, 1972, for a detailed review of this phenomenon.)[218] The kindling effect appears to be restricted to limbic system stimulation and the tendency to kindling appears to be directly related to the number of connections with the amygdala. Goddard concludes that the kindling effect is a relatively permanent transsynaptic change resulting from neuronal stimulation and is unrelated to such factors as tissue damage, edema (excessive fluid in the tissues), or gliosis (an overgrowth or tumor in the connecting cells of the brain). There do not appear to be detectable histological differenes between the brains of animals with low seizure thresholds from repeated stimulation and control animals that had the implants but not the stimulation. At least one case has been reported in which a human patient was stimulated in the *lateral amygdala* (4-5 and 6-3) daily for a three-month period with no report of a lowered seizure threshold.[377]

Kindling only results when the stimulation is brief and intermittent, usually separated by a twenty-four-hour period. It has been shown in the rat that if the stimulation is massed, that is, given at intervals of less than twenty minutes, the animals seldom develop convulsions. Further, if animals, previously kin-

133

dled, are given continuous stimulation for many hours, they appear to adapt to the stimulation and cease having convulsions.

Thus, it is possible that the kindling effect may be circumvented by massing the stimulation but, until much more is known about that effect, procedures involving repeated electrical stimulation of the brain of the human can hardly be considered risk-free.

Kindling results from repeated electrical brain stimulation. However, one study has shown that a single application of 1 mg. of acetylcholine chloride bilaterally to the basolateral portion of the *amygdala* (4-5 and 6-3) of cats resulted in relatively permanent abnormalities in the electrical activity of the brain. Within four minutes of the stimulation electrophysiological seizure activity was recorded from the point of stimulation. Overt motor seizures appeared within ten to fifteen minutes that were quite similar to epileptic attacks in humans. The behavioral seizures disappeared during the next twenty-four- to forty-eight-hour period but highly abnormal discharge patterns persisted during the five months of observation. Immediately after the seizure the animals were hypersensitive to all stimuli and made unprovoked but well-coordinated attacks on other cats and the experimenter. The "wild cat" behavior also persisted for the entire observation period. The formerly tame cats continued unprovoked attacks on conspecifics and on people and resisted all attempts at taming. Behavioral effects of chemical stimulation in others areas studied, including the *hypothalamus* (Fig. 3), *midbrain* (3-10) *reticular activating system* (3-11), *thalamus* (2-6), and *amygdaloid regions* (4-5 and 6-3) did not persist for more than thirty to sixty seconds.[236]

Aside from this single study essentially nothing is known about this phenomenon. It is not known whether other brain areas can be affected in the same way by a single stimulation, nor is it known whether the abnormalities will persist indefinitely. However, the possibility that a single stimulation of the brain of humans could result in convulsions, permanently wild behavior, and abnormal electrical spiking in the brain is indeed frightening. At least one human patient has shown delayed and prolonged increases in violent aggressive behavior from a single session of electrical stimulation in the *amygdala* (4-5 and 6-3). That patient showed an apparent recovery of this prestimulation, well-controlled behavior after a twenty-four-hour period. However, it is not possible to determine whether there were long-term changes because the patient died (from other causes) soon after the stimulation session.

There is another side effect about which even less is known. It has been reported that one patient (and only one as of this date) has become addicted to electrical stimulation of the *amygdala* (4-5 and 6-3).[174,378] The patient was a thirty-three-year-old engineer who had periodic attacks of extreme violence. He also presented symptoms of multiple pains, worry, dejection, and intense feelings of anxiety and tension. Bipolar stimulation of the lateral portions of the amygdaloid complex on either side resulted in symptom relief after a ten- to thirty-second latency and a feeling of superrelaxation. Stimulation was given several times weekly for an unspecified period and the patient developed an "addiction" to the stimulation. He insisted on being stimulated and when the procedure was stopped for ten days he became irritable, depressed, and manifested his earlier symptoms. Placebo stimulation had no effect and stimulation of other sites did not relieve the symptoms.

The addictive process implies that some kind of positive affect may have been produced. In addition to the so-called addiction, the continuous electrical activation of positive areas may involve a number of as yet unrecognized psychological problems. Valenstein puts it succinctly when he says, "The belief that anyone could adjust in this world if a spontaneous orgasm followed by mental calmness was programmed at ten, two, and six o'clock seems ludicrous" (p. 173).[601] It is not clear what to make of this single case, and nothing is known about the possible mechanisms underlying the addiction, if that is, indeed, what it is. However, the case raises a red flag of caution for electrical brain stimulation in humans. We are also cautioned by the delayed violence produced by electrical stimulation.

In at least one case in humans, the aggression suppression effects of brain stimulation lasted for months.[563] If the effect was indeed due to the stimulation and if further work results in sufficient understanding of the mechanisms so that a reasonable prediction of success can be made, it may be possible to facilitate an individual's ability to deal with his hostile impulses by a single series of amygdaloid stimulations, after which the electrode can be removed. It should be emphasized that such a procedure, although relatively safe surgically, is highly experimental and the possible long-term, and even short-term consequences, are not at all understood.

Many patients have an intense desire to gain mastery over their irrational impulsive aggressive behavior. It is now technologically feasible, although it may not be desirable, for them to do so through the stimulation of their own brains. Heath[260] has developed a transistorized self-contained unit the individual can wear on his belt. The unit generates a preset train of stimulus pulses each time it is activated. This stimulator could be connected to an electrode implanted in an aggression suppressor area, and the patient would then have his own "antihostility button" which he could press to calm himself down whenever his irrational feelings of hostility occurred. This device has already been used with a narcoleptic patient who, whenever he felt himself drifting off to sleep, could reach down and press his "on button" and once again become alert. His friends soon learned that they could press the button to get him back into the conversation if he fell asleep too rapidly to press it himself.[255]

Based on earlier work with animals, R. G. Heath showed that stimulation of the center of the *cerebellum* (6-5) tends to block neural activity in the aversive neural mechanism, activity in the *hippocampus* (6-4) and parts of the amygdala. In addition to the suppression activity of those structures, it also increased the amount of EEG activity in the *septal region* (3-5). That region had been shown to be related to the activation of pleasurable states of mind. Thus, there was a feedback mechanism that operated to block aversive feelings when the pleasurable mechanisms were working and vice versa. This confirms what is common knowledge, that one does not generally experience pain and pleasure at the same time. A rare exception occurs in certain circumstances with the ingestion of LSD. Subjects report that they experience love and hate and aversion and pleasure at the same time.

Heath developed a cerebellar pacemaker.[258] The pacemaker was then used on forty patients. Twelve of those were subject to bouts of violent behavior. According to Heath, this behavior could be successfully treated with long-term intermittent stimulation that was given at five minutes on and five minutes off. These patients were followed up for four and a half years during which their progress was frequently checked.

The following case is, according to Heath, representative:

This 19-year-old man was selected because he was considered to be the most severely ill patient in our state hospital system at that time. Slightly retarded from birth, he was first hospitalized when he was 13 years old. Following private treatment, he was hospitalized at several state institutions and, finally, at the East Louisiana State Hospital, where he was confined on a ward for severely disturbed patients. He had slashed his wrists and arms on numerous occasions during episodes of violence, and on one occasion, he had attempted to kill his sister. Despite administration of huge quantities of numerous drugs (lithium, imipramine, thioridazine, chlorpromazine, trihexyphenidyl, diazepam, phenobarbital, and anti-Parkinsonism medication), he had to be kept in physical restraints much of the time. All attending physicians had declared it hopeless that he would ever return to his home. A cerebellar pacemaker was

136

implanted in March, 1976. The patient's postoperative course was turbulent because of the necessary withdrawal of large quantities of drugs and because of drug-induced tardive dyskinesia. Before the pacemaker was activated, it was necessary to use large quantities of sedatives and to continue to use restraints. He was so disturbing to the entire ward that other patients petitioned to have him removed.

From the day the pacemaker was activated, one month after its implantation, the patient had no further outbursts of violence. His tardive dyskinesia gradually diminished, and his behavior continued to improve. He became a pleasant and sociable young man. Psychological tests, including intelligence quotient, showed significant improvement, and he was able to cope adequately with the vicissitudes of everyday life. Clinically, the patient had a complete remission and required no medication. He was enlisted in a vocational rehabilitation program.

The pattern of improvement continued until the Spring of 1978, when he began to be irritable and negativistic, both at home and at school. A check of the external power source—at that time techniques were not available to check the implanted equipment—failed to reveal a problem. But the patient grew more irascible until he viciously assaulted both parents, severely injuring his father. A neighbor who intervened was also severely injured before the police arrived. The patient was subdued with great difficulty and taken to a local hospital, where he injured some of the personnel and destroyed furniture before adequate sedation was achieved. Transferred to the University Hospital, roentgenograms showed a break in the wires between the receiver and the brain electrodes. In June, 1978, the original electrodes were removed and a new system was implanted. Symptoms again promptly remitted, and improvement has continued without further episodes of violence to the present time. In August, 1980, the patient's original receiver was replaced with the implanted power source (p. 188-89).[259]

It may ultimately be possible to provide brain stimulation in limited subcortical areas without open surgery. Although this development may not be in the immediate future, the implications are of such importance that it should at least be mentioned. A stereotaxic instrument is now available* that can produce

*CDV Stereotaxic Ultrasonic System, from Baltimore Instrument Company, Inc., 716 West Redwood Street, Baltimore, Maryland 21201.

lesions as small as 0.5 to 0.1 mm. by using low-frequency ultrasonic energy without opening the skull. It may ultimately be possible to use the ultrasonic source of energy at a lower level as a stimulator. C. W. Dickey, who developed the device, has already given some thought to that possibility (personal communication). Delgado[143] has been using an electromagnetic source which he indicates permits stimulation at specific brain sites (personal communication).

In order to eliminate the need for restraint and the necessity for connecting wires to the head, a technique was developed by which the brain of the subject could be stimulated by remote, radio control.[135,138,139,140,141,472] The monkey wore a small stimulating device on its back that was connected by leads under the skin to the electrodes which were implanted in various locations in the brain. The leads were connected through a very small switching relay which would be closed by an impulse from a miniature radio receiver that was bolted to the animal's skull. The radio receiver could then be activated by a transmitter which was some distance away. With this system it was possible to study the monkeys while permitting them to roam free in the caged area.

In one experiment the subject was the aggressive boss monkey that dominated the rest of the colony with his threatening behavior and overt attacks. A radio-controlled electrode was implanted in the monkey's *caudate nucleus* (4-1). When the radio transmitter was activated the boss monkey received stimulation to the caudate nucleus with the result that his spontaneous aggressive tendencies were blocked. His territoriality diminished and the other monkeys in the colony reacted to him differently. They made fewer submissive gestures and showed less fear of the boss. When the caudate nucleus was being stimulated, it was possible for the experimenter to enter the cage and catch the monkey with his bare hands.

During one phase of the experiment described above, the button for the transmitter was placed inside the cage near the feeding tray and thus made available to all of the monkeys in the colony. One small monkey learned to stand next to the button and watch the boss monkey. Every time the boss would start to threaten and become aggressive the little monkey would push the button and calm him down. This may be the first experimental evidence of St. Matthew's prediction that the meek shall inherit the earth.

A number of humans have now been equipped with such a device. Even though the unit just described weighs only about 70 g., there are still some obvious difficulties. It must be worn under bandages on the head (although one patient was able to hide the device completely with a wig) and it is necessary for the leads to the electrodes to penetrate the skin, thus producing a constant source of irritation as well as the ever-present possibility of infection. There are also psychological problems in that the patients feel conspicuous with radios on their heads.

However, even these difficulties have been resolved by the recent developments in electronic microminiaturization. At a symposium in 1969, Delgado reported that an entire stimulation unit had been reduced in size and shaped so that it could be implanted under the skin. It would therefore be possible for an individual to have an electrode implant in an aggression-inhibiting area attached to one of these devices.[142] As soon as his hair grew back, he would not look different from any other individual. He could then return to all normal activities as long as he stayed within the range of the transmitter. Obviously, the range would depend on the transmitter's power. It would also be possible to give the subject a small, relatively inexpensive, transistorized radio transmitter similar to the units used for the remote opening of garage doors. He could then carry his transmitter with him in his pocket and as long as he possessed the initiative to inhibit his own unacceptable impulses, the reduction of that behavior would be available to him. It would also be possible to make transmitter units available to responsible individuals for use during periods when the subject's violence was dangerous but not subject to his own wish to block it. The ethical implications of this type of device will be discussed.

In Michael Crichton's superb book *The Terminal Man*[117] the main character, because of his inability to deal with his violent impulses, has had an electrode implanted in his brain. He also had a microminiaturized computer implanted subdermally and connected to the electrode. The computer senses, on the basis of characteristic brain waves, when Mr. Benson is about to become aggressive and provides stimulation in an aggression suppression area. Mr. Benson can then lead a normal life. However, things go awry, and thereby a very fine tale is told. How close is the *"terminal man"*? Closer than many would like to believe. Like all good science fiction writers, Dr. Crichton had done his homework well.

Delgado reported in 1969 that he had implanted electrodes in the brain of a chimpanzee and connected them to a miniaturized transmitter-receiver bolted to the animal's head. With this device it was possible to make EEG recordings from depth electrodes as well as to provide remote stimulation of deep brain sites. It was then determined that spontaneous spindles (a particular wave form in the electroencephalogram) from the *amygdala* (4-5 and 6-3) were correlated with excitement and attack behavior, and that stimulation in the area of the *central gray* (3-9) resulted in a negative response in the chimp. A computer was then programmed to differentiate the spindle waves from other EEG responses to activate the electrode implanted in the central gray (3-9) on the occurrence of the amygdaloid spindles. A reduction in the amount and frequency of spindle waves from the amygdala resulted. Within two hours the amount of spindling was reduced by one-half and after a few days the spindles were essentially eliminated. The chimpanzee's behavior also changed. He became considerably more docile, had less appetite, and became somewhat lethargic. The behavior change persisted for a two-week period without further stimulation.

The interpretation of this experiment is not yet clear. Until the procedure is applied to humans it will not be possible to know what kinds of subjective experience are associated with either the spindles or the stimulation of the central gray. Central gray stimulation was negatively reinforcing for the chimp and has been associated with pain in humans and thus would be undesirable as a locus for stimulation in the inhibition of aggression. However, it has been shown that under certain circumstances violent behavior in humans is preceded and accompanied by particular EEG tracings from the depths of the temporal lobe, particularly the amygdaloid and hippocampal regions.[377] As indicated earlier, stimulation in several brain areas results in an inhibition of hostility with the substitution of some positive affect. Thus, it appears that the basic mechanisms for the computer-induced changes in hostility in humans have already been demonstrated. Once again, the hardware technology is available and much more is known about that aspect of the problem than is known about the brain mechanisms involved. The possible complications and side effects of such a procedure are at the moment completely unknown and may be legion.

## POTENTIAL FOR ABUSE

Brain stimulation for the production of changes in aggression is a highly experimental technique, and relatively little is known about potentially dangerous and irreversible side effects. The evidence clearly indicates that the procedure can prevent aggressive behavior or block that which is ongoing. Those findings are, of course, of considerable theoretical importance. As of yet, however, there are relatively few patients for whom the therapy would be appropriate. However, when all else fails and the only alternatives are years of physical restraint, solitary confinement in a barren room, or brain lesions, this measure may in time be preferred.

The greatest potential for abuse appears to be similar to that for lesioning procedures. The technique may be used prematurely when it is not warranted, or by individuals who are inadequately trained. The sophisticated achievements in electronic hardware may lure some individuals to use the techniques before some of the serious possible problems are understood and resolved. The suppression of aggressive behavior by brain stimulation is of considerable theoretical importance. However, it should be emphasized once again that it is a highly experimental technique with many unknown risks and is not yet a practical therapeutic procedure.

Like brain lesions, brain stimulation for aggression inhibition would not be a particularly good device for political suppression. There is no evidence that brain stimulation has any effect on instrumental aggression, and even if it were effective, the technical problems of controlling large numbers of individuals would be overwhelming. Further, this type of aggression inhibition is not needed to manipulate the aggressive tendencies of large numbers of people. Recall the controls that Hitler achieved with no more than verbal techniques.

# CHAPTER

# VIII

# Potential for the Inhibition of Aggression: Hormone and Pharmaceutical Interventions

It is clear from the material in Chapter IV that the tendency to certain kinds of aggressive behavior in humans is a function of particular hormone balances and that alterations in the individual's hormonal status result in a change in the aggression potential. Except for the endocrinopathies, where the obvious therapy is the normalizing of the endocrine balance, there are essentially two types of aggressive behavior that appear to respond to endocrine manipulations. The first is the very serious problem of sexual violence. The second is the much less serious but frequently troublesome irritability associated with fluctuations in the menstrual cycle.

## Sex Related Aggression

Aggressive behavior that is directly associated with sexual behavior, either heterosexual or homosexual, can frequently be reduced

143

by blocking the androgens in the bloodstream. (See Chapter IV for details.) The simplest and most obvious method of accomplishing this is through the operation of castration. There is now considerable evidence that this operative procedure is effective in reducing the level of sexual arousal regardless of its direction. This is, of course, a drastic therapy and a number of problems are connected with it. In cultures where manliness is commonly associated with sexual potency, the psychological effects of castration may be devastating. Almost one-third of a sample of castrates in Norway were extremely embittered after having undergone the operation.[74] Although some authors[252] consider the physiological effects to be minimal and to some extent even beneficial, Bremer[74] reported a variety of somatic complaints in thirty-seven of 215 castrated subjects. These problems included troublesome weight gain, exceptionally aged appearance, polydypsia, and polyuria, complaints of weakness and deterioration of general health.

Although the evidence is certainly not extensive, there appears to be good reason to believe that sex-related aggresssion can be controlled by estrogenic and antiandrogenic compounds. The problem of side effects must, of course, be considered. Most of the side effects of the estrogenic compounds, such as tenderness in the breast, loss of facial hair, redistribution of fat deposits, and so on, can be controlled by reduction or withdrawal of the medication. However, Laschet[331] suggests that prolonged treatment with estrogens or progestagens may lead to irreversible damage of the testicular cell functions.

If the potentially sexually violent individual is to be released into society, two other problems must be taken into consideration. First, there must be assurance that the individual receives the medication and, second, its effectiveness must be checked. When there is the possibility of a brutal child murder, self-medication obviously cannot be trusted. An individual may, under most circumstances, be very concerned about his violent tendencies and feel strongly about controlling them. However, as a therapeutic dose of a hormone or hormone inhibitor wears off and the state of extreme sexual arousal ensues, he may be unable to respond to his rational processes. Several attempts have been made to solve this problem with long-acting subcutaneous or intramuscular injections. Chatz[101] indicates that intramuscular depot injections of estradiol valerianate (Primogyn Depot Sherin Berlin) remain effective for a two-week period. The individuals are released into society and report to their personal physician or to the outpatient clinic every fourteen days for another injection. If a dangerous offender fails to report he is rearrested and either given the injection or returned to an institution. Estradiol B.P.C. has also been used as a long-acting sex suppressant.[192] It is implanted subcutaneously after the skin has been anesthetized. Implants of 100 mg. at a time are made until the goal of impotence or near impotence is reached. The dosage has varied from 100 to 1200 mg. In this study a two-year follow-up revealed that sexual reoffending was essentially eliminated. Two of the antiandrogens, cyproterone acetate and medroxyprogesterone acetate, are also available in depot form.[62,331]

Money reports the following results using Depo-provera:

> Suffice it to say here that the effective dosage, dependent on physique and body weight, appears to be between 300 to 400 mg., intramuscular every ten days. Within approximately a month, this dosage radically lowers plasma testosterone levels to those typical of the female, or lower. Concurrently, sexual potency and ejaculation are radically reduced, and may become zero. Both of these effects are reversed when the treatment is gradually tapered-off and terminated. . . . Some patients undergo sufficiently dramatic improvement that they can be weaned from treatment in a matter of months. Others may need a repeat series of "booster" injections if their behavior subsequently deteriorates. (p. 167) (Also, see Blumer et al.)[62,400]

During 1984, there was a resurgence of interest in the physiological methods for dealing with hypersexuality and rape. Judge C. Victor Pyle gave three convicted rapists the choice of a 30-year prison sentence or surgical castration. Faced with this choice, two of the men chose the castration while the other decided to go to prison.

The crime was a particularly brutal one involving six hours of torture of the victim as well as the triple rape. Her arms were burned with cigarettes, skin was rubbed from a portion of her arm. She was raped with a bottle, lost a considerable amount of blood and suffered a considerable tear in the vagina. Mark Vaughan who decided to go to prison thought that the sentence was particularly harsh. He said, "Well, I have never been regarded as an animal before in my life. I've never. I've always been an easy-going nice person. And one mistake, you're an animal. And that's not true."

The use of physiological methods to inhibit violent sexual behavior is obviously a social problem and one facet of the problem is the readiness of the population to accept such judgments. If the attitudes of the members of this small southern textile town in the heart of the Bible Belt is representative, and of course, it is not, the people are more than ready. Interviews by an

ABC reporter revealed some of their feelings about the case. One woman wanted them put in prison for life. Another suggested that the sentence was not tough enough. A man felt that castration was not enough, that they should be hung or shot or whatever they wanted to do. Another man said, "If it was me in there, I'd kill him myself. I wouldn't let the state do it: I'd kill him myself." Paul Harvey of ABC radio has interpreted the bumper sticker *Disarm the rapist* as meaning more than castration, it means amputation of the offending organ.

Obviously the legal options are not within the purview of a small and outraged community. These decisions will result from long and useful deliberations of the legal profession before the decision goes to the people. It is the opinion of Professor Alan Dershowitz of the Harvard Law School that the sentence is probably unconstitutional because it may be considered as cruel and unusual punishment.

A second therapy (or punishment, depending upon your point of view) is the use of Depo-provera to block testosterone levels. It has been called chemical castration. Because the treatment does not involve obvious mutilation it is more easily accepted and the treatment is reversible. Although there are a number of places that are using this technique to reduce the probability of sexual assault, one of the oldest is in the Johns Hopkins University Hospital. The program is under the direction of Dr. Fred Berlin. The patients get one shot a week and the shots can not be interrupted because if the subject stops taking the drug, the testosterone level returns to normal. For good reason, violent rapists and murderers are excluded from the program. Typical patients are the exhibitionists, voyeurs, and fondlers.

There are some serious problems with the use of Depo-provera, or cyproterone or other testosterone antagonists that will surely be developed. All of these medications wear off in time. That is an advantage because the effect is then reversible. It is also a disadvantage because the medication must be administered at specific intervals. In the case of Depo-provera, the injections must occur at about weekly intervals. This means that the violent men must return to the medical facility once a week. Many of the individuals involved in sex crimes welcome the treatment because, they say, they cannot otherwise deal with their behavior. They may be most distressed by their violence.

As is common with all physiological functions, there are vast individual differences in testosterone production and its effectiveness on the target organs. Thus, the amount of antiandrogen, or even the blood level of testosterone, is not a foolproof indicator of the patient's responsiveness to whatever it is that *turns him on.*

The sexual potential and directions in the male can be determined through the measurement of penile responsiveness with a device called a Phallometer.[202,205,206] Both volume and circumference have been measured. Sexual arousal patterns to sexual stimuli and responsiveness to the sexual act, including masochism, rape and other behaviors have been used.

The procedure consists of placing the measuring device on the subject. The measure of circumference is accomplished through the use of a partial metal ring. Changes of penile circumference causes changes in the ring which acts as a strain gauge and records the changes on a meter or an electrical recorder. The volume measurement consists of a plythmograph, an air filled sleeve placed around the penis. Volume changes are reflected in the air sleeve and are transmitted to a recorder.

Sexual stimuli consist of slides of nude females or nude males presented rapidly on a screen. Motion pictures have also been used. This technique can discriminate between heterosexuals and homosexuals as well as homosexual and heterosexual pedophilia [203, 204]. The subject shows a greater response to the stimuli that illustrate his particular sexual preference. The ease with which the subject is aroused can also be measured and can contribute to the decision to determine whether or not the individual should be released into society after either psychotherapy or antiandrogenic therapy.

In an experimental program at the maximum security prison in Saskatoon, Canada, Dr. Arthur Gordon is teaching violent sex criminals to "fake" a negative response to sexual stimuli. He suggests that sex crimes are committed in part because sexual stimuli produce a very high level of arousal in rapists, and they are unable to control their behavior. If the individual is taught to block the sexual arousal, the tendency to commit crimes of a sexual nature will be reduced. This work is in progress and has not yet been published. It will be interesting to see the results.

There is a problem with the idea of the release of sex criminals on the basis of the Phallometer. It has been shown that subjects can fake either positive or negative reactions to the stimuli.[334] They accomplished this by thinking about non-sexual material to fake decreased arousal and to engage in sexual fantasy to show a greater amount of arousal.

There is another serious problem with the use of antiandrogens to eliminate sexual violence. Although the evidence indicates that in the proper circumstance, the hormonal approach will reduce sexual and aggressive tendencies, there are specific conditions in which the therapeutic response will be minimal. As indicated earlier, there are a number of different kinds of aggression and the physiological basis of each is different. When a rapist

147

attacks and brutalizes a woman, he may be operating under a primarily sexual motivation. On the other hand, a rapist may be seeing his victim as a representative of all womanhood for whom he has learned a pathological hatred. If that is the case, neither hormones nor castration will have a therapeutic effect.

It has been frequently suggested that rape is not sexually motivated, but is a crime of violence and violation and nothing more. It is both possible and likely that an individual may behave under more than one motivational state. The probability of some rapists repeating their crime after castration is reduced to zero. This would lead one to conclude that he had been operating in large measure under sexual motivation.

The woman who continues to endure premenstrual irritability and tension month after month has a physician who either is not aware of the problem or has not kept up on the literature. A number of possible therapies are now available and, whereas a given therapy may not be satisfactory for a particular individual, there is a good probability of finding one that will control the symptoms without excessive side effects. These measures have been indicated in the discussion of the physiological basis of the syndrome and will not be covered in more detail here.

The complexity of the problem of the physiological control of hostility is well illustrated by the attempts to use drugs for that purpose. A single pharmacological agent may dramatically reduce the hostile tendencies of one individual. It may just as dramatically increase the expressions of aggression by a second individual and it may have no effect on these tendencies in a third. Kalina,[297] for example, has successfully used diazepam to eliminate the intense rage reactions of psychotic criminals. However, DiMascio et al.[150] report that the same drug may result in assaultive and destructive behavior. Previously quiet patients were seen to break up office furniture shortly after being placed on the drug. Cases of violence and even murder, presumably resulting from the "paradoxical rage reaction" induced by one of the benzodiazepines, have also been reported.

These results are not too surprising when one recognizes that there are a number of different kinds of aggressive behavior and that each of them has a different physiological basis. Similar results have also been reported in many animal studies.[602] There is no general anti-aggression drug that will provide relief to all patients suffering from unwanted and uncomfortable feelings of hostility. That emotional state and behavioral tendency may be caused by a variety of physiological dysfunctions. Depression may serve as an example (although depression is also not a single disorder). One of the components of depression symptomatology is an intense feeling of irritability and hostility. Generally drugs

## TABLE 2
## MENTAL DISORDERS IN WHICH AGGRESSION OCCURS

| Origins of Violence | Drugs of Choice |
| --- | --- |
| Schizophrenic psychosis | Antipsychotics |
| Acute brain syndrome | Benzodiazepines |
| Chronic brain syndromes | Antipsychotics |
| | Antihistamines |
| Mental retardation | Antipsychotics |
| Seizures and dyscontrol syndromes | Anticonvulsants |
| Mania | Benzodiazepines |
| | Lithium |
| | Anticonvulsants |
| | Lithium |
| Depression | Trycyclic |
| | Antidepressants |
| Sexual violence | Lithium |
| | Antidepressants |
| | Antiandrogens |

such as the Valium or Librium which are useful for aggression inhibition in some patients are of little value to the person beset with depression. However, if one of the commonly used anti-depressive drugs such as Elavil or Tofranil is given, the depression will generally abate in two to three weeks and the irritability will go with it. Table 2 lists some of the drugs that will have a high probability of reducing aggression in some of the disorders in which hostile behavior is a common symptom.

Because aggression has many causes and can result from a variety of neural and endocrine dysfunctions, the problem of predicting which drug will be effective in the inhibition of hostility of a given individual is difficult. There are some guidelines. Weintraub et al.[615] show how the violent individual can be dealt with, and offer a twenty-five-item table of disorders that may, if conditions are right, produce violent behavior, and the drugs used to "bring the patient down." They report the following case study.

A 26-year-old unmarried male was brought in an agitated state to the emergency department by his family. Earlier in the day he had attacked a younger sibling who had asked an innocuous question. The patient worked at an institution for the mentally retarded, where, in the last month, he had made sexual advances toward several adolescent female clients. According to the family, he had boundless energy, never stopped talking, stayed out late at night, and was easily angered. The patient was the only sibling of five who didn't finish college; he dropped out after 2 years of study because of "problems with drugs and inability to concentrate." In the emergency department he paced incessantly, occasionally pounding his fists against the wall and screaming "help me."

The patient received 10 mg. of haloperidol intramuscularly. An hour later he was still remarking ominously on his pent-up feelings of explosive rage. The dose of haloperidol was repeated, and within a half hour, the patient was resting quietly in a chair while his family made arrangements for admission. The haloperidol dosage was converted to the oral form and set at 15 mg. Further observation over the next two days coupled with the patient's history confirmed the diagnosis of manic-depressive disorder. Lithium carbonate was added to the patient's regimen. He made rapid progress during the next three weeks and the haloperidol was gradually withdrawn. The patient was discharged on lithium carbonate, 600 mg. bid, and when last seen, he was preparing to resume his college studies.

There are as yet no diagnostic tests that permit a rational pharmacotherapeutic approach to hostility reduction. However, in spite of this lack of perfect predictability in the matching of a particular drug to a particular patient, the large number of substances capable of blocking both overt aggression and feelings of hostility are a valuable adjunct to the therapeutic measures available to relieve human misery. In many areas of medicine a lack of knowledge of the details of the therapeutic process dictates that a search must be made for the most efficacious drug. The simple dictum is, if the first drug does not work, try the next one on the list. The lists are suggested in Eichelman and Weintraub papers. A wide selection of pharmaceutical agents are now available that have hostility reduction as a significant component of their effects and that have limited serious side effects. Thus there is a high probability that irrational, incapacitating, discomforting, aggressive behavior can be kept within bounds through the use of drugs.

There is a general misconception in the popular literature and among a surprising number of physicians that the drugs manifesting an antihostility effect, as well as psychotropic drugs in general, produce their effects by reducing the individual's general level of awareness, making him stuporous, stupid, and unable to respond adjustively to the relevant stimuli in his environment.

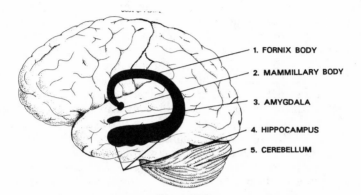

1. FORNIX BODY

2. MAMMILLARY BODY

3. AMYGDALA

4. HIPPOCAMPUS

5. CEREBELLUM

FIGURE 6. *Amygdala-hypothalamus relationship.*

Individuals are frequently described as "drugged," implying the glazed look and general apathy of the heroin addict "on the nod." Research (and there is now a large body of literature on the problem) does not support that interpretation.

The most general finding has been that patients improve on various tests of intellectual functioning during the drug trials, or those processes are unaffected by the drugs. Baker [28] has reviewed eighty-nine studies on the effects of psychotropic drugs on test performance and finds relatively few deleterious effects. The interested reader is referred to Baker for details, but the general finding in regard to chlorpromazine is that it is an effective agent. The effectiveness of the drug enables anxious and highly agitated patients to direct their attention in the testing situation, with the result that they do significantly better on tests of intellectual functioning. Anxious subjects treated for six weeks with 800 and 1600 mg. of meprobamate do significantly better on a digit symbol test than do placebo controls. The performance of normal subjects has generally been reported to be unaffected, except for one study in which the individuals received a dose of 1600 mg. per day and did more poorly on the digit symbol test than controls.

The results of other studies not covered by Baker[28] yield similar results. Dilantin sodium not only reduced the irritability of institutionalized epileptics, it also resulted in a general improvement in intelligence rating, which was particularly reflected in memory, reasoning and planning, and recognition of verbal absurdities.[476]

It is, of course, possible to give a large enough dose of any of the antiaggression drugs to reduce alertness. If the dose is high enough to interfere with the individual's general adjustment, there is a good possibility that a better agent may be found. It is also true that drowsiness is sometimes a side effect to which the patient habituates with continued treatment or with dosage reduction.

All the drugs used in the inhibition of aggression may also have, in some individuals, unwanted physiological side effects, and the therapist must obviously be aware of them and be attentive to the possibility of an idiosyncratic reaction by particular individuals to certain of the drugs. Exactly the same precautions must be taken in the prescription of antihostility agents as with any other drug. The possible side effects of the various drugs are listed in most of the manuals of drug use, such as the *Physician's Desk Reference*, and will not be covered here.

Although some drugs appear to facilitate aggressive behavior, many more tend to inhibit both overt aggression and feelings of hostility. There is currently no drug that is a completely specific

152

antihostility agent; however, a significant number of preparations are available that do reduce aggressive tendencies as one component of their action. It is not possible here to provide a complete and exhaustive coverage of the now vast literature on drug inhibition of aggression, but a number of studies are covered.

Some kind of a measure for aggressiveness is a part of the battery of screening tests used in the initial evaluation of psychotropic drugs on animals and many standard drugs are being evaluated for antiaggression effects. A review article by Valzelli[602] provides some notion of the extent of these investigations. He reported 204 animal studies dealing with drug-aggression interaction. Eight of these studies reported drugs that produced an increase in aggressiveness; twenty-four reported no effect on the particular behavior studied. Of the eighty drugs covered in the studies reported by Valzelli, seventy-four of them inhibited some form of aggression in some animals studied. Thus the potential for the development of aggression-inhibiting drugs is very great. It is important, however, to recognize that drug effects may be both species-specific and situation-specific. Valzelli[602] is one of the few authors who makes an attempt to discriminate among the different kinds of aggressive behavior. His table of drug effects shows that some drugs tend to block one kind of aggression and facilitate another within the same species and that a given drug may block aggression in one species but facilitate it in another. In addition, there are wide individual differences in susceptibility to the taming effects of various drugs.

All the preceding factors are significant to an understanding of drug effects on hostile tendencies in humans. Aggressive behavior has many causes, and can result from overactivity or dysfunction in a number of different neural systems. It is therefore not surprising that a specific drug may be effective in reducing the hostility of some individuals and have no effect on others with similar symptoms.

Although there can be little doubt that a variety of drugs can have profound effects on the neural substrates for aggression, much of the evidence at this time is sketchy and limited to clinical studies using nonblind procedures in which suggestion can and sometimes does have a larger impact on the dependent variable than the drug. Many of these clinical reports should be considered as hypothesis-generating rather than hypothesis-testing studies. They suggest the design of careful, well-designed experiments. There are, however, some pitfalls in research designs on drugs that must be understood in evaluating the results. A good double-blind crossover study showing that a given drug or drug combination decreases aggressive tendencies as indicated by some reliable measure is potent evidence for believing that the preparation has some antihostility actions. However, a good double-blind crossover study showing no antiaggression effect is not good evidence, and this goes beyond the obvious principle that one cannot prove the null hypothesis. Because there are different kinds of aggression, which, according to our model at least have different neurological bases, and because there are wide individual differences in susceptibility to all types of pharmaceutical agents, it is quite possible for a given drug to have potent antihostility effects that do not reach statistical significance in a particular study even though that study was well designed. Many studies use a large, heterogeneous sample of patients composed of neurotics, schizophrenics, manic-depressives, sex deviants, and whatever other type of patient happens to be available to the experimenter. With this kind of sample it is conceivable that a given drug may have a real and profound antihostility effect on a small percentage of individuals and no effect at all on a large percentage of patients. The high variability in the data then washes out any possibility of statistical significance. If there are good clinical or theoretical reasons for believing that a particular drug should have aggression reduction properties, the negative finding in the initial study should be followed up by a study of the responders in which each subject serves as his own control with, of course, all the appropriate research controls and cautions. This is obviously an arduous and time-consuming task, but there is no way around it.

The advent of the widespread use of phenothiazines led to a significant reduction in psychotic hostility. Kline[317] suggests that "wards formerly filled with screaming denudative, assaultive patients now have window curtains and flowers on the table." Quantitative estimates of the reduction of destructive, assaultive behavior are difficult to find, but Kline[317] offers one that is dramatic in its simplicity. In 1955 prior to the use of the major tranquilizers in the Rockland State Hospital, there were 8,000 windowpanes broken and three full-time glaziers were needed to keep the windows in repair. By 1960, when full use was being made of the psychotropic drugs, window pane breakage was down to 1,900 panes a year. It has been suggested that the sedative action of the phenothiazines alone could account for the improved picture in the mental hospitals. However, it must be recognized that potent sedative hypnotics such as chloral hydrate and paraldehyde have been known and used for three-quarters of a century.

The phenothiazines, or major tranquilizers, all appear to have a taming effect over and above their sedative action.[29,223] They are the drug of choice for self-referred violent patients who report to Massachusetts General Hospital because they have

154

what they perceive as uncontrollable destructive or homicidal tendencies.[347] Cole et al.,[112] reporting on a number of controlled studies on the phenothiazines used for schizophrenic patients, conclude that hostility and uncooperativeness are more frequently controlled than are anxiety, tension, and agitation.

Perphenazine alone, or in combination with the antidepressant, Amitriptyline, has been useful in reducing the aggressive tendencies of depressed patients,[447] aggressive mental defectives,[398] sex-deviated criminals,[84] and aggressive alcoholics.[45] In one study using a double-blind crossover design to compare the psychological effect of perphenazine and a placebo, the investigators reported a significant reduction of the median scores on hostility for sixteen of twenty patients when they were on perphenazine.[228]

The hostile tendencies of a wide variety of patients, from epileptic psychotics,[300,444,637] to disturbed adolescents,[474] mentally retarded patients,[1,7] and hyperactive children,[5] have been successfully reduced with thioridazine. A survey of the studies on thioridazine is given by Cohen.[109]

Other phenothiazines on which there is clinical evidence for the particular control of aggressive and combative behavior are propericiazine,[290,594] trifluoperazine,[533,570,603] and fluphenazine.[586,646]

A brief survey of some of the other drugs that are useful for the inhibition of hostile-feeling, aggressive acting-out will be found in Appendix A. These include Dilantin, Haldol, the benzodiazepines (including Librium and Valium), the propendiols, and tethahydrocannabinol (marihuana).

The antihostility drugs discussed above function to raise the threshold for hostile feelings and thus for hostile behavior. They are therefore useful in providing the individual with a measure of control that is unavailable without them. In a sense they help to control his environment in that he is an active participant in interpersonal interactions. Hostility evokes hostility that evokes further hostility. Drugs with an anti-aggression action contribute to the breaking of that type of vicious circle, since the patient is less easily angered. In some cases that action in and of itself may be all that is needed. However, anger frequently results from an inappropriate interpretation of the environmental stimuli. That is, the individual has learned to respond with anger in situations that would not arouse that affective state in most people in his culture. Psychotherapy in one form or another is necessary to help the patient learn to interpret the cues in his environment differently and more appropriately. The drug therapy may make the patient more accessible to psychotherapy and facilitate the learning process. Therefore, for many patients the optimal therapeutic approach is a combination of both drug and psychotherapy.

There is probably more potential for abuse (i.e., the inappropriate use) of drugs for aggression control than for any of the other physiological methods. Currently, all the drugs with an antihostility component to their action require a prescription signed by a physician. None of them give a very satisfactory "high" so they are unlikely to be abused by the same group of individuals who abuse the various mood elevators. However, the ease with which drugs can be administered means that they can be prescribed inappropriately without adequate evaluation of the optimal therapy.

With drugs there is a *potential* for political abuse. I have suggested[410] that it might ultimately be possible to put antihostility drugs or a combination of drugs in the water supply and that we should be concerned about it. In April of 1974 a panel at the Seventh International Water Quality Symposium considered the question. "Shall we add lithium to drinking water?" As of this writing the conclusions of the panel are not available, but it is clear that the unequivocal answer is NO!!, and that "no" applies to lithium and any other psychotropic drug. There are obvious ethical considerations, which will be discussed later, and there are practical considerations almost too obvious to mention. These relate to dosage, distribution, side effects, and a general ignorance of the effects of mass distribution that would almost undoubtedly bring to light a large number of unpredicted idiosyncratic and possibly paradoxical reactions.

As a political tool for the control of the masses of people to keep them happy with a given administration or political system, it would not be very useful. At best, the wide distribution of antihostility drugs, whether via water, milk, bread, or any other system, would reduce the probability of some kind or kinds of aggression. Intellectual, unemotional dissent (i.e., instrumental aggression) would not be controlled.

CHAPTER

# The Limitations of Physiological Methods of Aggression Reduction

The physiological methods of aggression reduction cannot be effectively used against a person like Speleni (the hired killer in Chapter 1), or a bomber pilot over the Persian Gulf. Both are engaged in instrumental aggression and neither may have any feeling of hostility toward their victims. The bomber pilot may be essentially at peace with the world. He has had a good breakfast of steak and eggs and a very pleasant morning ride high above the clouds, which are bathed in sunshine far below. When his radar indicates that it is time to press a bomb release button, he may do so without the slightest feeling of antagonism. His bombs may destroy the homes and lives of hundreds of people. He has behaved as he has been trained to behave and emotional responses may not be involved at all. The "trigger man" (Speleni) kills because he is financially rewarded for killing. He may not know his victim and may feel no animosity toward him whatsoever. Scott[506] (p. 38) was quite correct when he said "we still have no drug that will selectively erase the effect of training." It should be added that there is no other physiological manipulations that can selectively modify the effects of training. Further, with the current state of the art, no such method is likely to be found in the near future. That type of control change must await major, and as yet, quite unpredictable breakthroughs.

It is important to differentiate learned aggressive behavior from learned feelings of anger. Learned aggressive behavior, instrumental aggression, is similar to any other complex learned response such as driving an automobile. Once the response pattern is learned, there is little if any affective component connected with it. And, just as there is no physiological method of selectively manipulating the learned response of driving behavior, there is none for the learned response of aggressive behavior. It is true that a number of procedures may reduce general awareness, interfere with neuromuscular coordination, and through sedation interfere with performance. They do not, however, affect learning.

In addition to learning to respond aggressively to particular situations in order to gain some satisfaction or reinforcements, it is also possible to learn to become angry. Frustration, deprivation, or some other anger-evoking phenomenon becomes associated with the cues of a particular situation or individual. Those cues are then capable of eliciting a feeling of anger or hostility. The feeling of anger is subject to physiological manipulation because that feeling is dependent on a particular set of neural pathways in the limbic system that are subject to the various methods of physiological reduction considered in this chapter. It is possible to raise the threshold for feelings of anger, with the result that greater provocation is necessary before the individual feels the appropriate emotion.

The distinction between instrumental aggression and aggressive behavior containing an affective component has important implications for the abuse potential of the physiological control of aggression. As indicated briefly in connection with each method, none of them are particularly valuable as political tools, since they are capable only of reducing the intensity of, or the threshold for, the affective component. They may, in fact, be counterproductive for an individual who wishes to control the rebellious tendencies of a particular population. One reaction to oppression, political or otherwise, is to become angry and, as a result of that anger, to evolve a plan, which may involve aggressive behavior, to alleviate the oppression. Another reaction to oppression is to recognize it as such intellectually and to come to the conclusion that the oppression must be eliminated. A plan, which may involve aggressive behavior, is then worked out. Antihostility drugs in the water supply will affect only the anger; they will have no influence on the intellectual processes involved in the aggressive plans. In fact, if the anger is controlled, the plans may be more effective because they will not involve the impulsive quality that often results from the urgency of anger. Further, because the emotional component will not function as a distractor, the intellectual processes may function more efficiently.

In 1971 Kenneth B. Clark started a monumental controversy when he suggested that the necessary resources in terms of scientific personnel and research facilities be mobilized "to reduce human anxieties, tensions, hostilities, violence, cruelty, and destructive power irrationalities of man which are the basis of wars (p. 1055)."[106] He further suggested that world leaders accept and use the first form of psychotechnological biochemical intervention that would reduce or block the possibility that they would use their power destructively. He implies that the adequate use of the new physiological technology of hostility inhibition could eliminate destructive wars. Since, as this book has shown, a great deal is now known about hostility control and the potential for further developments in those types of reductions is great, it is important to attempt to relate these developments to Clark's proposal.

If one makes the assumption that modern wars result from the impulsive behavior of world leaders who are acting in anger, Clark's proposal would be a reasonable one, and adequate antiaggression therapy for world leaders would, in fact, significantly reduce the possibilities of armed conflict. Further, given the current status of our understanding, it is highly likely that a concentrated research program could develop pharmaceutical agents that, either singly or in combination, could eliminate feelings of anger and hostility and the irrational decision based on those feelings. A number of drugs are available now but considerable research is needed to establish the types of aggressive behavior affected and more needs to be known about possible side effects. When these drugs are perfected, as they certainly will be, and we know with some assurance that there are minimal risks of such effects as paradoxical reactions, I agree with Kenneth Clark that they should be taken by those who hold positions of political power. The world can ill afford the luxury of world leaders who are subject to fits of anger that may result in impulsive and irrational aggressive behavior.

However, the unfortunate fact is that although the psychotechnical revolution may ultimately reduce feelings of anger and its resultant behavior, it is not likely to eliminate destructive war. Much, if not most, of the aggression involved in war is instrumental, that is, it is directed at achieving certain gains, the acquisition of territory, the settlement of disputed boundaries, the expansion of a sphere of influence, or the economic exploitation of another country. Those motives may have essentially no emotional component and anger may play no role. Once again, it should be emphasized that no known physiological manipulation can selectively influence particular learned behaviors. The psychotechnological revolution is not even close to being able to influence those kinds of behavior; thus, war based primarily on nonemotional motivations will not be curtailed by physiological manipulations.

Kenneth Clark's proposal implies the use of some kind of pressure to convince world leaders to take advantage of the predicted psychotechnical advances. William G. Scott,[507] however, proposes that, "Mind techniques will be used by the elite doing significant jobs to changes themselves into significant people." His argument runs, in part, that the elite are overworked and constantly striving to improve their efficiency. Such factors as anxiety and unreasonable feelings of hostility interfere with clear thinking and the most efficient performance. Various types of mind control ultimately offer the possibility of reducing these distracting states of mind. Scott indicates that the moral grounds for the use of mind control techniques by "significant people" stem from the significance of their jobs, the superior execution of which will benefit large numbers of people. This is an interesting proposal, which time will test.

## Ethical Problems

As indicated, there are now large numbers of methods that are useful for the inhibition of aggressive behavior. These methods may be highly beneficial to individuals in terms of their own adjustment, happiness, and efficiency. They may also be beneficial to society in protecting it from the depredations of the irrationally hostile individual. However, controls always imply the limitation of freedom, and the limitation of freedom is the justifiable concern of most of humankind. The issues are complex but they cannot be ignored for the reason. The possibility of highly effective control of the aggression of individuals is here now, and the methods can only become more effective and efficient in the future. It is therefore critical that some of the problems be examined and some tentative suggestions for guidelines offered.

Harris[249] has considered the general ethical problems of research with humans. His major points are well-summarized below.

1. . . . each and every person should be regarded as worthy of sympathetic consideration, and should be so treated; 2. . . . no

person should be regarded by another as a mere possession; or used as a mere instrument or treated as a mere obstacle, to another's satisfaction; and 3. . . . persons are not and ought never be treated in any undertaking as mere expendables.

However, a more detailed consideration of the problem is also needed.

Many individuals who exhibit aggressive behavior do not want to behave in that way but insist that they cannot help it. The annals of crime contain many cases of pathological murderers who plead with the police to catch them before they commit another murder. Many of the patients discussed here actively seek help in controlling their impulsive aggressiveness. Mark and Ervin[377] indicate that half of a sample of 150 of their violent patients were driven to attempted suicide because of their despair over their uncontrollable violence.

The ethical problems involved in dealing with the self-referred patient appear to be relatively uncomplicated. As long as the patient gives *informed* consent, it would appear that any of the available therapies could be used as long as the welfare of the patient is paramount and the individual administering the therapy does not have a conflict of interest in the case. The patient, it is true, must have a certain amount of trust in the therapist because some of the therapies are highly complex and require a considerable background of knowledge before they can be reasonably well understood and evaluated. Further, as has been emphasized repeatedly, aggressive behavior is most generally episodic and the individual's tendency to give consent, either informed or otherwise, may vary considerably as a function of where he or she is in the cycle. Charles Whitman actively desired help in the control of his globally hostile impulses and did seek such help from a psychiatrist. However, once he was engaged in the violent episode, it is clear that he was unwilling to consent to any control over his behavior.

The problem is dramatically illustrated by a case study presented informally at a symposium on the identity and dignity of man. This quotation is presented in full because it dramatizes so well the dilemmas involved in informed consent and the problems in the outer reaches of behavior control. The exchange is between Robert V. Bruce and Frank Ervin.

*Bruce:* May I ask Dr. Ervin if he has ever been tempted to press a button to make the patient reasonable enough to understand the explanation of why the button should be pressed?

*Ervin:* This leads to a very interesting kind of paradox. I will give you a specific example. We had a patient whom we had in fact operated on. We had done the diagnostic procedure and had wires in his brain. A guy who had a very dramatic "flip-flop" in his personality state, he was either aggressive, paranoid, litigious, difficult to deal with or he was a very sweet, reasonable, passive, dependent kind of neurotic. These were his two modes of existence. Long before he had also happened to have epilepsy which is why he had come to us. In fact, there were two patients. I had a choice as to which one to deal with. These two patients were a great stress on the wife of the single body in whom they were contained. On this occasion she broke down and wept and said, "Who are you, honey? I don't know who you are." He had gotten extremely upset on the ward. We could not hold him against his will in the hospital since our hospital is a voluntary hospital and he could only be there by his own choice. He threatened to leave and was, in fact, in the process of leaving, ostensibly to kill his wife. At least that is what he said he was going to do, and I rather believed him. In the course of the day, we managed to get him into the laboratory and stimulate this part of the brain that Hudson Hoagland mentioned this morning.* He took a deep breath and said, "You know you nearly let me get out of here?"

*Bruce:* If I may quote history instead of the Bible for a change, you appealed from Alexander drunk to Alexander sober.

*Ervin:* Precisely, and I said, "Yes, I couldn't have held you." He said, "You've got to do something to keep me from getting out of here. I think if you had the nurse hide my pants, I wouldn't have left." I thought that was a good suggestion and followed it. We had a very reasonable discussion and he was grateful for my having stopped him. I said, "Well, I guess we won't have to go through this very much longer because tomorrow morning we have planned to make the definitive lesion and I wanted to talk to you about that. What we are going to do is burn out this little part of the brain that causes all the trouble." He said, "Yeah, that's great." Well, the next morning about 9:00, he was brought down and he said, "You're going to burn what out of my brain? Not on your bloody life you're not!" He would easily at the earlier point have signed anything I asked for. He was guilty; he was sweet; perhaps he was reasonable. But which of those two states I should deal with posed a real problem for me. So informed consent isn't all it's cracked up to be. Voluntary understanding has its problems.[173]

---

*This reference is to the amygdala (4-5 and 6-3).

Ervin's dilemma over whether the patient was being reasonable before or after the electrical stimulation is an exaggeration of the same problem in the normal person who sometimes makes decisions during a state of anger or during a state of calm. When the neural substrates for anger are activated by external stimuli, the individual may make a decision to shout at his wife, beat her, or kill her. If he is restrained from any of these activities by circumstances and has an opportunity to calm down so that those neural substrates are no longer active, or are, in fact, inhibited by the activity in one of the neural substrates for positive affective behavior, his decision on how to behave toward his wife may be very different. He may be extremely grateful for the circumstances that prevented him from carrying out his decision during his anger state. I am obviously not suggesting in any sense that individuals should be aided in their decision-making processes by direct amygdaloid stimulation, I merely wish to point up the fundamental similarity. In the case of Ervin's patient, the aggressive mental state was blocked directly by a handy electrode. It is conceivable that the patient's mood could have been changed by the manipulation of the external environment, calm therapeutic counseling, and so on.

The problems involved in the use of brain stimulation as a method of aggression control were discussed earlier. This case is used merely to point up the problem with the concept of informed consent. In spite of the difficulties, however, the principle of informed consent appears to be a useful guide in deciding on the types of therapy to be used for those individuals who actively seek help in controlling their hostile feelings and actions.

The more difficult problem from an ethical standpoint lies in the control of aggression when the aggressor actively rejects the idea that his behavior should be controlled. When, under what circumstances, and by whom should controls be imposed from without?

Obviously, this problem did not arise with the development of the recent behavioral and physiological control methodologies. People have always been controlling others, and since the Code of Hammurabi in 1780 B.C., laws have been used to limit that control. Law must ultimately limit the use of more sophisticated controls developed by technology.

Society must and will protect itself from the depredations of violent individuals regardless of the origin of their violence. It already has an elaborate, although frequently ineffective, system for protecting itself while protecting the civil rights of the individuals being restrained. Technology has now provided society with much more powerful tools for the control of aggressive individuals. Because these techniques have been developed only recently, there is no body of common law regarding them. Because they are powerful, they are subject to misuse and thus potentially threaten individual civil rights.

It should be recognized, however, that the techniques now available, or potentially available, provide the individual with considerably better alternatives than the traditional ones in general use. Some of the techniques discussed here are irreversible and, because of that, their use should certainly be limited and subject to the most stringent types of controls. However, it is not clear that they should be completely rejected on the basis of their irreversibility. Drugs, hormones, electrical stimulation, and lesions do make changes in the brain, some more permanent than others. However, it should be obvious that current prison management techniques also make changes in the brain and those changes are frequently permanent. It would be naive to believe that prison conditions as described by many individuals (see Menninger's *Crime of Punishment*)[393] do not have a permanent and deleterious effect on the behavior and the emotional stability of those incarcerated. Experience, and particularly traumatic experience, has its own powerful effects on the neural mechanisms that control our behavior.

The ideal technique for dealing with the violent individual is one that protects society and enables the individual to gain some control over his actions. As indicated earlier, a number of disorders that are readily diagnosed result in behavior ranging from minor social disruption to murder. Persons subject to these disorders frequently break laws and are subject to the judicial process. Their tendency to violent behavior can frequently be readily eliminated by a physiological manipulation, and they are benefited little, if any, by incarceration. The uncontrollably hostile individual with a septal or temporal lobe tumor can regain normal behavior when the tumor is removed. Some psychomotor epileptics with episodic dyscontrol can have their periodic outbursts of violence eliminated when they are given adequate doses of Dilantin. Certainly most people would agree that physiological techniques should be used in those instances. These are "medical" problems, which should be dealt with medically. They require careful and complete diagnosis and therapy and although it may be necessary to take careful security precautions, the treatment should be handled by physicians and in a medical rather than penal facility.

Many other violent individuals, however, who do not have readily diagnosable physical disorders may nevertheless be helped by physiological techniques. Special precautions must be taken to assure their rights are not abused by the misuse of modern technology. A number of actions are possible to assure such protection.

One of the potential problems is that the decisions to use drastic therapies may be made by individuals who have a particular vested interest in having the individual brought under control. Family members, prison officials, and some governmental units may find their purpose well-served if the aggressive person can no longer express his hostility, and their concerns may very well not be in the best interest of the one whose behavior is to be altered. In order to minimize that risk, it would be useful to have an independent review board approve all procedures that are not a part of the traditional correction methodologies. The board should be composed of physicians, lawyers, ethicists, laymen, and prisoner advocates.

In addition to the review board that must ultimately pass on whether or not a given procedure can be used in a particular case, the principle of informed consent should be utilized within the constraints set down by the judicial process. Obviously, consent, informed or otherwise, is not required before a person can be confined, even in solitary, for prolonged periods. However, even though some of the physiological techniques of behavior control are far less drastic than prolonged solitary confinement, informed consent should be required at least until those procedures have the sanction of prolonged usage. Informed consent in a prison situation leaves much to be desired. There are many pressures, some subtle and some blatant, that can be brought to bear on prisoners to induce them to agree to a given procedure. It is for this reason that the prisoner's consent is not sufficient of itself for permission to be granted. The review board indicated earlier must help to protect the individual from those pressures. However, at this stage of knowledge, it seems that the greatest protection of civil rights would be served by not permitting the use of nontraditional techniques without the consent of the recipient, and those designated to protect his rights.

The new therapies for the control of hostility are not equally risky and several criteria can be used to assess their relative desirability and priority of use. Clearly experimental techniques should not be used on a captive population that, because of the nature of its life-situation, cannot give a reliable informed consent. Mark and Neville[380] delineate two aspects of the concept of *experimental*. In the first sense a technique is experimental if it is done for the purpose of increasing fundamental knowledge and without the expectation that the recipient will derive benefit from it. In the second sense a procedure is experimental if "its effects are unpredictable, its mechanisms poorly understood, its risks highly variable, and its usefulness subject to widespread debate in the medical community" (p. 766). Mark and Neville go on to indicate that psychiatric neurosurgery is experimental in the latter sense even though there is now relatively little risk to life.

A procedure that provides the least amount of discomfort while providing the greatest amount of self-determination and that provides that least amount of risk of objectionable side effects is the most desirable. Finally, at this stage of technological development a procedure's desirability is partly a function of its reversibility. When these physiological procedures get beyond the experimental stage, nonreversibility may be a virtue. At the current stage of development, however, reversible effects are clearly preferred.

According to the preceding criteria, psychosurgery would be one of the least desirable techniques because it is clearly experimental and the effects are permanent. If there are any behavioral side effects, they are also frequently permanent. Aggression control by brain stimulation would also be undesirable because so little is known about it that it must be considered as highly experimental. Further, it is not yet clear what the possible side effects are, and whether they are transitory or relatively permanent. Castration as a treatment for sex crime would also be relatively less desirable than other types of treatment. The results are obviously permanent and, in some individuals at least, there are both psychological and phsyiological side effects that, although not critical, may be quite disturbing.

Hormone therapy and the use of pharmaceutical agents would seem to be a valuable addition to correctional procedures for specific kinds of critical violence as long as the safeguards previously outlined are provided. The effects of both of these procedures are readily reversed simply by withdrawing the medication. There is always the possiblity of undesirable side effects, but careful monitoring, particularly during the early phases of treatment, can usually prevent any serious damage and the side effects are generally eliminated by a reduction of the dosage or by discontinuing the treatment.

Finally, there is a general concern by some critics about all methods of physiological control over behavior. They suggest that aggressive behavior is an expression of the free will and that any direct physiological intervention that limits or prevents that expression is demeaning and degrading of human dignity. Mark and Neville[380] put it very well when they reply to this argument, "This view is particularly inappropriate not because free will is to be denied but because the quality of human life is to be prized" (p. 772). They point out, as had been repeatedly indicated in this book, that many hyperaggressive individuals are

166

most distressed by their own unacceptable behavior and their ability to control it and many are driven to the brink of suicide because of their deficiencies in impulse control. A physiological therapeutic measure that helps to alleviate an impulsive-aggressive syndrome provides the individual with more, not less, control over his own behavior and, "It enhances, and does not diminish, his dignity. It adds and does not detract, from his human qualities (p. 772)."[380]

# CHAPTER
# X
# Territoriality

## The Problem

"And ye shall hear of wars and
rumours of wars; . . .
For nation shall rise against nation and
kingdom against kingdom, . . .
*Matthew XXIV:6–7*

The causes of international aggression are complex. The interactions among those causes have a complexity currently beyond the human. Although there is little understanding of the multiplicity of the factors that lead humanity into the inhumanity of war, simplistic explanations can be rejected. It has been repeatedly suggested that wars occur and are the inevitable and inescapable destiny of the human race because a part of its heritage is the innate and universal behavior tendency of territoriality.

Territoriality is one of the most hallowed concepts of animal behavior. All animals from the anolis lizard to the King of Spain exhibit territorial behavior. It is said to have great explanatory power providing a better understanding of why a dog lifts its leg at a fire hydrant and why a nuclear war is inevitable.

In order to have a detailed understanding why this concept is of little value, it is necessary to go back to the extensive literature on animals from which this idea was derived.

In 1968 I suggested[410] that it might be useful to consider territorial aggression as a separate classification in which the major stimulus variables eliciting that behavior included a territory in which an animal had established itself as an intruder. It was implied further that this type of aggression had a separate physiological basis about which little was known, but which should ultimately be experimentally differentiable. However, further study has convinced me that this is not the case. It seems, in fact, that the term "territorial" may be misleading.

The literature on animals is replete with examples of vigorous fighting which occurs when one individual enters the home range of another. Schenkel,[495] for example, reports several instances in which an intruder lion has been killed when it was encountered in areas which were frequently visited by a given lion pride. In general, animals concentrate their activities in a particular spatial location. Periodically, however, they move out from the area in which they spend most of their time into less familiar grounds. If, during that foray, they enter the area in which a conspecific concentrates its activities, an aggressive display is likely to ensue. If the intruder does not leave, there is a high probability that a fight will occur. Further, the resolution of the conflict will generally involve the defeat and retreat of the animal which is on unfamiliar ground. The animal closest to the center of its own activity range is most likely to conduct the more vigorous attack and is also more likely to win the encounter and, it is likely to win even though the intruder is larger and, in other situations, may be more dominant and a more able and vigorous fighter.

The aggression scenario described above has been observed and reported so frequently and by so many investigators that there can be little doubt that it is a behavior pattern characteristic of a wide variety of species. However, many, if not most, reports on territoriality have involved a mixture of observations and inferences about those observations. Much of the theorizing about the meaning of these behaviors has further confused inference and observation with the result that a great deal more meaning has been attached to this particular aggressive interaction than the actual observations merit. One of the purposes of this section will be to attempt to separate observation from inference and put this behavior in perspective.

Territoriality is such a diverse phenomenon that a single definition seldom includes all of the behaviors considered relevant by all investigators. However, territoriality is generally considered to be different from *home range*. The latter concept, initially formulated by Burt[86] includes *the area, usually around a home site, over which the animal normally travels in search of food.*

Although one cannot know what an animal is searching for or even if it is searching at any given time as suggested by Burt's definition, the other uses of the home range concept are generally clear, observable, and can be agreed upon by independent observers. The definitions of territoriality and territorial aggression, however, are not so clear nor so easily agreed upon. Unobservables are inferred by almost all definitions of these constructs. Anthropomorphic motivational states are projected to the animal and are then treated as though they were established observations.

One of the earliest definitions[435] suggested that *territory is a defended area.* Many authors have adopted this definition.[18,47,81,263,264,289,423,481,556,612,639] It has been repeatedly pointed out that home ranges may overlap, but territories generally do not because the various animals under study *defend* their territories and *protect* them from encroachment by conspecifics, or by male conspecifics, or by any intruder. How intensive a *defense* the animal puts up depends on the species under consideration and on how broad the experimenter wishes to make the definition.

Motivational states are not only attributed to the territory-holder but they are also not uncommonly attributed to the intruder. For example, Stevenson-Hamilton (quoted in)[639] suggests that the blue Wildebeest (Gorgon *taurinus*) *strongly resents* encroachment on its grazing land. He also describes an instance in which intruders are chased by a territory-holding bull and then says, *"Not the least remarkable phase of the incident was the sense of wrong-doing exhibited by the trespassers, which displayed not the smallest tendency to offer any resistance."*

*Defend, protect, resent* are all terms which are descriptive of human motivational states. When these terms are applied to animals they are inferred from the behavior, and there can be no assurance that the animal has any mental process even remotely similar to those implied by such words. Observation indicates only that many kinds of animals live within certain restricted areas and that some of them sometimes engage in fighting behavior. It can also be said that, in general, the closer they are to the center of their home range, the more likely they are to react to another animal with threatening gestures and fighting responses. It is really no more reasonable to suggest that an animal is *defending* its territory than it is to believe that the intruder is defending its God-given right to territorial expansion. Crook[118] makes the important point that, *"In animal societies, individu-*

*als do not fight because they have territories, they have territories because, among other things, they fight."*

It contributes very little to our understanding of the phenomenon to suggest that certain animals have an innate tendency for territorial defense. Understanding will come only when we can specify the variables of which this behavior is a function. We need to spell out specifically the stimulus characteristics that elicit this kind of behavior in a given animal. Further, since many animals engage in aggression within the home range only at particular times in the seasonal or life cycle, it is necessary to specify the physiological state of the animal during that aggressive period.

Although it is certainly true that a wide variety of animals in diverse circumstances do engage in aggressive behavior near the center of their home range, there is little evidence that there is any kind of unitary instinct or innate tendency for *territorial defense*. The conditions under which home range fighting occurs are highly variable and differ on a wide variety of dimensions. Carpenter[96] expresses it well when he says, *"Territorial behavior apparently has great variations; these are related to population pressures, to social organization, to fluctuations of food supplies, to predation, and many other factors."* He indicates further that, *". . . territoriality is of the nature of higher order, complex and dependent behavior systems which are organized upon numerous subsystems and behavorial determinants."* It is, in fact, (although this is not suggested by Carpenter) the case that such a catchall term for such a wide variety of behaviors has little value as a unifying construct.

There have been some attempts to classify different kinds of territoriality on the basis of presumed function. Nice,[434] in reference to territories in birds, has suggested seven classes based on combinations of feeding, breeding, and nesting grounds, as well as roosting. Others have included communal territories.[250] Burt,[86] writing about mammals, has also suggested a classification based on function. These include territories concerned with breeding and rearing of young and with food and shelter. He indicates further that these classes can be subdivided. Territoriality, because it is so diverse, could, of course, be classified in a variety of other ways.

In order to appreciate the many different response patterns which have been referred to as territorial, some of the characteristics of this phenomenon in different species must be reviewed. This is not an attempt to survey the vast literature on the topic, but to cite examples of animals that show the different behaviors. Since I wish to avoid the imputation of unknowable motives to animals, I will refer to what is often called territorial defense as *central home range fighting.* "Central home range" refers to the geographical area most frequented by the animal in question. This review deals primarily with mammals because they are most relevant for an increased understanding of humans. However, there is probably much more information available on *territoriality* in birds.

There is considerable variability among the species in regard to what types of stimulus animals will elicit threat or attack by an individual within its own central home range. Some species such as the vole are so solitary that a vigorous fight will occur when another vole is encountered whether it be male or female, young or old, except during a restricted mating period.[39] Among wildebeests, the fighting age occurs generally at thirty-four to forty months. At this time some of the males confine their activities to a particular geographical location. Other male wildebeests that approach the area will be attacked in the characteristic *tournament behavior.* Females, however, are neither threatened nor attacked.[177] Similar behavior is found in the Uganda kob.[83]

Lions do not restrict their attacks to males. Either a male or a female lion may be attacked and in some instances killed if it is encountered within the central home range of another animal.[493,495] The lion like many other animals does not live in isolation. Thus, the home ranges, including the central home ranges may overlap with many other animals of the same species. Lions live in prides of from four or five members up to fifteen adults and two cubs. These animals meet and interact with one another with the occurrence of remarkably little agonistic behavior within the colony. However, if a lion which has its central home range in a different geographical location wanders into the home range of the colony, it will be attacked. Thus, it is a conspecific with which the attacker has had little experience that is the object of the aggressive encounter.

Territory is sometimes defined as that area in which a given animal will not tolerate another member of the same species.[47,164] However, in many animals the tendency to attack within the central home range is not limited to conspecifics.

Hediger[264] describes the case of a lemur, which would permit only its keeper in its cage, that severely bit a volunteer assistant. Hediger suggests that in *territorial defense,* even small birds and animals can be dangerous to humans.

According to Barnett[39] a lion is not particularly dangerous to humans if it has escaped from captivity and is encountered in the street. It can be driven away fairly easily. However, if the animal is in its home cage or home range, it may instantly strike down a human intruder. Thus, Barnett suggests, the wise lion

173

tamer has the animal driven into an area already occupied by the tamer.

In many species from the mouse to the Uganda kob, fighting behavior is the particular province of the male. However, there are also many species in which the female shows the same aggressive proclivity as does the male when another animal appears in the central home range. The female gibbons are as hostile as the male.[95] Rhesus monkeys and lions are also examples of fighting females.[495]

The tendency for an animal to threaten* or fight in its home range is highly variable depending on both the environmental conditions and the internal physiological process of the individual. Under laboratory conditions of high population density, mice do not restrict their activities to specific areas. Although they do fight, the fighting is not geographically localized.[502] However, it has been shown that under more natural conditions where space is available, some species of mice do live in colonies within restricted areas and do attack non-colony members who enter the area.[120,160] Several factors may contribute to a shift from geographically localized fighting to a dominant subordinate relationship within a group of animals. These include insufficient space, a lack of opportunity to emigrate, inadequate escape cover as well as a high population density.[17] A number of animals restrict their activities to a particular geographical area only during certain times of the year, frequently during the breeding season. This is true of a number of the Pinnipedia such as the southern fur seal, the grey seal, sea lions, and elephant seals.[639] It is also true of the Uganda kob, the wildebeest,[177] and in part, the red deer.[127]

Fighting by females near the nest area in some animals depends on whether or not the animal is lactating.[314] The area adopted for the home range is also dependent on the season and the availability of food. The deer[127] and the elk[419] have home ranges in the mountains during the summer but migrate to the lower ranges during the winter. The home range of howler

---

*The term "threat" refers to species specific behavior that occurs when the animal encounters a conspecific within its home range. It generally involves responses that make the responder appear larger. This is accomplished by ruffling the feathers of a bird, or having the hair stand up if the subject is a mammal. Threat is complex response involving a series of movements in addition to those that make the animal appear larger. The term "threat" is not meant to imply any thought processes such as the animal being fearful, or angry or the wish to drive the intruder away. The threat response can be observed and different individuals can agree on the response. That is not true of the unobservables such as "fear, anger or wishes."

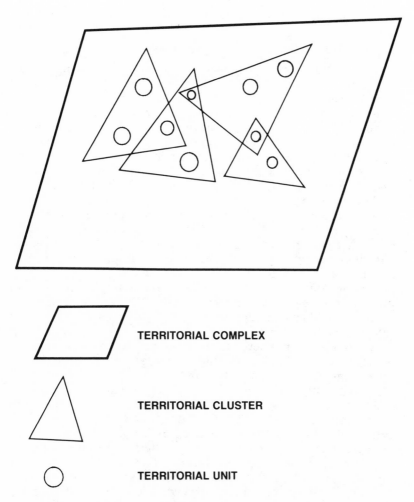

**TERRITORIAL COMPLEX**

**TERRITORIAL CLUSTER**

**TERRITORIAL UNIT**

*FIGURE 7. Complexity of human territorial behavior. (Modified from D. Stea, Space, Territory, and Human Movements, Landscape, 1965, 15, No. 1.)*

monkeys is dynamic and shifts over the years and within the seasons.[94] Restriction of range and intensity of fighting within that range in small carnivores depends both on the amount of food available and on the number of competing animals.[354]

A number of different animals from birds[381] to humans,[240,537] under certain conditions, prevent the close approach of conspecifics. The infringement of this individual distance or personal space results in either avoidance or attack by the animals involved. Crook[118] suggests that territoriality is a special case of spatial defense which cannot be easily separated from the maintenance of personal space. However, the tendency to maintain an individual distance may also be combined with the tendency to fight within a given home range. Carpenter[95] indicates that gibbons have a personal space that cannot be violated but they also fight as a group against other groups which intrude into their home range.

Among some species, the moose[10] for example, the mother maintains a *ring of sliding territoriality* [10] (p. 245) or a personal space around herself and the young, and will behave aggressively toward any approaching animal.

Although a number of authors are impressed by how widespread territoriality is among vertebrates,[18,96] it is by no means universal. Even among closely related species, some show an attachment, a tendency to stay within a particular geographical location and a tendency to fight within it, while other species do not. Heller,[268] for example, studied four species of chipmunk. Two of these species, *Eutamias alpinus* and *E. amoenus* behaved aggressively within their home range whereas *e. minimus* and *E. speciosus* did not. The Indian rhinoceros is highly aggressive and remains within a specific geographical location throughout the year. However, the white rhino does not have a well-differentiated land area to which it confines its activities and is much less aggressive.[107] The black rhinoceros does not appear to be territorially inclined.[496] As indicated above, many seals and related animals have well-defined areas of activity during the breeding season. However, seals of the genus *Phoca* as well as some others do not manifest this behavior and do not react aggressively to conspecifics.[639]

The home ranges of nutria *Myocastor coypus* overlap extensively and although adults may be highly aggressive, there is no indication that this hostile behavior is restricted to a given location except that a mother with offspring is aggressive in the nesting area.[483] Lowe[363] has reported aggressive behavior among red deer on the island of Rhum but he indicates that marked animals may be found in different groups at different times and that there is no evidence of group territorial behavior.

Many herding animals, primarily the ungulates, show neither the restriction of activity to a given land space nor hostile tendencies.[639] Among the subhuman primates which are most closely related to humans, many do not show aggression when encountering a strange conspecific. Among the Rhodesian baboons, for example, the habitual daily routines tend to keep the different troops apart but the ranges of the troops overlap to a considerable extent in some cases. There is no evidence that these animals fight with other troops when they meet.[612] The monkeys of the forest fringes and the savannahs (*Cercopithecus* and *Macaca*) also do not show central home range fighting.[118] Chimpanzees are organized into troops, but interchanges in membership are not uncommon and several troops may use the same home range.[465]

## Scent Marking and Its Meaning

A large number of animals are equipped with specialized anatomical structures which produce species-specific chemical substances. These scents are distributed around the animal's home range through a variety of behaviors. Antelopes have scent glands located beside the eye.[262] In the gerbil, the midventral sebaceous gland produces a scent.[574] Badgers and martens have scent glands under the bases of their tails.[164] Scent glands are located in the flanks of voles[81] and hamsters.[164] Rabbits have scent glands located under the chin.[425] Lions can release a scent along with the urine[493] and many animals are said to utilize urine and fecal material for *marking purposes*.[90,157]

The act of depositing the scent in the environment is referred to as marking and many investigators refer to this behavior *as territorial marking*. Cloudsley-Thompson,[107] suggests that some of the scent glands have evolved specifically for the purpose of marking territory and Eibl-Eibesfeldt[164] says in a quotation from G. Goethe[219] that scent markings are chemical property signs. The term scent marking is descriptive of a given animal's behavior. That is, the marmoset rubs the circumgenital area against some item in the environment, or the gerbil rubs its ventral sebaceous gland against a peg, or the dog deposits a few drops of urine on a fire plug. The result of this behavior is the deposition of a scent which can be detected and reacted to by other animals. However, to refer to this behavior as *territorial marking* imputes to the animal a motivation. (It *wants* to mark a territory to warn conspecifics that this land is occupied so that they will avoid it. Lorenz,[358] for example, compares scent marking in the dog to the song of the nightingale. The dog deposits scent in its territory in order to ward off intruders.) Such a teleological explanation is neither necessary nor particularly useful and can, in fact, be misleading. Marking may be associated with aggressive behavior and it may frequently occur within the animals home range. However, it is also associated with other behavior patterns.

Marking is a response to certain types of stimuli in the environment and those stimuli need not necessarily be associated with the animals central home range or *territory*. Any dog owner knows that it is possible to take his pet half a world away from its home range and that dog will readily mark any post in the environment even though that post has been previously marked by local dogs. Many members of the Canidae family do mark familiar and conspicuous objects on which they have previously deposited a scent, but marking is also elicited by entirely new and unfamiliar objects.[315] Marking in gerbils is actually less frequent in the central home range where the stimuli are most familiar. The highest rate of ventral marking in this species occurs in a moderately novel environment[35] and olfaction appears to be of prime importance because olfactory ablation essentially eliminates the marking response.[35,575] Golden hamsters (*Mesocricetus auratus*) have been shown to spend significantly more time engaged in flank marking in the cage of strange hamsters than they do in their own cage.[421]

If marking is territorial in nature and designed to warn conspecifics away from the area, it would be expected that the scent marks would elicit an avoidance response from other members of the same species. In many cases, however, just the opposite reaction occurs. Gerbils show a preference for objects marked by conspecifics, that is, they will choose as nesting material paper that has been marked by another gerbil.[35] When gerbils mark an environment which is new to them, they show neither preference for, nor a tendency to avoid, pegs which have been previously marked by a strange gerbil.[575]

Marmosets approach and mark a perch in their cages that has been previously marked by another marmoset significantly more than they do a neutral perch or one marked with mouse urine.[170] Both mice and rats follow regular pathways and trails in their daily excursions through their home range. These trails are well-scent-marked with urine. If a given population is experimentally eliminated, the home range will be taken over by immigrants from surrounding areas. These newcomers actually utilize the marked trails and paths of the previous population to find their way around the area and show no evidence of being repelled by the earlier scent markings.[163,569]

In some species there appears to be a tendency to avoid the

marked areas of other individuals. Schaller[493] implies that lions avoid marked areas but he provides little evidence that they do. It has been suggested[315] that the avoidance of marked areas is due to the novelty of the scent of the stranger. However, an interesting experiment on gerbils suggests that the avoidance of a particular scent is a learned reaction because that scent has been associated with the negative reinforcement of defeat. If gerbils are given an opportunity to nest in boxes which contain either clean shavings or shavings which have been soiled by other gerbils, they show no preference. However, if these animals are placed in the home area of a group of gerbils and are attacked and defeated, they show a clear cut preference for nesting in clean shavings in preference to shavings which have been soiled by the antagonists which had defeated them earlier.[573] When gerbils are given a choice in a maze, they will reliably avoid the odor of an animal that has recently defeated them.[438]

Although there is relatively little evidence that a strange scent produces an automatic avoidance response, it does frequently affect the animals' behavior. A strange scent frequently elicits a considerable increase in the marking in a number of different species, including the sugar glider, rabbit, hamster, marmoset, duiker.[457] Some of these animals, including the rabbit,[425] hamster,[160] and marmoset,[170] display a threat response in connection with this increased marking.

It should also be pointed out that scent marking is said to have a number of functions which do not relate to territory. It may help to define a *safe* area and promote colony cohesio.[42] It may be important as sexual communication,[170] and may help to reassure the animal in a strange territory.[315] It may also be a mechanism for defining trails or paths.[164] Ralls[457] lists several other possible functions including, as alarm signals, for individual or group recognition, for species or subspecies recognition and as a primer pheromone which influences reproductive processes.

Population dispersal as well as the limitation of individuals and groups to restricted geographical locations appears to be due in part to a variety of vocal signals. There is evidence that a number of mammals, although by no means all, tend to avoid areas in which conspecifics are emitting particular calls.

The chipmunk (*Tamias striatus*) produces several kinds of vocalizations. Although home ranges of these animals overlap completely, a given chipmunk is usually dominant to others in the core area which centers around its burrow entrance. The particular sound called *chipping* occurs only in that immediate area and it has been suggested the chipping may function as an agonistic signal that inhibits the approach of other chipmunks.[154]

Roaring by lions is said to function as a signal that informs conspecifics of the location of a local pride and thus keeps them at a distance.[495] This function of roaring has not, however, been experimentally demonstrated. Experimental work has shown that barking by the larger male sea lions (*Zalophus californianus*) functions to restrict both the movements and the amount of vocalization by other smaller males.[498]

Although there are exceptions, primates very rarely show inter-animal or inter-group aggressive behavior in relation to their home range or core areas. In general, however, they do restrict their activities to definable geographic areas and family groups or troops are usually isolated from one another even though their home ranges may overlap.[47] The groups appear to be separated by spacing mechanisms. A number of observations indicate that spacing is accomplished by a mutual repulsion or avoidance rather than as a result of actual aggression.[147,382] Many primates, including the howler monkey,[97] gibbon,[95] the northern India languor,[287] and the Callicebus,[383] produce vocalizations that are loud enough to be audible at a considerable distance and which may contribute to the spacing process. These long range calls occur frequently during the early morning and in the absence of any particular external triggering situations.[382] To refer to these calls as territorial markers[383] or threats, seems unwarranted. The calls may serve as *spatial location markers* [47] which provide other members of the same species with information concerning the whereabouts of conspecifics. They may then react by avoiding that location, and contribute to the dispersal of those animals. For the sake of completeness, it should be pointed out that long distance calls of some primate species do not necessarily elicit avoidance reactions. They do some times result in approach tendencies.[382]

## Territorial Mechanisms Reviewed

It can be seen from the foregoing discussion that *territoriality* refers to a complex of behavior patterns that vary widely across species and within species depending on the animal's sex, the characteristics of the intruder, the season of the year, the developmental stage of the animal, as well as a variety of environmental variables. There is evidence, of course, that animals do confine their activities to particular geographical locations and within a given location many animals spend greater amounts of time in so-called core areas. There is also abundant evidence that many animals engage in intraspecific fighting within home ranges and that many species tend to win encounters that are fought close to their core area—that is to say, the animals on unfamiliar ground are chased away, infrequently injured, and on very rare occasions killed.

It is of little explanatory value to suggest that the large variety of factors contributing to fighting within an animal's home range are related to an innate tendency or need to defend a territory. The fact that the animal closest to the center of its home range is more likely to be successful in an encounter with an intruder is certainly not evidence that territorial "defense" is involved. Barnett,[40] for example, has suggested that aggressive behavior in the rat is territorial because the animal must be on familiar ground before it will attack a conspecific. By the same reasoning, one should refer to territorial sexual behavior and territorial eating behavior.

Animals are more *successful* in all of their behaviors when they are on familiar ground. If one wishes to study sexual behavior, predation, or simply eating and drinking, it is essential that the animal be adapted to the environment. In a strange area, the predominant behavior of most animals is cautious investigation which is incompatible with aggressive, sexual, or consummatory behavior. Exploratory behavior will override eating or drinking even under conditions of extreme deprivation. It has been repeatedly reported that a mouse in its home cage will be more likely to initiate and to win a fight against an introduced intruder. However, Urich[599] observed in 1938 that the stranger spends most of its time investigating the unfamiliar cage while the home cage mouse concentrates on fighting.

There are a variety of stimulus conditions which facilitate the tendency for one male to attack another.[410] There is also a tendency on the part of most animals to investigate and/or escape from unfamiliar situations. There is also evidence that the neural systems underlying escape behavior may very well function to inhibit the neural substrates for some kinds of aggressive behavior. Thus, the neural system for aggression (of whatever kind) is less likely to be fully active in an animal that is on unfamiliar ground. If under the pressure of attack, the animal flees to the familiar stimuli of its own core area, the activity in its neural substrates for escape or investigation decreases, and the stimulus of its attacker elicits full and uninhibited activity in the neural substrate for aggression. (See Moyer, 1973[413] for a complete exposition of this point.) It is now more likely to win an encounter with the aggressor who is now itself on unfamiliar ground and has escape and investigation tendencies to compete with its hostile behaviors. In a series of chases and counterchases, it would be expected that the animals might end up at the borders of their home ranges manifesting a combination of escape and

181

aggressive behaviors which are frequently components of the threat response.

Since, as Carpenter[96] suggests, the so-called territorial behavior is a higher order construct which results from the action of a variety of subsystems, it is not possible to attribute this behavior to particular physiological mechanisms. In different seasons and in different species, fighting in relation to a geographical location may be primarily between males, as in the Uganda kob *inter-male aggression*, or restricted to a nest area and confined to lactating females, as in certain female mice (*maternal aggression*), or related to the herding of a harem as in the Pinnipedia (*sex-related aggression*). The amount and intensity of fighting must also undoubtedly be a function of the success or failure of these various aggressive interactions and is therefore partly *instrumental aggression*. The physiological substrates of each of these different kinds of aggression have been considered in some detail elsewhere in this book.

## Human Aggression and the Territorial Imperative

The application of the concept of territorial aggression to humans has resulted primarily from an attempt to extrapolate findings from animal research to the human condition. Thus, if the construct is of dubious value in understanding animals, it may be even less useful in understanding humans. The question, of course, is not whether humans are territorial, but whether that territoriality is imperative.

There is little need to document man's tendency to become attached to geographical locations and possessions. National boundaries do exist; property lines are carefully drawn; and there are well-established legal mechanisms in our culture for establishing title to and exclusive use of property and possessions. Mental patients establish definable territories on the ward and defend them;[176] children establish and defend territories in a playroom[443] and my neighbor down the street becomes upset if I step on his lawn. Significant portions of a number of books have been devoted to the experimental and literary exploration of the human tendency to territoriality.[18,175,240,404,455,537]

Humans not only establish and defend territories but they do so with far greater complexity than is apparent in lower animals. As Stea's[549] analysis indicates, a single individual may have a *territorial unit* in his place of employment, another one at home, and a third at his vacation cabin. The same individual also has a territorial domain which he shares with other persons, each of whom also has several *territorial units* of which only some are shared by two or more individuals. This shared territory is the *territorial cluster*. Each worker, for example, has an individual territorial unit which may be the area immediately surrounding his desk or machine but he shares with others the territorial cluster of the department. Further, a number of territorial clusters may be grouped into a *territorial complex* such as a business, or a political unit which large numbers of individuals perceive as their own and are willing, to some extent, to protect and defend.

Although it is dubious to use the concepts of *protect, defend,* and *resent* in relation to animal behaviors, such motivational constructs are readily applied to humans and can be inferred from the individual's verbal behavior as well as directly observed in one's own introspection. The real question is not whether many humans establish and defend a complexly organized set of territories but whether such a tendency is innate or built-in as it has been said to be, but actually is not in animals. Humans do, of course, have internal impulses to aggression,[411,412] but there is little evidence that the expression of these impulses is innately related to the remarkably complex and abstract construction of territory. Certainly, there is no need to invoke an *instinct* to territoriality as an explanatory principle. The analysis earlier in this section appears to make such an explanation untenable for animals, and it seems even less likely for humans. There is abundant opportunity for humans to learn an aggressive reaction to the invasion of their many territories. Such an invasion frequently involves threat, inconvenience, frustration, and deprivation. Successful aggressive action terminates these negative states with the result that the aggressive behavior is rewarded. In the early social development of humans, conflict potential was considerably enhanced as the concept of ownership of property, tools, livestock, etc, began to develop. It seems reasonable to suggest, as does Crook,[118] that cultural patterns of behavior would develop to regulate interactions regarding property. These behaviors would then be codified into laws of property, its use and exchange.

However, even if, for the sake of argument, the concept of instinctive territorial defense in humans were to be granted, it would not mean that the resultant behavior would be ineradicable as is frequently implied.[18,360,556] Powerful internal impulses of all kinds are modifiable through learning and through manipulations of the environment. Some cultures such as the Arapesh[50] and the Zunibs,[390] although manifesting other kinds of aggressive behavior, do not show territorial tendencies.

It is generally agreed that the Indians on Manhattan Island received a very bad business deal because the Dutch gave them fish hooks and trinkets worth sixty guilders for the entire island.

However, it was the Dutch that were defrauded. First, the Indians did not own the land they sold. Second, they had no understanding of the concept of land ownership. Thus, they had no concept of territorial defense.

Further, *instinctive territorial defense* is not particularly useful in helping us to understand modern war. At best, such an instinct could be offered to explain a defensive war, or why countries tend to win a defensive war. They don't, of course, as the downfall of Ethiopia in 1936, and the fall of most of western Europe in the '40s, will testify. An *instinct* for territorial acquisition would have to be invoked to explain the expansionist policies of many national bodies.

In summary, many humans manifest a wide variety of highly complex territorial tendencies but there is little evidence that territorial defense is any more instinctive, innate, inevitable, or ineradicable than any other complex learned behavior. The superficial similarities between the territorial behavior of animals and that of man are analogous rather than homologous.

# Appendix A

## Drugs and Aggression Inhibition

### ANTICONVULSANT—DILANTIN

Dilantin [sodium diphenylhydantoin[ is a drug that has been used with considerable success in the control of seizures. Some years ago it came into popular prominence because of its apparent tendency to control hyperexcitability and hostility in nonepileptic patients.[475] Zimmerman,[645] as early as 1956, studied two hundred children with severe behavior disorders and reported that seventy percent of them improved under sodium diphenylhydantoin therapy showing less excitability, as well as less frequent and less severe temper tantrums.

Turner[593] in a study of seventy-two subjects seen in psychiatric practice found that eighty-six percent showed drug-related improvement particularly in relation to anger, irritability, and tension. (See also Maletzky.)[370] The drug is effective with individuals having both abnormal and normal EEG records.[476] There seems to be little question that Dilantin is useful in treating persons with a wide variety of disorders, including neurotics, psychotics, psychopaths, and emotionally disturbed children. The behavioral syndrome that seems to be common in such a diverse group of patients includes explosiveness, low frustration tolerance, irritability, impulsive behavior, compulsive behavior, aggressive behavior, erratic behavior, inability to delay gratification, mood swings, short attention span, undirected activity, and similar symptoms.[463]

Some double-blind studies, one on male delinquents[114,335] and one on children with severe temper tantrums,[356] have not found Dilantin to be superior to a placebo in the control of aggressive behavior. As indicated earlier, a double-blind study showing lack of effect of a drug is not good evidence by itself that the preparation does not have antihostility properties. Other studies, equally well controlled, have reported that the drug's effect on those behaviors was significant. Stephens and Shaffer,[551] in a double-blind crossover study of neurotic outpatients, found it to be effective in reducing symptoms relating to anger, irritability, impatience, and anxiety. Resnick[463] also reported that Dilantin significantly improved the hostile behavior of selected prisoners and juvenile delinquents. He gives revealing excerpts from tape recordings of interviews with the prisoners during the study that reveal the potency of the drug in manipulating negative affect.

## HALDOL

### Haloperidol

A number of studies have now shown that Haloperidol can be used effectively to moderate the aggressive tendencies of several different types of individuals. LeVann[342] compared the effectiveness of Haloperidol and chlorpromazine in a double-blind study on mentally retarded children and concluded that haloperidol reduced the severity of hostility and aggressiveness in significantly more patients than did chlorpromazine. Adverse reactions were minimal. The same author[341] reported that the drug significantly reduces hyperactivity, assaultiveness, and self-injury in hospitalized children and adolescents with behavioral disorders. These results are accomplished with no loss of mental alertness.

Psychotic patients also have reduced tendencies to hostility under haloperidol medication. Haward[251] reports a significant reduction in verbal hostility and Darling,[128] who treated thirty chronically assaultive patients, indicates that twenty of them improved substantially. Phenothiazines had been tried on these patients without success. The drug is also therapeutically effective for agitated, overactive, and hostile elderly patients suffering from chronic brain syndromes.[561]

Finally, Haloperidol appears to be particularly effective in controlling the rather strange disorder Gilles de la Tourette's disease in which the individual has bouts of involuntary swearing and using of profanities and obscenities.

## THE BENZODIAZEPINES

### Librium, Valium and Others

Although there is good evidence that the benzodiazepines increase aggressive tendencies in some individuals, they have also been shown to have an antihostility effect on a wide variety of persons, from neurotic outpatients to raging psychotic criminals. Librium (chlordiazepoxide) has been shown significantly to reduce "hostility outward" (statements of destructive or aggressive intent) and "ambivalent hostility" (statements blaming or criticizing others) in a group of juvenile delinquent boys. The study was done double-blind and the hostility measures were taken on the Gottschalk scale.[216] Podobnickar[453] has also reported on the effectiveness of Librium in the control of hyperaggressiveness in a double-blind study of private patients suffering from various forms of anxiety and neurotic hyperaggression. Several clinical studies have also shown Librium[144,373] and Valium (diazepam)[44] to be useful in the reduction of irritability in neurotic patients. Monroe[402] used Librium alone and in combination with primidone added to a basic phenothiazine regimen to reduce the aggressiveness in psychotic patients, eighty percent of whom had been relegated to the disturbed ward of a state hospital because of uncontrolled aggressive outbursts. Both Librium and Valium in combination with primidone were effective. Valium has been used with "remarkable success" in eliminating the destructive rampages of psychotic criminals.[297,298] Kalina indicates that schizophrenia is unaffected by the drug, but the aggressive and destructive elements that make the patient difficult and dangerous to manage are eliminated.

## LITHIUM

Chronic mania, which frequently involves considerable hostility and episodic hyperaggressiveness, can be successfully treated with lithium carbonate.[210,497] A number of clinical reports (summarized by Tupin[589]—also see)[516] seem to indicate that this drug may be useful in the treatment of a variety of disorders having aggressiveness as a symptomatic component. These studies combined with the evidence that lithium reduces aggressiveness in animals[520,521,522,616] have led some investigators to utilize lithium in the reduction of excessive aggressiveness in selected prisoners. Tupin and Clanon,[590] studied ten prisoners whose behavior was characterized by significant outbursts of violence and who had spent long periods in solitary confinement because of their uncontrollable aggressiveness. They found a reduction in aggression while the prisoners were on the drug. The subjects took lithium for a three-month period during which time all except two were free of disciplinary infraction related to violence. It was also reported that the men showed a noticeable increase in frustration tolerance and were able to work in the prison program. Tupin et al.[591] reported similar results in a population of prisoners with a long history of violent behavior.

In a single-blind study in a maximum security prison, twelve chronically assaultive prisoners with a record of violence in the prison setting were given a three-month trial of one month on lithium, one on placebo, and a return to lithium, during the final month.[523] Aggressiveness was significantly reduced during the lithium trials. The aggression measures included a self-rating scale, clinical ratings of verbal aggression during clinical interviews, and the number of "tickets" received for aggressive behavior. Although a single-blind design was used for the study, two of the assessment conditions, the self-rating scale and the number of tickets given by the prison staff, were, in fact, done blind, and both of them showed a significant difference between drug and placebo conditions.

For obvious reasons there have been fewer long-term studies on the use of drugs than there are acute studies. However, Tupin et al.[591] studied the long term use of lithium carbonate on the violent behaviors of twenty-seven criminals. The assessments of change were the incidence of and type of diciplinary actions and the number, as well as the subjective reports, of the prison personnel. A control period of the same length was compared with the time that the subject took the drug. Their findings are interesting. The number of disciplinary actions for violent behavior decreased significantly whereas the average number of disciplinary actions for non-violent behavior did not decrease significantly. Individually considered, subjects received fewer disciplinary actions for violence. Security classifications improved. Subjective reports included: 1. an increased capacity to reflect on the consequences of actions; 2. increased capacity to deal with angry feelings when provoked; 3. diminished intensity of angry affect; and 4. generally a more reflective mood. The authors conclude that the results strongly suggest that lithium may be effective in long-term reduction of aggressive behavior.

A case study may be useful to give the reader some insight into the reactions of a patient using lithium.

### Case Example

A 27-year-old mentally retarded man was referred for treatment because of worsening temper outbursts that had intermittently plagued his life. He had always been a hyperactive child and demonstrated much psychomotor restlessness and impulsivity that led to many physical altercations at home with family members. Throughout the years, a number of medications had been tried without success, including tranquilizers, sedatives, and stimulants. The patient's mother remarked that his rage attacks seem to occur within a several month period. After that time, a few months would occur when he demonstrated reduced temper outbursts. Thus, it appeared that the aggressive problem was almost cyclic, though there was no history of mood swings, nor any family history of cyclic mood disorders.

The patient was hospitalized and demonstrated, on admission, some tangential thinking and definite psychomotor restlessness, and agitation. While no physical outbursts occurred on the ward, the patient was accusatory, and made covert verbal threats. However, he was not paranoid but responded more to other staff and patients in the manner of a child, demanding relief from a multitude of somatic concerns and seeking attention continuously by insistent demands.

188

Neurological examination revealed external Strabismus of the left eye. Minimal athetosis and dystonicity were noted on movement of the extremities. No other focal findings were evident. An EEG was normal. Psychological testing revealed the patient to be functioning within the mental defective range of adult intelligence, with a full scale I.Q. of fifty-two. He was distractable, and showed an inability to think abstractly and to distinguish essential from nonessential details. Testing suggested mental deficiency of an endogenous type. Other laboratory tests were unremarkable. The etiology of the mental retardation remained obscure.

Because of the cyclic nature of the aggressive outburst, it was decided to try the patient on lithium carbonate. Accordingly, he was begun on 300 mg. TID. The dosage was increased to a total of 1800 mg. a day, yielding a blood level of 1.2 Meq./L. On this dosage, he was calm, and displayed reduced psychomotor activity, restlessness, insomnia, and looseness of associations. He was uneventfully discharged and a follow-up revealed a clear reduction in aggressiveness at home.[345]

Most of the studies on this drug have not attempted to use the double-blind procedure.* Marini et al.[376]found that individuals giving the drug were unable to tell which patients received the lithium and which had received the placebo. However, the patients on lithium had no difficulty making the discrimination because of the side effects. A total of sixteen left the experiment and fourteen of those were taking the drug. Those that withdrew did so because of side effects, most frequently nausea.

It is generally agreed by those who have prescribed lithium and those who have studied the literature that this drug is effective in reducing aggressiveness in humans. It does work, but how it works is not yet known. Marini and Sheard[375] rejected most of the hypotheses about the mechanism, but are not able to offer a better one.

Both Sheard and Tupin are continuing their studies of the usefulness of lithium in aggression reduction in humans under more controlled conditions. Although the initial studies indicate that lithium is another drug that may have a reasonably specific antihostility action, further work is clearly needed.

---

*That type of study is, of course, the best but it also has problems. In the double blind procedure neither the patient nor the person who administers the drug knows which is the placebo and which has the active drug. This reduces psychological effects that may occur due to the patient's or the drug administrator's expectations.

# THE PROPENDIOLS

### Miltown and Similar Drugs

The propendiols [meprobamate and tybamate] should be mentioned, not because they have a predominantly antihostility effect but because they are so widely used. Miltown was one of the first of the minor tranquilizers introduced in the early 1950s and it is still used by thousands for the control of anxiety. Ban[29] surveys the literature on this drug class and concludes that the propendiols in general, and meprobamate in particular, are indicated for various psychoneuroses in which psychic tension and anxiety are associated with irritability.

# TETRAHYDROCANNABINOL

### Marihuana

Perhaps the most controversial drug in the current scene is marihuana or, more specifically, tetrahydrocannabinol [THC], which is the active ingredient of the hemp plant. It has been suggested that THC under certain circumstances can precipitate violent reactions. Murphy[420] concludes that violence may occur when the user is less familiar with the drug, or is in an unfamiliar, nonsupportive environment. If all of those conditions are met, "Acute toxic psychosis or panic reaction may develop in certain users who become agitated and feel threatened by everything."

All of these conditions are rarely met and more recent research clearly indicates that there need be little concern about marihuana as the *violent weed*. The first report of the National Commission on Marihuana[430] concludes that the use of marihuana does not lead to violent crime. Instead, it tends to inhibit aggression expression.[426]

A well-controlled experiment by Taylor et al.[568] supports this position. College students served as his subjects. After ingestion of one or two doses of pure THC they were provoked by shock in a pseudo-experiment and then were given an opportunity to set the shock level to be administered to other students in the experiment. The results showed a small but consistent trend for the THC to show less physical aggression.

# Appendix B

## Glossary

***Ablation:*** The removal of a portion of the brain.

***Abulia:*** Loss of will power.

***Acetylcholine:*** A neurotransmitter in the central nervous system also liberated by the preganglionic and postganglionic endings of the parasympathetic fibers and from the preganglionic fibers of the sympathetic nervous system.

***Addison's Disease:*** Chronic adrenocortical insufficiency.

***Adrenal Androgen:*** Androgenic substances that originate in the adrenal cortex, including dehydroepiandrosterone, androstenedione, and possibly testosterone.

***Agnosia:*** Loss of sensory ability to recognize objects.

***Amitriptyline:*** Elavil. An antidepressant drug that also has a tranquilizing effect that helps to control the anxiety and agitation often found in depression.

***Amygdalectomy:*** A surgical procedure in which the amygdalae are excised.

***Amygdalotomy:*** A surgical procedure in which the amygdalae are partially removed.

***Androgens:*** A generic term for an agent, usually a hormone (e.g., testosterone or androsterone) that stimulates the activity of the accessory sex organs of the male, encourages the development of the male sex characteristics.

***A-Norprogesterone:*** A recently developed antiandrogenic substance that "blocks" male hormones.

***Arousal:*** As the term implies, the person is in a state of tension with a readiness to act. See Reticular Activating System.

***Arrest Phenomenon:*** A condition in which opposing muscles tighten. This blocks all movement.

***Athetosis:*** A pathological condition in which there is constant movement of a writhing and involuntary nature. It most commonly involves the hands and fingers but may also affect the feet and toes.

***Atrophic Lesion:*** A lesion produced by a gradual wasting away, sometimes due to inadequate nutrition.

***Automatism:*** A state in which the individual's behavior occurs independent of his own willful processes. The behaviors are involuntary and are often purposeless and may be foolish or harmful.

***Autonomic System:*** That portion of the peripheral nervous system that regulates those body functions not usually under

191

voluntary control, such as the visceral changes that occur during emotion. It includes the sympathetic and parasympathetic divisions.

**Benzodiazepines:** A group of drugs used for their antihostility, anti-convulsant, and skeletal-muscle-relaxing properties. The most commonly used are chlordiazepoxide (Librium), diazepam (Valium), and oxazepam (Serex). Used for control of tension, irritability, anxiety, and related symptoms.

**Bilateral:** Refers to both sides as of the body or of the brain.

**Cerebral Arteriosclerosis:** A degeneration of the blood vessels in the brain.

**Chlormadinone Acetate:** A progesterone derivative. With estrogen, it is used as an oral contraceptive.

**Chlorpromazine:** Thorazine. The first major tranquilizer developed. Used in the control of agitation, anxiety, tension, and confusion, associated with the neuroses and such psychotic conditions as schizophrenia, manic phase of the manic-depressive states and senile psychosis. Has a definite antihostility effect.

**Chromosome:** A rodlike body in the nucleus of the cell that contains the genes responsible for hereditary traits.

**Cyproterone Acetate:** A synthetic steroid that blocks the action of androgens.

**Depot Injection:** An injection that deposits a large amount of a drug that is gradually absorbed into the bloodstream.

**Diuretic:** Any agent that promotes urine secretion.

**Dopamine:** Hydroxytyramine. An intermediate in tyrosine catabolism. The precursor of norepinephrine and epinephrine.

**Dystonicity:** A condition in which muscle tone functions incorrectly.

**Electroencephalograph [EEG]:** An apparatus consisting of a cathode ray oscillograph which is integrated with a writing device. Leads are attached to the scalp. Alternating currents of the brain are recorded.

**Encephalization:** Progressive development of the more complex areas of the brain, particularly the cortex, from the lowest species to the highest, humans.

**Endocrine Glands:** Ductless glands that secrete hormones directly into the bloodstream.

**Endocrinopathy:** Malfunctions of the endocrine system.

**Endogenous:** Occurring within the body.

*Estrogen:* A general term for all estrus–producing hormones.
*Etiology:* The origin or basis of a condition.

**Gonadotropic Hormone:** A hormone that promotes gonadal growth and function.

**Huntington's Chorea:** A hereditary disorder of a chronic nature that usually begins between the ages of thirty and fifty years. It is characterized by irregular spasmodic movements of the limbs and facial muscles. It is accompanied by a gradual loss of mental capacity.
**Hyperinsulinism:** A condition of excess insulin in the bloodstream. Results in hypoglycemia.
**Hypoglycemia:** An inadequate concentration of glucose in the circulating blood for normal functioning.

*Ictal:* Relating to or produced by an epileptic seizure.
**Islands of Langerhans:** Cells in the pancreas that secrete insulin directly into the bloodstream.
**Intramuscular:** Inside the muscle. In giving shots, the needle is plunged directly into the muscle.

**Kluver & Bucy Syndrome:** A group of symptoms produced by extensive lesions in the temporal lobes. It involves an inability to recognize familiar objects, hypersexuality, and a dramatic increase in tameness.
**Korsakoff's Syndrome:** A disorder characterized by hallucinations, loss of memory, and imaginary reminiscences. Frequently involves marked agitation.

**Law of Effect:** The law states that if an individual is rewarded for a given behavior he has an increased tendency to behave in the same way in a similar situation.
*Lesion:* Circumscribed tissue damage.
**Levarteranol bitartrate:** L-Norepinephrine bitartrate. See Norepinephrine.
**Librium:** One of the early minor tranquilizers in the benzo-diazepine class.
**Limbic System:** The limbic system as proposed as a complex of directly and indirectly connected brain structures that underlie emotional feelings and thus influence emotional behavior.
**Lithium Carbonate:** A drug with anithostility properites. Usually used in the treatment of manic-depressive states.

**Medroxyprogesterone:** A progesterone-type substance that is effective orally as well as parenterally. It is more potent than progesterone. Used with estrogens as an oral contraceptive.

**Motor Aphasia:** A loss in the ability of verbal expression by either writing or speaking.

**Neural System:** A large number of neurons that tend to function together.

**Neuron:** The neuron is the basic unit of the nervous system. It is a single cell.

**Oligophrenia:** Feeblemindedness.

**Parkinson's Disease:** (Paralysis Agitans) A neurological disorder caused by degeneration of the basal ganglia (see Figure 4), characterized by rhythmical tremor, rigidity, poor movement, and masklike face.

**Pedophilia:** Unnatural desire to have sexual relations with a child.

**Perphenazine:** Trilafon. A phenothiazine similar to chlorpromazine in action.

**Phallometer:** A device that measures the volume of the penis.

**Pituitary:** A two-lobed endocrine gland that lies at the base of the brain just below the hypothalamus. Secretes a large number of hormones that affect the other endocrine glands.

**Placebo:** An inert substance used to duplicate an active drug in a controlled drug study. Sometimes used in medicine to effect changes caused by suggestion.

**Plethysmograph:** An instrument for recording changes in volume in any portion of the body.

**Pneumoencephalography:** A diagnostic procedure in which the cerebrospinal fluid is replaced by air and an X-ray picture is taken of the brain.

**Polydypsia:** Pathological thirst resulting in excessive drinking.

**Polyuria:** Excessive production of urine.

**Progesterone:** A hormone secreted by the corpus luteum. Used to correct abnormalities in the menstrual cycle.

**Psychometrist:** An individual who administers psychological tests.

**Radiculitis:** Inflammation of a spinal nerve root at the point of entrance to the spinal column.

**Reciprocal Inhibition:** The inhibition of a given set of muscles when the antagonistic set is activated.

**Reticular Activating System (RAS):** That portion of the central nervous system that is responsible for the wake-sleep cycle.

The level of arousal reflects, in part, activity of the RAS.

*Rhinencephalic:* Refers to the rhinencephalon or olfactory brain. In humans, this includes the rudimentary olfactory lobe, which consists of the olfactory bulb and peduncle, the paraolfactory area, the subcallosal gyrus, and the anterior perforated substance.

*Schizophrenia:* The worst of the psychoses. Symptoms include loss of contact with reality as well as delusions and hallucinations.

*Scotoma:* An isolated area within the visual field where vision is absent or blurred.

*Sebaceous Glands:* Glands in the skin that produce an oily, fatty substance known as sebum.

*Senile Dementia:* Loss of mental capacity that comes with old age.

*Sensory Aphasia:* Loss of the ability to comprehend printed or spoken words.

*Somatic:* Refers to the body.

*Sphenoidal Leads:* Attached to the base of the skull.

*Strabismus:* A condition in which the eyes squint and one or both eyes turn inward or outward.

*Subcortex:* The area just below the covering of the brain (cortex). The subcortex is generally "white matter" composed of projections from one group of cells to another.

*Subcutaneous:* Below the skin.

*Synapse:* The place where a nerve impulse is transmitted from one neuron to another.

*Synaptic Resistance:* Nerve impulses are transmitted from one neuron to another through chemicals found in the transmitting cell. Synaptic resistance is a function of a number of variables including the number of cells at that synapse and the types of chemicals (neuro-transmitters) available.

*Theta Waves:* EEG waves of four to seven cycles-per-second. These have been interpreted as a possible sign of inhibitory activity.

*TID:* Three times a day. Used in the writing of prescriptions.

*Uncus:* The hooked portion of the hippocampal gyrus that lies on the basal surface of the brain medial to the temporal lobe.

*Unilateral:* Referring to one side of the body.

*Wechsler Adult Intelligence Scale:* A test battery for intelligence. Also called Wechsler-Bellevue Scale and WAIS.

***X-Chromosome:*** A sex-determining chromosome. XX produces a female.

***XYY Syndrome:*** A chromosome abnormality in which the sex-chromosome constitution is XYY. These individuals are tall and are said to have problems with impulse control.

***Y Chromosome:*** A sex-determining chromosome carried by the male. An XY produces a male.

# References

1. Abbott, P., Blake, A., & Vincze, L. "Treatment of mentally retarded with thioridazine." *Diseases of the Nervous System 26* (1965), 583–585.
2. Abrahamson, E. M., & Pezet, A. W. *Body, mind, and sugar.* Holt, Rinehart & Winston, New York, 1951.
3. Aird, R. B., & Yamamoto, T. "Behavior disorders of childhood." *Electroencephalography and Clinical Neurophysiology 21* (1966), 148–156.
4. Aldersberg, D., & H. Dolger. "Medico-legal problems of hypoglycemia reaction in diabetes." *Annals of Internal Medicine 12* (1938–1939), 1804–1815.
5. Alderton, H., & Hoddinott, B. A. "A controlled study of the use of thioridazine in the treatment of hyperactive and aggressive children in a children's psychiatric hospital." *Canadian Psychiatric Association Journal 9* (1964), 239–247.
6. Allen, A. A. "Sex rhythm in the ruffed grouse [Bonasa umbellus L.] and other birds." *Auk 51* (1934), 180–199.
7. Allen, M., Shannon, G., & Rose, D. "Thioridazine hydrochloride in the behavior disturbances of retarded children." *American Journal of Mental Deficiency 68* (1963), 63–68.
8. Allison, T. S., & Allison, S. L. "Time-out from reinforcement: Effect on sibling aggression." *Psychological Record 21* (1971), 81–86.
9. Alpers, B. J. "Relation of the hypothalamus to disorders of personality." *Archives of Neurology and Psychiatry 38* (1937), 291–303.
10. Altman, M. Naturalistic studies of maternal care in the moose and elk. In H. L. Rheingold, Ed., *Maternal behavior in mammals,* Wiley, New York, 1963, pp. 233–253.
11. Altman, M., Knowles, E., & Bull, H. D. "A psychosomatic study of the sex cycle in women." *Psychosomatic Medicine 3* (1941), 199–225.
12. Anderson, E. W. "Psychiatric complications of hypoglycemia in children." *Lancet 2* (1940), 329–331.
13. Anderson, R. "Psychological differences after amygdalotomy." *Acta Neurologica Scandinavica, Supplement 46* (1970), 94.
14. Andy, O. J., & Jurko, M. F. Hyperresponsive syndrome. In E. Hitchcock, L. Laitinen, & K. Vaernet, Eds., *Psychosurgery,* Thomas, Springfield, Ill. 1972, pp. 117–126.
15. Anonymous. "Massed killer kissed wife and children goodbye." *The Pittsburgh Press 101* (July 20, 1984), 1.
16. Arai, N., Shibata, Y., & Akahene, A. "Electroencephalographic analysis of behavior problem children." *Acta Criminologiae et Medicina Legalis Japonica 32* (1966), 143–152.
17. Archer, J. Effects of population density on behaviour in rodents. In J. H. Cook, Ed., *Social behaviour in birds and mammals,* Academic Press, London, 1970, pp. 169–210.
18. Ardrey, R. *The territorial imperative.* Atheneum, New York, 1966.

197

19. Ardrey, R. *African genesis: A personal investigation into the animal origins and nature of man*. Atheneum, New York, 1968.
20. Arthurs, R. G., & Cahoon, E. B. "A clinical and electroencephalographic survey of psychopathic personality." *American Journal of Psychiatry 120* (1964), 875–877.
21. Augenstein, L. *Come, let us play God*. Harper & Row, New York, 1969.
22. Ax, A. "The physiological differentiation of fear and anger in humans." *Psychosomatic Medicine 15* (1953), 433–442.
23. Azrin, N. H. Aggression. Paper presented at the meeting of the American Psychological Association. Los Angeles, September, 1964.
24. Azrin, N. H., Hutchinson, R. R., & Hake, D. F. "Extinction induced aggression." *Journal of the Experimental Analysis of Behavior 9* (1966), 191–204.
25. Bach-Y-Rita, G., Lion, J. R. & Ervin, F. R. "Pathological intoxication: Clinical and electroencephalographic studies." *American Journal of Psychiatry 127* (1970), 698–703.
26. Bach-Y-Rita, G., & Lion, J. R. "Episodic dyscontrol: A study of 130 violent patients." *American Journal of Psychiatry 127* (1971), 1473–1478.
27. Bailey, P. Discussion. In M. Baldwin & P. Bailey, Eds., *Temporal lobe epilepsy*, Thomas, Springfield, Ill., 1958, p. 551.
28. Baker, R. R. "The effects of psychotropic drugs on psychological testing." *Psychological Bulletin 69* (1968), 377–387.
29. Ban, T. A., *Psychopharmacology*. Williams & Wilkins, Baltimore, 1969.
30. Banay, R. S. "Pathologic reaction to alcohol, Vol. I. Review of the literature and original case reports." *Quarterly Journal of Studies on Alcohol 4* (1944), 580–605.
31. Bandler, R. J., & Moyer, K. E. "Animals spontaneously attacked by rats." *Communications in Behavioral Biology 5* (1970), 177–182.
32. Bandura, A. Analysis of modeling processes. In A. Bandura, Ed., *Theories of modeling*, Atherton Press, New York, 1970.
33. Bandura, A., *Aggression: A social learning analysis*. Prentice-Hall, Englewood Cliffs, N.J., 1973.
34. Bandura, A. & Huston, A. C. "Identification as a process of incidental learning." *Journal of Abnormal and Social Psychology 63* (1961), 311–318.
35. Baran, D., & Glickman, S. E. "Territorial marking in the Mongolian gerbil: A study of sensory control and function." *Journal of Comparative and Physiological Psychology 71* (1970), 237–245.
36. Barbeau, A. Dopamine and mental function. In S. Malitz, Ed., *L-DOPA and behavior*, Raven Press, New York, 1972, pp. 9–33.
37. Bardwick, J. M. *Psychology of women*. Harper & Row, New York, 1971.
38. Barnett, S. A. Social stress. In J. D. Carthy & C. L. Duddington, Eds., *Viewpoints in biology*, Butterworth, London, 1964, pp. 170–218.
39. Barnett, S. A. "The biology of aggression." *Lancet 8* (1964), 803–807.

40. Barnett, S. A. Grouping and dispersive behavior among wild rats. In S. Gaattini & E. B. Sigg, Eds., *Aggressive behavior*, Wiley, New York, 1969, pp. 3–14.
41. Baron, R. A. *Human aggression*. Plenum Press, New York, 1977.
42. Baran, D., & Glickman, S. E. "Territorial marking in the Mongolian gerbil: A study of sensory control and function." *Journal of Comparative and Physiological Psychology 71* (1970), 234–245.
43. Barrett, J. E., & DiMascio, A. "Comparative effects on anxiety of the 'Minor Tranquilizers' in 'high' and 'low' anxious student volunteers." *Diseases of the Nervous System 27* (1966), 483–486.
44. Barsa, J., & Saunder, J. C. "Comparative study of chlordiazepoxide and diazepam." *Diseases of the Nervous System 25* (1964), 244–246.
45. Bartholomew, A. A. "Perphenazine [Trilafon] in the immediate management of acutely disturbed chronic alcoholics." *Medical Journal of Australia 1* (1963), 812–814.
46. Bassoe, P. "The auriculotemporal syndrome and other vasomotor disturbances about the head: 'Auriculotemporal syndrome' complicating diseases of parotid gland; angioneurotic edema of brain." *Medical Clinics of North America 16* (1932), 405–412.
47. Bates, B. C. "Territorial behavior in primates: A review of recent field studies." *Primates 11* (1970), 271–284.
48. Bayrakal, S. "The significance of electroencephalographic abnormality in behavior-problem children." *Canadian Psychiatric Association Journal 10* (1965), 387–392.
49. Beeman, E. A. "The effect of male hormone on aggressive behavior in mice." *Physiological Zoology 20* (1947), 373–405.
50. Benedict, R. *Patterns of culture*. Houghton Mifflin, Boston, 1934.
51. Bennett, R. M., Buss, A. H., & Carpenter, J. A. "Alcohol and human physical aggression." *Quarterly Journal of Studies on Alcohol 39* (1969), 870–876.
52. Berkowitz, L. *Aggression: A social psychological analysis*. McGraw-Hill, New York, 1962.
53. Berkowitz, L. Experiments on automatism and intent in human aggression. In C. O. Clementy & D. B. Lindlsey, Eds., *Aggression and defense: Neural mechanisms and social patterns*, Vol. V, Brain Function. University of California Press, Los Angeles, 1967, pp. 243–266.
54. Billig, H. E., Jr., & Spaulding, C. A. "Hyperinsulinism of menses." *Industrial Medicine, 16* (1947), 336–339.
55. Bingley, T. "Mental symptoms in temporal lobe epilepsy and temporal lobe gliomas." *Acta Psychiatrica et Neurologica Scandinavica Supplementium 120 33* (1958), 1–151.
56. Blau, A. "Mental changes following head trauma in children." *Archives of Neurology and Psychiatry 35* (1937), 723–769.
57. Bleicher, S. J. Hypoglycemia. In M. Ellenberg & H. Rifkin, Eds., *Diabetes mellitus, theory and practice*, McGraw-Hill, New York, 1970, pp. 958–989.
58. Blum, R. H. *Mind-altering drugs and dangerous behavior: Alcohol.*

U. S. Government Printing Office, Washington, D. C., 1967. Task Force Report on narcotics and drug abuse. pp. 29–49.

59. Blum, R. H. Drugs and violence. In *D. J. Mulvihill, M. M. Tumin & L. A. Curtis, Eds., Crimes of violence,* U. S. Government Printing Office, Washington, D. C., 1969, pp. 1462–1523. A staff report to the National Commission on the Causes and Prevention of Violence.

60. Blumer, D. "The temporal lobes and paroxysmal behavior disorders." *Szondiana 7* (1967), 273–285.

61. Blumer, D. "Hypersexual episodes in temporal lobe epilepsy." *American Journal of Psychiatry 126* (1970), 1099–1106.

62. Blumer, D., & Migeon, C. Treatment of impulsive behavior disorders in males with medroxy-progesterone acetate. Paper presented at the annual meeting of the American Psychiatric Association, May, 1973.

63. Boelkins, C. R., & Heiser, J. F. Biological bases of aggression. In D. N. Daniels, M. F. Gilula & F. M. Ochberg, Eds., *Violence and the struggle for existence,* Little, Brown, Boston, 1970, pp. 15–52.

64. Bolton, R. "Aggression and hypoglycemia among the Qolla: A study in psychobiological anthropology." *Ethnology 12* (1973), 227–257.

65. Bonkalo, A. "Electronencephalography in criminology." *Canadian Psychiatric Association Journal 12* (1967), 281–286.

66. Boshka, S. C., Weisman, H. M., & Thor, D. H. "A technique for inducing aggression in rats utilizing morphine withdrawal." *Psychological Record 16* (1966), 541–543.

67. Bostow, D. E., & Bailey, J. B. "Modification of severe disruptive and aggressive behavior using brief timeout and reinforcement procedures." *Journal of Applied Behavior Analysis 2* (1969), 31–37.

68. Bowden, N. J. Studies on the manner in which sex steroids influence aggressiveness. In: Musculus, L. Unpublished Ph.D. dissertation: The University of Wales.

69. Brain, P. F. "Hormones and aggression." *Annual Research Reviews 2* (1979), 170. Eden Press, Montreal.

70. Brain, P. F., Evans, C. M., & Poole, A. E. "Studies on the effects of cyproterone acetate administered both in early life and to adults on subsequent fighting behavior and organ weight changes in male albino mice." *Acta Endocrinologica, and Supplementium 177* (1973), 286.

71. Breamish, P., & Kiloh, L. "Psychosis due to amphetamine consumption." *Journal of Mental Science 106* (1960), 337–343.

72. Breggin, P. R. Psychosurgical procedures for the control of violence: A critical review. In *From neural bases of violence and aggression,* Warren, St. Louis, 1975.

73. Breiner, S. J. "Psychosocial Aspects of Violence," USA Today 107 (1978), 22–29.

74. Bremer, J. *Asexualization.* Macmillan, New York, 1959.

75. Brewer, C. "Homicide during a psychomotor seizure: The importance of airencephalography in establishing insanity under

200

McNaughten rules." *Medical Journal of Australia 1* (1971), 857–859.

76. Brigs, J. L. The origins of nonviolence: Inert management of aggression. In A. Montague, Ed., *Learning non-aggression*. Oxford, New York, 1978, pp. 54–93.

77. Brill, H. *Postencephalitic psychiatric conditions*. Vol II Basic Books, New York, 1959. American Handbook of Psychiatry. pp. 1163–64.

78. Brill, H. "Drugs and aggression." *Medical Counterpart 1* (1969), 33–38.

79. Brown, R. Z. "Social behavior, reproduction, and population changes in the house mouse." *[Mus musculus L.] Ecological Monographs 23* (1953), 217–240.

80. Brown C. *Manchild in the promised land*. Macmillan, New York, 1965.

81. Brown, L. E. Home range and movement of small mammals. In P. A. Lewell & C. Loizos, Eds., *Play, exploration and territory in mammals*, Academic Press, London, 1966, pp. 85–107.

82. Bucher, B., & Lovaas, O. I. Use of aversive stimulation in behavior modification. In M. R. Jones, Ed., *Miami symposium on the prediction of behavior, 1967: Aversive stimulation*, University of Miami Press, Coral Gables, FL., 1968, pp. 77–145.

83. Buechner, H. K. "Territorial behavior in the Uganda kob." *Science 133* (1961), 698–699.

84. Buki, R. A. "The use of psychotropic drugs in the rehabilitation of sex-deviated criminals." *American Journal of Psychiatry 120* (1964), 1170–1175.

85. Burgess, A. *A Clockwork Orange*. Norton, New York, 1962.

86. Burt, W. H. "Territoriality and home range concepts as applied to mammals." *Journal of Mammalogy 24* (1943), 346–354.

87. Buss, A. *The psychology of aggression*. Wiley, New York, 1961.

88. Buss, A. H., & Durkee, A. "An inventory for assessing different kinds of hostility." *Journal of Consulting Psychology 21* (1957), 343–349.

89. Calhoun, J. B. "A comparative study of the social behavior of two inbred strains of house mice." *Ecological Monographs 26* (1956), 81–103.

90. Calhoun, J. B. The ecology and sociology of the Norway rat. U. S. Department of Health, Education and Welfare, publication No. 1008. Washington, D. C.: U. S. Government Printing Office.

91. Campbell, H. E. "The violent sex offender: A consideration of emasculation in treatment." *Rocky Mountain Medical Journal 64* (1967), 40–43.

92. Campbell, M. B. Allergy and behavior: Neurologic and psychic syndromes. In F. Speer, Ed., *Allergy of the nervous system*, Thomas, Springfield, IL, 1970, pp. 28–46.

93. Campbell, M. B. Allergy and epilepsy. In F. Speer, Ed., *Allergy of the nervous system*, Thomas, Springfield, IL, 1970, pp. 59–78.

94. Carpenter, C. R. "A field study of the behavior and social relations

of howling monkeys." *Comparative Psychology Monographs 10* (1934), 1–168.

95. Carpenter, C. R. "A field study in Siam of the behavior and social relations of the gibbon." *Comparative Psychology Monographs 16* (1940), 1–212.

96. Carpenter, C. R. Territoriality: A review of concepts and problems. A. Roe & G. G. Simpson, Eds., In *Behavior and evolution*, Yale University Press, New Haven, 1958, pp. 224–250.

97. Carpenter, C. R. *Naturalistic behavior of nonhuman primates.* Pennsylvania State University Press, University Park, PA, 1964.

98. Carstairs, G. M. Overcrowding and human aggression. Violence in America: Historical and Comparative, National Commission on the Causes and Prevention of Violence, 1969, Vol. II. pp. 593–601.

99. Cazzullo, C. L. "Psychiatric aspects of epilepsy." *International Journal of Neurology 1* (1959), 53–65.

100. Chagnon, N., "Yanomamo: The fierce people. Holt, Rinehart & Winston. New York, 1968.

101. Chatz, T. L. "Management of male adolescent sex offenders." *International Journal of Offender Therapy 2* (1972), 109–115.

102. Christian, J. J. "Social subordination, population density, and mammalian evolution." *Science 168* (1970), 84–90.

103. Christian, J. J., & D. E. Davis. "Endocrine, behavior, and population." *Science 146* (1964), 1550–1560.

104. Christiansen, K. O. A review of studies of criminality among twins. In *Biosocial bases of criminal behavior*, Mednick S. A. & K. O. Christiansen, Eds., Gardner Press, Inc., New York, 1977, pp. 45–88.

105. Clapham, B. "An interesting case of hypoglycemia." *Medico-Legal Journal 33* (1965), 72–73.

106. Clark, K. B. "The pathos of power: A psychological perspective." *American Psychologist 26* (1971), 1047–1057.

107. Cloudsley-Thompson, J. L. *Animal conflict and adaptation.* Dufour, Chester-Springs, PA, 1965.

108. Coca, A. F. *The Pulse Test: The secret of building your basic health.* Lyle Stuart, New York, 1959.

109. Cohen, S. "Thioridazine [Mellaril]: Recent developments." *Journal of Psychopharmacology 1* (1966), 1–15.

110. Cohen, S. Abuse of centrally stimulating agents among juveniles in California. In F. Sjoqvist & M. Tuttle, Eds., *Abuse of Central Stimulants*, Raven Press, New York, 1969, pp. 165–180.

111. Cohn, R. & Nardini, J. E. "The correlation of bilateral occipital slow activity in the human EEG with certain disorders of behavior." *American Journal of Psychiatry 115* (1958), 44–54.

112. Cole, J. O., Goldberg, S. C., & Davis, J. M. Drugs in the treatment of psychosis: Controlled studies. In P. Solomon, Ed., *Psychiatric drugs*, Grune & Stratton, New York, 1966, pp. 153–180.

113. Connell, P. H. *Amphetamine psychosis.* Oxford University Press, London, 1958.

114. Conners, C., Kramer, R., Rothschild, G., Schwartz, L., & Stone, A. "Treatment of young delinquent boys with diphenylhydantoin

sodium and methylphenidate." *Archives of General Psychiatry* 24 (1971), 156–159.

115. Coppen, A., & Kessel, N. "Menstruation and personality." *British Journal of Psychiatry* 109 (1963), 711–721.

116. Crabtree, J. M., & Moyer, K. E. "Sex differences in fighting and defense induced in rats by shock during morphine withdrawal." *Physiology and Behavior* 11 (1973), 337–343.

117. Crichton, M. *The Terminal Man*. Bantom Books, New York, 1972.

118. Crook, J. H. The nature and function of territorial aggression. In M. F. A. Montague, Ed., *Man and aggression*, Oxford University Press, London, 1968, pp. 141–178.

119. Crook, W. G., Harrison, W. W., Crawford, S. E., & Emerson, B. S. "Systemic manifestations due to allergy: Report of fifty patients and a review of the literature on the subject." *Pediatrics* 27 (1961), 790–799.

120. Crowcroft, P. "Territoriality in wild house mice, [Mus musculus]." *Journal of Mammalogy* 36 (1955), 299–301.

121. Currier, R. D., Little, S. C., Suess, J. F., & Andy, O. "Sexual seizures." *Archives of Neurology* 25 (1971), 260–264.

122. Dalton, K. "Menstruation and acute psychiatric illness." *British Medical Journal* 1 (1959), 148–149.

123. Dalton, K. "Schoolgirls' misbehavior and menstruation." *British Medical Journal* 2 (1960), 1647–1649.

124. Dalton, K. "Menstruation and crime." *British Medical Journal* 3 (1961), 1752–1753.

125. Dalton, K. *The premenstrual syndrome*. Thomas, Springfield, IL, 1964.

126. Daniels, D. N., Gilula, F. M., & Ochberg, F. M. *Violence and the struggle for existence*. Little, Brown, Boston, 1970.

127. Darling, F. F. *A herd of red deer: A study in animal behaviour*. Oxford University Press, London, 1937.

128. Darling, H. F. "Haloperidol in 60 criminal psychotics." *Diseases of the Nervous System* 32 (1971), 31–34.

129. Davis, F. C. "The measurement of aggressive behavior in laboratory rats." *Journal of Genetic Psychology* 43 (1933), 213–217.

130. Davison, H. M. "Allergy of the nervous system." *Quarterly Review of Allergy and Applied Immunology* 6 (1952), 157–188.

131. DeHaas, A. M. *Lectures on epilepsy*. Elsevier, Netherlands, 1958.

132. DeHaas, A. M. "Epilepsy in criminality." *British Journal of Criminology* 3 (1963), 248–257.

133. Delgado, J. M. R., Hamlin, H. & Chapman, W. P. "Technique of intracerebral electrode placement for recording and stimulation and its possible therapeutic value in psychotic patients." *Confinia Neurologia* 12 (1952), 315–319.

134. de la Vega Llamosa, A. Los equivalentes del delito y su importancia en nuestro medio. Thesis presented at Universidad Nacional Autonoma de Mexico, Mexico City, 1966.

135. Delgado, J. M. R. "Modification of social behavior induced by remote controlled electrical stimulation of the brain." XXI International Congress of Physiological Science 75 (1959).

136. Delgado, J. M. R. "Cerebral heterostimulation in a monkey colony." *Science 141* (1963), 161–163.
137. Delgado, J. M. R. *Evolution of physical control of the brain.* The American Museum of Natural History, New York, 1965.
138. Delgado, J. M. R. "Evoking and inhibiting aggressive behavior by radio stimulation in monkey colonies." *American Zoologist 5* (1965), 642.
139. Delgado, J. M. R. "Chronic radio stimulation of the brain in monkey colonies." *Proceedings of the International Union of Physiological Sciences 4* (1965), 365–371.
140. Delgado, J. M. R. "Aggressive behavior evoked by radio stimulation in monkey colonies." *American Zoologist 6* (1966), 669–681.
141. Delgado, J. M. R. Aggression and defense under cerebral radio control. In C. D. Clemente & D. B. Lindsley, Eds., *Aggression and defense: Neural mechanisms and social patterns, Vol. V brain function,* University of California Press, Los Angeles, 1967, pp. 171–193.
142. Delgado, J. M. R. Aggression in free monkeys modified by electrical and chemical stimulation of the brain. Paper presented at the Symposium on aggression, Interdepartmental Institute for Training in research in the Behavioral and Neurologic Sciences, Albert Einstein College of Medicine, New York, 1969.
143. Delgado, J. M. R. Personal Communication.
144. Denham, J. "Psychotherapy of obsessional neurosis assisted by Librium. Topical problems of psychotherapy." *Supplementum ad Acta Psychotherapeutica et Psychosomatica 4* (1963),195–198.
145. Denton, R. K. Notes on childhood in a nonviolent context: The Semai case [Malaysia]. In A. Montague, Ed., *Learning non-aggression,* Oxford, New York, 1978, pp. 94–143.
146. Deutsch, H., *The psychology of women.* Grune & Stratton, New York, 1944.
147. DeVore, I. Comparative ecology and behavior of monkeys and apes. In S. L. Washburn, Ed., *Classification and human evolution,* Wenner-Gren Foundation, New York, 1963, pp. 301–319.
148. DeVore, I. *Primate behavior: Field studies of monkeys and apes.* Holt, Rinehart and Winston, New york, 1965.
149. DiMascio, A., & Barrett, J. E. "Comparative effects of oxazepam in high and low anxious student volunteers." *Psychomatics 6* (1965), 298–302.
150. DiMascio, A., Shader, R. I., & Harmatz, J. "Psychotropic drugs and induced hostility." *Psychomatics 10* (1969), 27–28.
151. Dinnen, A. "Homicide during a psychomotor seizure." *Medical Journal of Australia 1* (1971), 1353.
152. Dollard, J., Doob, L. W., Miller, N. E., Mowrer, O. H., & Sears, R. R. *Frustration and aggression.* Yale University Press, New Haven, CT, 1939.
153. Duncan, G. G. "The antidotal effect of anger in a case of insulin reaction [hypoglycemia] in a diabetic." *Canadian Medical Association 33* (1935), 71.

154. Dunford, C. "Behavioral aspects of spatial organization in the chipmunk *[Tamias striatus].*" *Behaviour 36* (1970), 215–231.
155. Dunn, G. W. "Stilbestrol induced testicular degeneration in hypersexual males." *Journal of Clinical Endocrinology 1* (1941), 643–648.
156. Edwards, D. A. "Effects of cyproterone acetate on aggressive behaviour and the seminal vesicles of male mice." *Journal of Endocrinology 46* (1070), 477–481.
157. Egan, O., Royce, J. R., & Poley, W. "Evidence for a territorial marking factor of mouse emotionality." *Psychonomic Science 27* (1972), 272–274.
158. Egger, M. D. & Flynn, J. P. "Effect of electrical stimulation of the amygdala on hypothalamically elicited attack behavior in cats." *Journal of Neurophysiology 26* (1963), 705–720.
159. Ehrlich, P. R. *The population bomb.* Ballantine Books, New York, 1968.
160. Eibl-Eibesfedt, I. "Zur ethologie des hamsters [Cricetus cricetus L.]." *Zeitschrift fur Tierpsychologie 10* (1953), 204–254.
161. Eibl-Eibesfeldt, I. *Love and hate.* Holt, Rinehart, and Winston, New York, 1972.
162. Eibl-Eibesfeldt, I. *The biology of peace and war.* Viking Press, New York, 1979.
163. Eibl-Eibesfeldt, I. "Beitrage zur Biologie der Haus- und der Ahrenmaus nebst einigen Beobachtungen an andere Nagern." *Zeitschrift fur Tierphychologie 7* (1950), 558–587.
164. Eibl-Eibesfeldt, I. *Ethology: The biology of behavior.* Holt, Rinehart, and Winston, New York, 1970.
165. Elias, M. "Serum cortisol, testosterone and testosterone binding globulin responses to competitive fighting in human males." *Aggressive Behavior 7* (1981), 215–224.
166. Ellingson, R. J. "Incidence of EEG abnormality among patients with mental disorders of apparently non-organic origin: Critical review." *American Journal of Psychiatry 114* (1955), 263–275.
167. Ellinwood, E. H. "Amphetamine psychosis: I. Description of the individuals and process." *Journal of Nervous and Mental Diseases 144* (1967), 273–283.
168. Ellinwood, E. H. "Assault and homicide associated with amphetamine abuse." *American Journal of Psychiatry 127* (1971), 1170–1176.
169. Ellis, D. P., & Austin, P. "Menstruation and aggressive behavior in a correctional center for women." *Journal of Criminal Law Criminology and Police Science 62* (1971), 388–395.
170. Epple, G. "Quantitative studies on scent marking in the marmoset *[Callithrix jacchus].*" *Folia Primatologica 13* (1970), 48–62.
171. Epstein, A. W. "Disordered human sexual behavior associated with temporal lobe dysfunction." *Medical Aspects of Human Sexuality* (1969), 62–68.
172. Ervin, F. The biology of individual violence: An overview. In D. J. Mulvahill, M. M. Tumin & L. A. Curtis, Eds., *Crimes of violence,* Vol. 13, U. S. Government Printing Office, Washington, D. C.,

205

1969. A staff report submitted to the National Commission on the Causes and Prevention of Violence.

173. Ervin, F. R. Discussion in workshop on regulation of behavior. In P. N. Williams, Ed., *Ethical issues in biology and medicine*, Schenkman, Cambridge, MA, 1973, pp. 179–180.

174. Ervin, F. R., Mark, V. H., & Stevens, J. Behavioral and affective response to brain stimulation in man. In J. Zubin & C. Shogass, Eds., *Neurobiological aspects of psychopathology*, Grune & Stratton, New York, 1969, pp. 54–65.

175. Esser, A. H., (Ed.), *Behavior and environment: The uses of space by animals and men*. Plenum, New York, 1971.

176. Esser, A. H., Chamberlain, A. S., Chapple, E. D., & Kline, N. S. Territoriality of patients on a research ward. In F. Wortis, Ed., *Recent advances in biological psychiatry*, Plenum, New York, 1965, pp. 36–44.

177. Estes, R. D. "Territorial behavior of the wildebeest [Connochaetes taurinus Burchell]." *Zeitschrift fur Tierpsychologie 26* (1969), 284–370.

178. Evans, D. R. "Specific aggression, arousal and reciprocal inhibition therapy." *Western Psychologist 1* (1970), 125–130.

179. Evans, D. R., & Hearn, M. T. "Anger and systematic desensitization: A follow-up." *Psychological Report 32* (1973), 569–570.

180. Fabrykant, M., & Pacella, B. L. "Association of spontaneous hypoglycemia with hypocalcemia and electrocerebral dysfunction." *Archives of Internal Medicine 81* (1948), 184–202.

181. Falconer, M. A. The pathological substrates of temporal lobe epilepsy and their significance in surgical treatment. In E. Hitchcock, L. Laitinen & K. Vaernet, Eds., *Psychosurgery*, Thomas, Springfield, IL, 1972, pp. 46–54.

182. Falconer, M. A. "Reversibility by temporal-lobe resection of the behavioral abnormalities of temporal-lobe epilepsy." *New England Journal of Medicine 289* (1973), 451–455.

183. Falconer, M. A., Hill, D., Meyer, A., & Wilson, J. L. Clinical, radiological, and EEG correlations with pathological changes in temporal lobe epilepsy and their significance in surgical treatment. In M. Baldwin & P. Bailey, Eds., *Temporal lobe epilepsy*, Thomas, Springfield, IL, 1958, pp. 396–410.

184. Falconer, M. A., Meyer, A., Hill, D., & Mitchell, W. "Treatment of temporal lobe epilepsy by temporal lobectomy: A survey of findings and results." *Lancet 268* (1955), 827–835.

185. Farris, R. E. L. *Social disorganization*. Ronald, New York, 1955. [2nd edition].

186. Feldman, P. E. "Analysis of the efficacy of diazepam." *Journal of Neuropsychiatry 3* (1962), 62–67.

187. Fenton, G. W., & Udwin, E. L. "Homicide, temporal lobe epilepsy and depression: A case report." *British Journal of Psychiatry 11* (1965), 304–306.

188. Ferinden, W. E. "Behavioristic psychodrama: A technique for modifying aggressive behavior in children." *Group Psychotherapy and Psychodrama 24* (1971), 102–106.

206

189. Feshbach, S. "The function of aggression and the regulation of the aggressive drive." *Psychological Review 71* (1964), 257–272.

190. Feshbach, S. "Dynamics of morality of violence and aggression: Some psychological considerations." *American Psychologist 26* (1971), 281–291.

191. Feshbach, N., & Feshbach, S. "The relationship between empathy and aggression in two age groups." *Developmental Psychology 1* (1969), 102–107.

192. Field, L. H., & Williams, M. "The hormonal treatment of sexual offenders." *Medicine, Science and the Law 10* (1970), 27–34.

193. Foote, R. M. "Diethylstilbestrol in the management of psychopathological states in males." *Journal of Nervous and Mental Diseases 99* (1944), 928–935.

194. Foxx, R. M., & Azrin, N. H. "Restitution: A method of eliminating aggressive-disruptive behavior of retarded and brain damaged patients." *Behaviour Research & Therapy 10* (1972), 15–27.

195. Frederichs, C., & Goodman, H. *Low Blood sugar and you.* Constellation International, New York, 1969.

196. Freud, S. *New introductory lectures on psychoanalysis.* Norton, New York, 1933.

197. Freed, H. *The chemistry and therapy of behavior disorders in children.* Thomas, Springfield, IL, 1962.

198. Freeman, W. "Psychosurgery." *American Journal of Psychiatry 121* (1965), 653–655.

199. Freeman, W. & Williams, J. M. "Human sonar: The amygdaloid nucleus in relation to auditory hallucinations." *Journal of Nervous and Mental Disease 116* (1952), 456–462.

200. Fregly, A. R., Bergstedt, M., & Graybiel, A. "Relationships between blood alcohol, positional alcohol nystagmus and postural equilibrium." *Quarterly Journal of Studies on Alcohol 28* (1967), 11–21.

201. Freud, S. *On narcissism: An introduction.* Hogarth Press, London, 1914. Standard edition.

202. Freund, K. "A laboratory method of diagnosing predominance of homo- or hetero-erotic interest in the male." *Behaviour Research and Therapy 1* (1963), 85–93.

203. Freund, K. "A laboratory method of diagnosing predominance of homo- or hetero-erotic interest in the male." *Behaviour Research and Therapy 3* (1965), 229–234.

204. Freund, K. "Erotic preferences in pedophilia." *Behaviour Research and Therapy 5* (1967), 339–348.

205. Freund, K. "A note on the use of the phallometric method of measuring mild sexual arousal in the male." *Behaviour Therapy 2* (1971), 223–228.

206. Freund, K., Chan, S. & Coulthard, R. "Phallometric diagnosis with 'non-admitters'." *Behaviour Research and Therapy 17* (1979), 451–457.

207. Gardos, G., & DiMascio, A., Salzman, C., & Shader, R. I. "Differential actions of chlordiazepoxide and oxazepam on hostility." *Archives of General Psychiatry 18* (1968), 757–760.

208. Gastaut, H. "Interpretation of the symptoms of 'psychomotor'

epilepsy in relation to physiologic data on rhinencephalic function." *Epilepsia 3* (1954), 84–88.

209. Gastaut, H., Roger, J., & Lesevre, N. "Differentiation psychologique des epileptiques en fonction des formes electro-cliniques de leur maladie." *Revue de Psychologie Appliquee 3* (1953), 237–249.
210. Gattozzi, A. A. Lithium in the treatment of mood disorders. U. S. Department of Health, Education, and Welfare. Washington, D. C., U. S. Government Printing Office.
211. Gibbens, T. C., Pond, D. A., & Stafford-Clark, D. A. "Follow-up study of criminal psychopaths." *Journal of Mental Science 105* (1959), 108–115.
212. Gibbs, F. A., Amador, L., & Rich, C. Electroencephalographic findings and therapeutic results in surgical treatment of psychomotor epilepsy. In M. Baldwin & P. Bailey, Eds., *Temporal lobe epilepsy*, Thomas, Springfield, IL, 1958, pp. 358–367.
213. Gillies, H. "Murder in West Scotland." *British Journal of Psychiatry 111* (1965), 1087–1094.
214. Glaser, G. H., Neuman, R. J. & Schafer, R. Interictal psychosis in psychomotor-temporal epilepsy: An EEG psychological study. In G. H. Glaser, Ed., *EEG and behavior*, Basic Books, New York, 1963, pp. 345–365.
215. Glass, G. S., Heninger, G. R., Lansky, M., & Talan, K. "Psychiatric emergency related to the menstrual cycle." *American Journal of Psychiatry 128* (1971), 705–711.
216. Gleser, G. C., Gottschalk, L. A., Fox, R., & Lippert, W. "Immediate changes in affect with chlordiazepoxide." *Archives of General Psychiatry 13* (1965), 291–295.
217. Gloor, P. In C. D. Clemente & D. B. Lindsley, Eds., discussion of a paper by Eibl-Eibesfeldt, I. Ontogenetic and maturational studies on aggressive behavior. In *Aggression and defense: Neural mechanisms and social patterns*, Vol. V, University of California Press, Los Angeles, 1967, pp. 57–94.
218. Goddard, G. V. Long term alteration following amygdaloid stimulation. In B. Eleftheriou, Ed., *The neurobiology of the amygdala*, Plenum, New York, 1972, pp. 581–596.
219. Goethe, F. "Beobachtunger uber das absetzen von witterungsmarken beim baummarder." *Deut Jager 13* (1938).
220. Goldstein, J. H., & Arms, R. L. "Effects of observing athletic contests on hostility." *Sociometry 34* (1971), 83–90.
221. Goldstein, A., Carr, E. G., Davidson, W. S., Wehr, P. *In response to aggression*. Pergamon Press, New York, 1981.
222. Golla, F. L., & Hodge, R. S. "Hormone treatment of the sexual offender." *Lancet 256* (1949), 1006–1007.
223. Goodman, L. S., & Gilman, A. *The pharmacological basis of therapeutics*. Macmillan, New York, 1965.
224. Gottlieb, P. M. Neuroallergic reactions to drugs. In F. Speer, Ed., *Allergy of the nervous system*, Thomas, Springfield, IL, 1970, pp. 134–142.
225. Gottlieb, P. M. Allergic neuropathies and demyelinative disease. In

F. Speer, Ed., *Allergy of the nervous system*, Thomas, Springfield, IL, 1970, pp. 79–121.

226. Gottschalk, L. A. Phasic circulating biochemical reflections of transient mental content. In A. J. Mandell & M. P. Mandell, Eds., *Psychochemical research in man*, Academic Press, New York, 1969, pp. 357–378.

227. Gottschalk, L. A., Gleser, G. C., & Springer, K. J. "Three hostility scales applicable to verbal samples." *Archives of General Pschiatry* 9 (1963), 254–279.

228. Gottschalk, L. A., Gleser, G. C., Springer, K. J., Kaplan, S., Shanon, J., & Ross, W. D. "The effects of perphenazine on verbal behavior: A contribution to the problem of measuring the psychologic effect of psychoactive drugs." *Archives of General Psychiatry* 2 (1960), 632–639.

229. Graham, H. D. & Gurr. T. R. *Violence in America: Historical and comparative perspectives*. 1969. A report to the National Commission on the Causes & Prevention of Violence.

230. Graziano, A. M., & Kean, J. E. "Programmed relaxation and reciprocal inhibition with psychotic children." *Proceedings of the 75th Annual Convention of the American Psychological Association* (1967), 253–254.

231. Greenbaum, J. V., & Lurie, L. A. "Encephalitis as a causative factor in behavior disorders of children." *Journal of the American Medical Association 136* (1948), 923–930.

232. Green, J. R., Duisberg, R. E., & McGrath, W. B. "Focal epilepsy of psychomotor type: A preliminary report of observation on effects of surgical therapy." *Journal of Neurosurgery 8* (1951), 157–172.

233. Greene, R., & Dalton, K. "The premenstrual syndrome." *British Medical Journal 1* (1953), 1007–1014.

234. Greenhill, J. P., & Freed, S. C. "The mechanism and treatment of premenstrual distress with ammonium chloride." *Endocrinology 26* (1940), 529–531.

235. Greenwood, J. "Hypoglycemia as a cause of mental symptoms." *Pennsylvania Medical Journal 39* (1935), 12–16.

236. Grossman, S. P. "Chemically induced epileptiform seizures in the cat." *Science 142* (1963), 409–410.

237. Gross, M. D., & Wilson, W. C. "Behavior disorders of children with cerebral dysrhythmia." *Archives of General Psychiatry 11* (1964), 610–619.

238. Gunn, J., & Fenton, G. "Epilepsy, automatism and crime." *Lancet 1* (1971), 1173–1176.

239. Guttmacher, M. The normal and the sociopathic murderer. In M. Wolfgang, Ed., *Studies in homicide*, Harper & Row, New York, 1967, pp. 114–135.

240. Hall, E. T. *The hidden dimension*. Doubleday, Garden City, N. Y., 1966.

241. Hall, C. S., & Klein, S. J. "Individual differences in aggressiveness in rats." *Journal of Comparative and Physiological Psychology 33* (1942), 371–383.

242. Hamburg, D. A. "Recent research on hormonal factors relevant to

human aggressiveness." *International Social Science Journal 23* (1971), 36–47.

243. Hamburg, D. A., & Lunde, D. T. Sex hormones in the development of sex differences in human behavior. In E. Macoby, Ed., The development of sex differences in human behavior. Stanford University Press, Palo Alto, Calif, 1966, pp. 1–24.

244. Hamburg, D. A., Moos, R. H., & Yalom, I. D. Studies of distress in the menstrual cycle and postpartum period. In R. P. Michael, Ed., *Endocrinology and human behaviour*, Oxford University, London, 1968, pp. 1–349.

245. Hamburg, D. A., & Turdeau, M. B., [Eds.]. *Biobehavioral aspects of aggression*. Alan R. Liss, New York, 1981.

246. Hampton, W. H. "Observed psychiatric reactions following use of amphetamine and amphetamine-like substance." *Bulletin of the New York Academy of Medicine 37* (1961), 167–175.

247. Harlan, H. "Five-hundred homicides." *Journal of Criminal Law and Criminology 25* (1950), 736–752.

248. Harris, S., Jr. "Hyperinsulinism." *Southern Medical Journal 37* (1944), 714–717.

249. Harris, E. E. Respect for persons. In R. T. DeGeorge, Ed., *Ethics and society*, Anchor Doubleday, Garden City, 1966, pp. 113.

250. Hatch, J. "Collective territories in Galapagos mockingbirds with notes on other behavior." *Wilson Bulletin 78* (1066), 198–207.

251. Haward, L. R. Differential modifications of verbal aggression by psychotropic drugs. In S. Garattini & E. B. Sigg, Eds., *Aggressive behaviour*, Wiley, New York, 1969, pp. 317–321.

252. Hawke, C. C. "Castration and sex crimes." *American Journal of Mental Deficiency 55* (1950), 220–226.

253. Heath, R G. "Correlations between levels of psychological awareness and physiological activity in the central nervous system." *Psychosomatic Medicine 17* (1955), 383–395.

254. Heath, R. G. Brain centers and control of behavior in man. In J. H. Nodine & J. H. Mayer, Eds., *Psychosomatic medicine: First Hahnemann Symposium*, Lea & Febiger, Philadelphia, 1962, pp. 228–240.

255. Heath, R. G. "Electrical self-stimulation of the brain in man." *American Journal of Psychiatry 120* (1963), 571–577.

256. Heath, R. G. "Developments toward new physiologic treatments in psychiatry." *Journal of Neuropsychiatry 5* (1964), 318–331.

257. Heath, R. G. Pleasure response of human subjects to direct stimulation of the brain: Physiologic and psychodynamic considerations. In R. G. Heath, Ed., *The role of pleasure in behavior*, Harper & Row, New York, 1964, pp. 219–244.

258. Heath, R. G. "Modulation of emotion with a brain pacemaker." *Journal of Nervous and Mental Disease 165* (1977), 300–317.

259. Heath, R. G., Llewellyn, R. C., & Rouchell, A. M. "The cerebellar pacemaker for intractable behavioral disorders and epilepsy: Follow-up reports." *Biological Psychiatry 15* (1980), 243–256.

260. Heath, R. G., et al. *Studies in schizophrenia*. Harvard University Press, Cambridge, MA, 1954, pp. 83–84.

261. Heath, R. G., & Mickle, W. A. Evaluation of seven years experience with depth electrode studies in human patients. In E. R. Ramey & P. S. O'Doherty, Eds., *Electrical studies on the unanesthetized brain*, Harper & Row, New York, 1960, pp. 214–247.

262. Hediger, H. "Saugetierterritorien und ihre Markierung." *Bijdr tot de Dierkde 28* (1949), 172–184.

263. Hediger, H. *Wild animals in captivity: An outline of the biology of zoological gardens.* Butterworks Scientific, London, 1950.

264. Hediger, H. P. The evolution of territorial behavior. In S. L. Washburn, Ed., *Social life of early man*, Aldine, Chicago, 1961, pp. 34–57.

265. Heimburger, R. F., Whitlock, C. C., & Kalsbeck, J. E. "Stereotaxic amygdalotomy for epilepsy with aggressive behavior." *Journal of the American Medical Association 198* (1966), 165–169.

266. Heino, F., Meyer-Bahlburg, L. & Ehrhardt, A. A. "Prenatal sex hormones and human aggression: A review and new data on progestogenic effects." *Aggressive Behavior 8* (1982), 39–62.

267. Heise, G. A., & Boff, E. "Taming action of chlordiazepoxide." *Federal Proceedings 20* (1961), 393.

268. Heller, H. C. "Altitudinal zonation of chipmunks [Eutamias]: Interspecific aggression." *Ecology 52* (1971), 312–319.

269. Herreca, M. A. "El visteo." *Revista Del Instituto de Investigaciones y Docencia Criminologicas 9* (1965–1966), 85–92.

270. Herrell, J. M. "A use of systematic desensitization to eliminate inappropriate anger." *Proceedings of the Annual Convention of the American Psychological Association 6* (1971), 431–432.

271. Hetherington, E. M., & Wray, N. P. "Aggression, need for social approval and humor preferences." *Journal of Abnormal and Social Psychology 68* (1964), 685–689.

272. Hill, D. "Cerebral dysrhythmia: Its significance in aggressive behavior." *Proceedings of the Royal Society of Medicine 37* (1944), 317–328.

273. Hill, D. "EEG in episodic psychiatric and psychopathic behavior." *Electroencephalography and Clinical Neurophysiology 4* (1952), 419–442.

274. Hill, D., Pond, A., Mitchell, W. & Falaconer, M. A. "Personality changes following temporal lobectomy for epilepsy." *Journal of Mental Science 103* (1957), 18–27.

275. Hill, D., & Sargant, W. A. "A case of matricide." *Lancet 1* (1943), 526–527.

276. Hill, D. & Watterson, D. "Electro-encephalographic studies of pschopathic personalities." *Journal of Neurology and Psychiatry 5* (1942), 47–65.

277. Himmelhock, J., Pincus, J., Tucker, G., & Detre, T. "Sub-acute encephalitis: Behavioral and neurological aspects." *British Journal of Psychiatry 116* (1970), 531–538.

278. Hinde, R. A. "The nature of aggression." *New Society 9* (1967), 302–304.

279. Hokanson, J. E. "Vascular and psychogalvanic effects of experimentally aroused anger." *Journal of Personality 29* (1961), 30–39.

280. Hokanson, J. E., & Burgess, M. "The effects of status, type of frustration, and aggression on vascular processes." *Journal of Abnormal and Social Psychology 65* (1962a), 232–237.
281. Hokanson, J. E., & Burgess, M. "The effects of three types of aggression on vascular processes." *Journal of Abnormal and Social Psychology 64* (1962), 446–449.
282. Hokanson, J. E., & Gordon, J. E. "The expression and inhibition of hostility in imaginative and overt behavior." *Journal of Abnormal and Social Psychology 63* (1958), 327–333.
283. Hoobler, B. R. "Some early symptoms suggesting protein sensitization in infancy." *American Journal of Diseases of Children 12* (1916), 129–135.
284. Ivey, M. E., & Bardwick, J. M. "Patterns of affective fluctuation in the menstrual cycle." *Psychosomatic Medicine 30* (1968), 336–345.
285. Jacobs, T. J., & Charles, E. "Correlation of psychiatric symptomatology and the menstrual cycle in an outpatient population." *American Journal of Psychiatry 126* (1970), 148–152.
286. Janowsky, E. S., Gorney, R., & Mandell, A. J. "The menstrual cycle: Psychiatric and ovarian-adrenocortical hormone correlates: Case study and literature review." *Archives of General Psychiatry 17* (1967), 459–469.
287. Jay, P. The common langur of north India. In I. DeVore, Ed., *Primate behavior*, Holt, Rinehart and Winston, New York, 1965, pp. 197–249.
288. Jenkins, R. L., & Pacella, B. L. "Electroencephalographic studies of delinquent boys." *American Journal of Orthopsychiatry 13* (1943), 107–120.
289. Jewell, P. A., & Loizos, C. (Eds.) *Play, exploration and territory in mammals*. Academic Press, London, 1966.
290. Jirgl, M., Drtil, J., & Cepelak, J. "The influence of propericiazine on the behavior of difficult delinquents." *Activitas Nervosa Superior 12* (1970), 134–135.
291. Johnson, R. Aggression in man and animals. Saunders, Philadelphia, 1972.
292. Jonas, A. D. *Ictal and subictal neurosis: Diagnosis and treatment*. Thomas, Springfield, IL, 1965.
293. Jones, M. S. "Hypoglycemia in the neuroses." *British Medical Journal* (1935), 945–946.
294. Kahn, I. S. "Pollen toxemia in children." *Journal of the American Medical Association 88* (1927), 241–242.
295. Kahn, M. W. "The effect of severe defeat at various age levels on the aggressive behavior of mice." *Journal of Genetic Psychology 79* (1951), 117–130.
296. Kalant, O. J. *The amphetamines: Toxicity and addiction*. Thomas, Springfield IL, 1966.
297. Kalina, R. K. "Use of diazepam in the violent psychotic patient: A preliminary report." *Colorado GP 4* (1962), 11–14.
298. Kalina, R. K. "Diazepam: Its role in a prison setting." *Diseases of the Nervous System 25* (1964), 101–107.

299. Kalin, R., McClelland, D. C., & Kahn, M. "The effects of male social drinking on fantasy." *Journal of Personality and Social Psychology 1* (1965), 441–452.

300. Kamm, I., & Mandel, A. "Thioridazine in the treatment of behavior disorders in epileptics." *Diseases of the Nervous System 28* (1967), 46–48.

301. Karli, P. "The Norway rat's killing response to the white mouse." *Behavior 10* (1956), 81–103.

302. Kasanin, J. "Personality changes in children following cerebral trauma." *Journal of Nervous and Mental Diseases 69* (1929), 385–406.

303. Kastl, A. J. "Changes in ego functioning under alcohol." *Quarterly Journal of Studies on Alcohol 30* (1969), 371–383.

304. Kaufman, H. *Aggression and altruism.* Holt, Rinehart and Winston, New York, 1970.

305. Keating, L. E. "Epilepsy and behavior disorder in school children." *Journal of Mental Science 107* (1961), 161–180.

306. Kelly, J. F., & Hake, D. F. "An extinction-induced increase in an aggressive response with humans." *Journal of the Experimental Analysis of Behavior 14* (1970), 153–164.

307. Kennedy, F. "Cerebral symptoms induced by angioneurotic edema." *Archives of Neurology and Psychiatry 15* (1926), 28–33.

308. Kennedy, F. "Allergic manifestations in the nervous system." *New York Journal of Medicine 36* (1936), 469–474.

309. Kennedy, F. "Allergy and its effect on the central nervous system." *Archives of Neurology and Psychiatry 39* (1938), 1361–1366.

310. Kepler, E. J., & Moersch, F. P. "The psychiatric manifestations of hypoglycemia." *American Journal of Psychiatry 14* (1937), 89–110.

311. Killeffer, F. A., & Stern, E. "Chronic effects of hypothalamic injury." *Archives of Neurology 22* (1970), 419–429.

312. Kiloh, L. G., Gye, R. S., Rosenworth, R. G., Bell, D. S., & White, R. T. "Stereotactic amygdaloidotomy for aggressive behaviors." *Journal of Neurology, Neurosurgery and Psychiatry 37* (1974), 437–444.

313. King, H. E. Psychological effects of excitation in the limbic system. In D. E. Sheer, Ed., *Electrical stimulation of the brain*, University of Texas Press, Austin, 1961, pp. 447–486.

314. King, J. A. Maternal behavior in Peromyscus. In H. L. Rheingold, Ed., *Maternal behavior in animals*, Wiley, New York, 1963, pp. 58–93.

315. Kleiman, D. Scent marking in the Canidae. In P. A. Jewell & C. Loizos, Eds., *Play, exploration and territory in mammals*, Academic Press, London, 1966, pp. 167–177.

316. Kletschka, H. D. "Violent behavior associated with brain tumor." *Minnesota Medicine 49* (1966), 1853–1855.

317. Kline, N. "Drugs are the greatest practical advance in the history of psychiatry." *New Medical Materia* (1962), 49.

318. Kluver, H., & Bucy, P. C. "'Psychic blindness' and other symptoms following bilateral temporal lobectomy in Rhesus monkeys." *American Journal of Physiology 119* (1937), 352–353.

319. Knott, J. R. Electroencephalograms in psychopathic personality and murders. In W. Wilson, Ed., *Applications of electroencephalography in psychiatry*, Duke University Press, Durham, N.D., 1965, pp. 19–29.
320. Knott, J. R., & Gottlieb, J. S. "Electroencephalogram in psychopathic personality." *Psychosomatic Medicine 5* (1943), 139–142.
321. Kopp, M. E. "Surgical treatment as sex crime preventive measure." *Journal of Criminal Law and Criminology 28* (1938), 692–706.
322. Kosman, M. E., & Unna, K. R. "Effects of chronic administration of the amphetamines and other stimulants on behavior." *Clinical Pharmacology and Therapeutics 9* (1968), 240–254.
323. Krafft-Ebing, R. *Psychopathic sexaulis*. Davis, Philadelphia, 1892.
324. Kramer, J. C., Fischman, V. S., & Littlefield, D. C. "Amphetamine abuse." *Journal of the American Medical Association 201* (1967), 305–309.
325. Kreuz, L. E., & Rose, R. M. "Assessment of aggressive behavior and plasma testosterone in a young criminal population." *Psychosomatic Medicine 34* (1972), 321–332.
326. Kuehn, J. L., & Burton, J. "Management of the college student with homicidal impulses." *American Journal of Psychiatry 125* (1969), 1594–1599.
327. Lagerspetz, K. "Genetic and social causes of aggressive behavior in mice." *Scandinavian Journal of Psychology 2* (1961), 167–173.
328. Lagerspetz, K. "Studies on the aggressive behavior of mice." *Annales Academiae Scientiarum Fennicae 131* (1964), 1–131. Series B.
329. Lange, J. *Verbrechen als Schisksal*. Unwin Brothers, London, 1931. English edition.
330. Laschet, U. "Antiandrogentherapie der pathologisch gesteigerten und abartigen sexualitat des mannes." *Sonderdruck aus Klinische Wochenschrift 45* (1967), 324–325.
331. Laschet, U. Antiandrogen in the treatment of sex offenders: Mode of action and therapeutic outcome. In J. Zubin & J. Money, Eds., *Contemporary sexual behavior: Critical issues in the 1970's*. Johns Hopkins Press, Baltimore, 1973, pp. 311–319.
332. Laschet, U., Laschet, L., Fetzner, H. R., Glaesel, H. U., Mall, G., & Naab, M. "Results in the treatment of hyper- or abnormal sexuality of men with antiandrogens." *Acta Endocrinologica* (1967), 54. Suppl. 119.
333. Laties, V. G. "Modification of affect, social behavior and performance by sleep deprivation and drugs." *Journal of Psychiatric Research 1* (1961), 12–25.
334. Laws, D. R., & Rubin, H. H. "Instructional control of an autonomic sexual response." *Journal of Applied Behavior Analysis 2* (1969), 93–99.
335. Lefkowitz, M. M. "Effects of diphenylhydantoin in disruptive behavior: Study of male delinquents." *Archives of General Psychiatry 29* (1969), 643–651.
336. LeMaire, L. "Danish experience regarding the castration of sexual offenders." *Journal of Criminal Law and Criminology 47* (1956), 294–310.

337. Lennard, H. L., Epstein, L. J., Bernstein, A., & Randsom, D. C. "Hazards implicit in prescribing psychoactive drugs." *Science 169* (1970), 438–441.

338. Lennox, W. G., & Lennox, M. A. *Epilepsy and related disorders.* Little, Brown, Boston, 1960.

339. Lerner, L. J. Hormone antagonists: Inhibitors of specific activities of estrogen and androgen. In *Recent progress in hormone research,* Vol. 20, Academic Press, New York, 1964, pp. 435–490.

340. Lerner, L. J., Bianchi, A., & Borman, A. "A-Norprogesterone an androgen antagonist." *Proceedings of the Society for Experimental Biology and Medicine 103* (1960), 172–175.

341. LeVann, L. J. "Haloperidol in the treatment of behavioral disorders in children and adolescents." *Canadian Psychiatric Association Journal 14* (1969), 217–220.

342. LeVann, L. J. "Clinical comparison of haloperidol with chlorpromazine in mentally retarded children." *American Journal of Mental Deficiency 75* (1971), 719–723.

343. Lichtenstein, P. E. "Studies of anxiety II: The effects of lobotomy on a feeding inhibition in dogs." *Journal of Camparative and Physiological Psychology 43 (1950),* 419–427.

344. Lion, J. R. *Evaluation and management of the violent patient.* Thomas, Springfield, IL, 1972.

345. Lion, J. R., Azcarate, C. L., & Koepke, H. H. "Paradoxical rage reactions during psychotropic medication." *Diseases of the Nervous System 36* (1975), 557–558.

346. Lion, J. R., & Bach-Y-Rita, G. "Group psychotherapy with violent outpatients." *International Journal of Group Psychotherapy 20* (1970), 185–191.

347. Lion, J. R., Bach-Y-Rita, G., & Ervin, F. R. "The self-referred violent patient." *Journal of the American Medical Association 205* (1968), 503–505.

348. Lion, J. R., Bach-Y-Rita, G., & Ervin, F. R. "Violent patients in the emergency room." *American Journal of Psychiatry 125* (1969), 1706–1711.

349. Livingston, S. "Epilepsy and murder." *Journal of the American Medical Association 188* (1964), 172.

350. Lloyd, C. W. Problems associated with the menstrual cycle. In C. W. Lloyd, Ed., *Human reproduction and sexual behavior,* Lea & Febiger, Philadelphia, 1964, pp. 490–497.

351. Lloyd, C. W. Treatment and prevention of certain sexual behavioral problems. In C. W. Lloyd, Ed., *Human reproduction and sexual behavior,* Lea & Febiger, Philadelphia, 1964, pp. 498–510.

352. Lloyd, J. A., & Christian, J. J. "Relationship of activity and aggression to density in two confined populations of house mice *Mus musculus.*" *Journal of Mammalogy 48* (1967), 262–269.

353. Lloyd, C. W., & Weisz, J. Hormones and aggression. Paper presented at Houston Neurological Symposium on Neural Bases of Violence and Aggression, Houston, Texas, March 9–11, 1972.

354. Lockie, J. D. Territory in small carnivores. In P. A. Jewell & C.

Loizos, Eds., *Play, exploration and territory in mammals*, Academic Press, London, 1966, pp. 143–165.
355. Logan, J. C. "Use of psychodrama and sociodrama in reducing excessive Negro aggression." *Group Psychotherapy and Psychodrama 24* (1971), 138–149.
356. Looker, A., & Conners, C. K. "Diphenylhydantoin in children with severe temper tantrums." *Archives of General Psychiatry 23* (1970), 80–89.
357. Loomis, T. A., & West, T. C. "The influence of alcohol on automobile driving ability: An experimental study for the evaluation of certain medicolegal aspects." *Quarterly Journal of Studies on Alcohol 19* (1958), 30–46.
358. Lorenz, K., *Man meets dog*. Methuen, London, 1954.
359. Lorenz, K. Ritualized fighting. In J. D. Carthy & F. J. Ebling, Eds., *The natural history of aggression*, Academic Press, New York, 1964.
360. Lorenz, K. *On aggression*. Harcourt Brace Jovanovich, New York, 1966.
361. Lottier, S. "Distribution of criminal offenses in metropolitan regions." *Journal of Criminal Law and Criminology 29* (1960), 37–50.
362. Lovaas, O. I. "Effect of exposure to symbolic aggression on aggressive behavior." *Child Development 32* (1961), 37–44.
363. Lowe, V. P. Observations on the dispersal of red deer on Rhum. In P. A. Jewell & C. Loizos, Eds., *Play, exploration and territory in mammals*, Academic Press, London, 1966, pp. 211–218.
364. Ludwig, A. M., Marx, A. J., Hill, P. A., & Browning, R. M. "The control of violent behavior through faradic shock." *The Journal of Nervous and Mental Disease 148* (1969), 624–637.
365. Lyght, C. E. [Ed.] *The Merck manual of diagnosis and therapy*. Merck, West Point, Pa., 1966.
366. MacDonald, J. W. *The murderer and his victim*. Thomas, Springfield, Ill., 1961.
367. MacDonnell, M. F., & Flynn, J. P. "Attack elicited by stimulation of the thalamus of cats." *Science 144* (1964), 1249–1250.
368. Madden, D. J., & Lion, J. R. *Rage, hate assault and other forms of violence*. Spectrum, New York, 1976.
369. Malamud, N. "Psychiatric disorders with intracranial tumors of the limbic system." *Archives of Neurology 17* (1967), 113–123.
370. Maletzky, B. M. "The episodic dyscontrol syndrome." *Diseases of the Nervous System* (1973), 178–185.
371. Mandell, M. Cerebral reactions in allergic patients. Case histories and provocative test results. Paper presented at the 25th annual Congress, American College of Allergists, Section on Neurologic Allergy, Washington, D.C., April, 1969.
372. Mandell, A. J., & Mandell, M. P. "Suicide and the Menstrual cycle." *Journal of the American Medical Association 200* (1967), 792–793.
373. Mans, J., & Senes, M. "Isocarboxazid, RO 5-0690 or chlordiazepoxide and RO 4-0403 a thioxanthene derivative." [1909–1918. Study on their individual effects and their possibilities of combination.] *Journal de Medicine de Bordeau 141* (1964).

374. Marinacci, A. A. "A special type of temporal lobe psychomotor seizure following ingestion of alcohol." *Bulletin of Los Angeles Neurological Society 28* (1963), pp. 241–250.
375. Marini, J. L., & Sheard, M. H. "Antiaggressive effect of lithium ion in man." *Acta Psychiat. Scand. 55* (1977), 269–286.
376. Marini, J. L., Sheard, M. H., Bridges, C. I, & Wagner, E., Jr. "An evaluation of the double-blind design in a study comparing lithium carbonate with placebo." *Acta Psychiat. Scand. 53* (1976), 343–354.
377. Mark, V. H., & Ervin, F. R. *Violence and the brain.* Harper & Row, New York, 1970.
378. Mark, V. H., Ervin, F. R., & Sweet, W. H. *Deep temporal lobe stimulation in man,* in B. E. Eleftheriou Ed. The Neurobiology of the amygdala. Plenum, New York, 1972, pp. 485–507.
379. Mark, V. H., Ervin, F. R., Sweet, W. H. & Delgado, J. "Remote telemeter stimulation and recording from implanted temporal lobe electrodes." *Confinia Neurologica 31* (1969), 86–93.
380. Mark, V. H., & Neville, R. "Brain surgery in aggressive behavior." *Journal of the American Medical Association 226* (1973), 765–722.
381. Marler, P. R. "Studies of fighting in chaffinches. [3] Proximity as a cause of aggression." *British Journal of Animal Behaviour 4* (1956), 23–30.
382. Marler, P. Aggregation and dispersal: Two functions in primate communication. In P. Jay, Ed., *Primate,* Holt, Rinehart and Windston, New York, 1968, pp. 420–438.
383. Mason, W. A. Use of space by Callicebus groups. In P. Jay, Ed., *Primates,* Holt, Rinehart and Winston, New York, 1968, pp. 200–216.
384. Masserman, J. H. *Behavior and neuroses.* University of Chicago Press, Chicago, 1943.
385. Matthews, L. H. Overt fighting in mammals. In J. D. Carthy & F. J. Ebling, Eds., *The natural history of aggression,* Academic Press, London, 1964, pp. 23–32.
386. McCandless, B. B. *Children: Behavior and development [2nd Ed.].* Holt, Rinehart & Winston, Inc., New York, 1967.
387. McClearn, G. E. Biological bases of social behavior with particular reference to violent behavior. In D. J. Mulvihill, M. M. Tumin & L. A. Curtis, Eds., *Crimes of Violence,* U.S. Government Printing Office, Washington D.C., 1969, pp. 979–1016. [A staff report submitted to the National Commission on the Causes and Prevention of Violence.]
388. McCord, W., McCord, J. *Psychopathy and delinquency.* Grune & Stratton, New York, 1956.
389. McCord, W., McCord, J., & Howard, A. "Familial correlates of aggression in nondelinquent male children." *Journal of Abnormal and Social Psychology 63* (1961), 493–503.
390. Mead, M. *Sex and temperament in three primitive societies.* Morrow, New York, 1935.
391. Mednick S. A., & Christiansen, K. O. *Biosocial bases of criminal behavior.* Gardner Press, Inc., New York, 1977.
392. Megargee, E. I. A critical review of theories of violence. In D. J.

217

Mulvihill, M. M. Tumin & L. A. Curtis, Eds., *Crimes of violence,* U.S. Government Printing Office, Washington, D.C., 1969, pp. 1038–1115. [A staff report submitted to the National Commission on the Causes and Prevention of Violence.]

393. Menninger, K. A. *The crime of punishment.* Viking Press, New York, 1968.

394. Meuringer, C., & Michael, J. L. [Eds.] *Behavior modification in clinical psychology.* Appleton-Century-Crofts, New York, 1970.

395. Milgram, S. "The experience of living in cities." *Science 167* (1970), 1461–1468.

396. Miller, N. E. "The frustration-aggression hypothesis." *Psychological Review 48* (1941), 337–342.

397. Miller, R. E., Murphy, J. V., & Mirsky, I. A. "The modification of social dominance in a group of monkeys by interanimal conditioning." *Journal of Comparative and Physiological Psychology 48* (1955), 392–396.

398. Mises, R., & Beauchesne, H. "Essai de la perphenazine chez l'enfant, et l'adolescent." *Annales Medice Psychologiques 2* (1963), 89–92.

399. Molof, M. J. Differences between assaultive and non-assaultive juvenile offenders in the California Youth Authority. Research Report 51, Department of Youth Authority, February, 1967. State of California.

400. Money, J. "Use of an androgen-depleting hormone in the treatment of male sex offenders." *The Journal of Sex Research 6* (1970), 165–172.

401. Monroe, R. R. *Episodic behavioral disorders: A psychodynamic and neurophysiologic analysis.* Harvard University Press, Cambridge, Mass., 1970.

402. Monroe, R. R. Drugs in the management of episodic behavioral disorders. Paper presented at the Houston Neurological Symposium on the Neural Bases of Violence and Aggression, March 9–11, 1972.

403. Montagu, M. F. A. *On being human.* Hawthorn Books, New York, 1966.

404. Montagu, M. F. A. [Ed.]. *Man and aggression.* Oxford University Press, London, 1968.

405. Montague, A. F. A. *The nature of human aggression.* Oxford University Press, New York, 1976.

406. Moore, M. W. "Extra-respiratory tract symptoms of pollinosis." *Annals of Alergy 16* (1958), 152–155.

407. Moos, R. "The development of a menstrual distress questionnaire." *Psychosomatic Medicine 30* (1968), 853–867.

408. Morton, J. H. "Premenstrual tension." *American Journal of Obstetrics and Gynecology 60* (1950), 343–352.

409. Morton, J. H., Addition, R. G., Addison, L. Hunt, & Sullivan, J. J. "A clinical study of premenstrual tension." *American Journal of Obstetrics and Gynecology 65* (1953), 1182–1191.

410. Moyer, K. E. "Kinds of aggression and their physiological basis." *Communications in Behavioral Biology 2* (1968), 65–87.

218

411. Moyer, K. E. "Internal impulses to aggression." *Transactions of the New York Academy of Sciences 31* (1969), 104–114.
412. Moyer, K. E., *The physiology of hostility.* Markham, Chicago, 1971.
413. Moyer, K. E. The physiological inhibition of hostile behavior. In J. F. Knutson, Ed., *The control of aggression: Implications from basic research,* Aldine, Chicago, 1973.
414. Moyer, K. E., & Crabtree, J. M. *Bibliography of aggressive behavior: A reader's guide to the research literature.* Alan Liss, Inc., New York, 1981.
415. Mulder, D., & Daly, D. "Psychiatric symptoms associated with lesions of temporal lobe." *Journal of the American Medical Association 150* (1952), 173–176.
416. Muller, M. "Alcholoismo Y criminalidad." *Revista del Instituto de Investigaciones y Docencia Criminologicas 9* (1965–1966), 51–69.
417. Mulvihill, D. J., Tumin, M. M., & Curtis, L. A. [Eds.]. Crimes of violence. Vol. 12. U.S. Government Printing Office, 1969. Washington, D.C.
418. Murdoch, B. D. "Electroencephalograms, aggression and emotional maturity in psychopathic and non-psychopathic prisoners." *Psychologia Africana 14* (1972), 216–231.
419. Murrie, O. J. *The elk of North America.* Stackpole and Wildlife Management Institute, Washington, D.C., 1951.
420. Murphy, H. B. M. "The cannabis habit: A review of recent psychiatric literature." *Bulletin of Narcotics 15* (1963), 15–23.
421. Murphy, M. R., & Schneider, G. E. "Olfactory bulb removal eliminates mating behavior in the male golden hamster." *Science 167* (1970), 302–304.
422. Myer, J. S. "Associative and temporal determinants of facilitation and inhibition of attack by pain." *Journal of Comparative and Physiological Psychology 66* (1968), 17–21.
423. Myers, K., & Mykytowycz, R. "Social behaviour in the wild rabbit." *Nature 181* (1958), 1515–1516.
424. Myer, J. S., & White, R. T. "Aggressive motivation in the rat." *Animal Behaviour 13* (1965), 430–433.
425. Mykytowycz, R. "Territorial markings by rabbits." *Scientific American 218* (1968), 116–126.
426. Nahas, G. G. *Marihuana: The deceptive weed.* Raven Press, New York, 1973.
427. Narabayashi, H., Nagao, T., Saito, Y., Yoshido, M., & Nagahata, M. "Stereoataxic amygdalotomy for behavior disorders." *Archives of Neurology 9* (1963), 1–16.
428. Nash, H., *Alcohol and caffeine: A study of their psychological effects.* Thomas, Springfield, Ill, 1962.
429. Nathan, P. E., Zare, N. C., Ferneau, E. W., & Lowenstein, L. M. "Effects of congener differences in alcoholic beverages on behavior of alcoholics." *Quarterly Journal of Studies on Alcohol* (1970), 87–100. Supplement #5.
430. National Commission on the Causes and Prevention of Violence. To establish justice, to insure domestic tranquility. U.S. Government Printing Office, Washington, D.C., 1969.

431. Neuman, F., Von Berswordt-Wallrabe, R., Elger, W., & Steinbeck, H. Activities of antiandrogens: Experiments in prepuberal and puberal animals in foetuses. In J. Tamm, Ed., *Testosterone: Proceedings of the workshop conference, April 1967, Tremsbuettel,* Georg Thieme Verlag, Stuttgart, 1968, pp. 134–143.

432. Neuman, F., Steinbeck, H., & Hahn, J. D. Hormones and brain differentiation. In L. Martini, M. M. Mutta, & F. Fraschini, Eds., *The hypothalamus,* Academic Press, New York, 1970, pp. 569–603.

433. Newton, G. D., & Zimring, F. E. *Firearms and violence in American life.* National Commission on the Causes and Prevention of Violence, Washington, D.C., 1970.

434. Nice, M. M. "The role of territory in bird life." *American Midland Naturalist 26* (1941), 441–487.

435. Noble, G. K. "The role of dominance in the social life of birds." *Auk 56* (1939), 263–273.

436. Novaco, R. W. "The functions & regulation of the arousal of anger." *American Journal of Psychiatry* (1976).

437. Nuffield, E. J. "Neuro-physiology and behavior disorder in epileptic children." *Journal of Mental Sciences 107* (1961), 438–458.

438. Nyby, J., Thiessen, D. D., & Wallace, P. "Social inhibition of territorial marking in the Mongolian gerbil *[Meriones unguiculatus]." Psychonomic Science 21* (1970), 310–312.

439. Obrador, S. Observations and reflections on psychosurgery at different levels. In E. Hitchcock, L. Laitinin & K. Vaernet, Eds., *Psychosurgery,* Thomas, Springfield, Ill, 1972, pp. 83–86.

440. Ounsted, C. "Aggression and epilepsy rage in children with temporal lobe epilepsy." *Journal of Psychosomatic Research 13* (1969), 237–242.

441. Paddock, J. "Values in an antiviolent community." *Humanities 12* (1976), 183–194.

442. Paige, K. E. The effects of oral contraceptives on affective fluctuations associated with the menstrual cycle. Unpublished doctoral dissertation, University of Michigan, Ann Arbor, 1969.

443. Paluck, R. J., & Esser, A. H. "Controlled experimental modification of aggressive behavior in territories of severely retarded boys." *American Journal of Mental Deficiency 76* (1971), 23–29.

444. Pauig, P. M., Delucam M. A., & Osterheld, R. G. "Thioridazine hydrochloride in the treatment of behavior disorders in epileptics." *American Journal of Psychiatry 117* (1961), 832–833.

445. Penfield, W., & Jasper, H. *Epilepsy and the functional anatomy of the human brain.* Little, Brown, Boston, 1954.

446. Pennington, V. M. "Meprobamate [Miltown] in premenstrual tension." *Journal of the American Medical Association 164* (1957), 638–640.

447. Pennington, V. M. "The phrenotropic action of perphenazine & amytriptyline. *American Journal of Psychiatry 120* (1964), 1115–1116.

448. Persky, H., Smith, K. D., & Basu, G. K. "Relation of psychologic measures of aggression and hostility to testosterone production in man." *Psychosomatic Medicine 33* (1971), 265–277.

449. Piness, G., & Miller, H. "Allergic manifestations in infancy and childhood." *Archives of Pediatrics 42* (1925), 557–562.
450. Podolsky, E. "The chemistry of murder." *Pakistan Medical Journal 15* (1964), 9–14.
451. Plotnik, R., Mir, D., & Delgado, J. M. R. Aggression noxiousness and brain stimulation in unrestrained rhesus monkeys. In B. E. Eleftheriou & J. P. Scott, Eds., *The physiology of aggression and defeat*, Plenum, New York, 1971, pp. 143–222.
452. Pool, J. L. "The visceral brain of man." *Journal of Neurosurgery 11* (1954), 45–63.
453. Podobnikar, I. G. "Implementation of psychotherapy by Librium in a pioneering rural-industrial psychiatric practice." *Psychosomatics 12* (1971), 205–209.
454. Pounders, C. M. "The allergic child." *Southern Medical Journal 41* (1948), 142–146.
455. Proshansky, H. M., Ittelson, W. H., & Rivlin, L. G. [Eds.]. *Environmental psychology: Man and his physical setting*. Holt, Rinehart and Winston, New York, 1970.
456. Rada, R. T. & Kellner, R. "Plasma testosterone levels in the rapist." *Psychosomatic Medicine 38* (1976), 257–268.
457. Ralls, K. "Mammalian scent marking." *Science 171* (1971), 443–449.
458. Randall, L. O., Schallek, W., Heise, G. A., Keith, E. F., & Bagdon, R. E. "The psychosedative properties of methaminodiazepoxide." *Journal of Pharmacology and Experimental Therapeutics 120* (1960), 163–171.
459. Randolph, T. G. "Ecologic mental illness-psychiatry exteriorized." *Journal of Laboratory and Clinical Medicine 54* (1959), 936.
460. Randolph, T. G. *Human ecology and susceptibility to the chemical environment*. Thomas, Springfield, IL, 1962.
461. Reckless, W. C., *The crime problem*. Appleton-Century-Crofts, New York, 1967.
462. Reeves, A. C., & Blum, F. "Hyperphagia, rage and dementia accompanying a ventromedial hypothalamic neoplasm." *Archives of Neurology 20* (1969), 616–624.
463. Resnick, O. "The psychoactive properites of diphenylhydantoin: Experiences with prisoners and juvenile delinquents." *International Journal of Neoropsychiatry Supp. 2* (1967), 20–47.
464. Resnick, O. The use of psychotropic drugs with criminals. In W. O. Evans & N. S. Kline, Eds., *Psychotropic drugs in the year 2000: Use by normal humans*, Thomas, Springfield, IL, 1971, pp. 109–127.
465. Reynolds, V. "Some behavioral comparisons between the chimpanzee and the mountain gorilla in the wild." *American Anthropologist 67* (1965), 691–706.
466. Ribero, S. L. "Menstruation and Crime." *British Medical Journal 1* (1962), 640–641.
467. Richardson, L. F. *Statistics of deadly quarrels*. Boxwood, Pittsburgh, 1960.
468. Rickles, K., & Downing, R. W. "Chlordiazepoxide and hostility in

anxious outpatients." *American Journal of Psychiatry 131* (1974), 442–444.
469. Rimm, D. C., DeGroot, J. C., Boord, P., Heiman J., & Dillow, P. V. "Systematic desensitazation of an anger response." *Behavioral Research and Therapy 9* (1971), 273–280.
470. Roberts, W. W., & Kiess, H. O. "Motivational properites of hypothalamic aggression in cats." *Journal of Comparative and Physiological Psychology 58* (1964), 187–193.
471. Robins, L. N. *Deviant children grow up.* William & Wilkins, Baltimore, 1966.
472. Robinson, B. W., Alexander, M. & Bowne, G. "Dominance reversal resulting from aggressive responses evoked by brain telestimulation." *Physiology and Behavior 4* (1969), 749–752.
473. Rocky, S., & Neri, R. O. "Comparative biological properties of SCH 12600 (6-chloro 4, 6 pregnadien 16-methylene 17-α-01-3, 20-dione-17-acetate) and chlormadinone acetate." *Federation Proceedings 27* (1968), 624.
474. Rosenberg, B., Edwards, A. E., & Hill, R. A. "Relationship between peripheral vascular state, personality, and adaptive response under effects of alcohol." *Proceedings of the 74th Annual Convention of the American Psychological Association (1966), 207–208.*
475. Rosenfeld, A. "10,000-to-one payoff." *Life Magazine 63* (1967), 121–128.
476. Ross, A. T., & Jackson, V. A. B. "Dilantin sodium: Its influence on conduct and on psychometric ratings of institutionalized epileptics." *Annals of International Medicine 14* (1940), 770–773.
477. Rosvold, H. S., Mirsky, A. F., & Pribam, K. H. "Influences of amygdalectomy on social behavior in monkeys." *Journal of Comparative Physiological Psychology 47* (1954), 173–178.
478. Rowe, A. H. "Allergic toxemia and migraine due to food allergy." *California and Western Medicine 33* (1930), 785–793.
479. Rowe, A. H. "Clinical allergy in the nervous system." *Journal of Nervous and Mental Diseases 99* (1944), 834–841.
480. Rud, E. "Spontaneous hypoglycemia with peculiar psychic disturbance." *Acta Medica Scandinavica 91* (1937), 648–655.
481. Ruffer, D. G. "Agonistic behavior of the northern grasshopper mouse [Onychomys leucogaster breviauritus]." *Journal of Mammalogy 49* (1968), 481–487.
482. Rylander, G. Clinical & medico-criminological aspects of addiction to central stimulating drugs. In F. Sjoqvist, M. Tottu, Eds., *Abuse of central stimulants*, Raven Press, New York, 1969, pp. 251–271.
483. Ryszkowski, L. The space organization of nutria [Myocastor coypus]. In P. A. Jewell & C. Loizos, Eds., *Play, exploration and territory in mammals*, Academic Press, London, 1966, pp. 259–275.
484. Sands, D. E. "Further studies on endocrine treatment in adolescence and early adult life." *Journal of Mental Science 100* (1954), 211–219.
485. Sano, K. "Sedative neurosurgery: With special reference to posteromedial hypothalamotomy." *Neurologia Medico-Chirurgica 4* (1962), 112–142.

486. Sano, K. Sedative stereoencephalotomy: Fornicotomy, upper mesencephalic reticulotomy and posteromedial hypothalamotomy. In K. Sano, Ed., *Progress in brain research*, Vol. 21B, Correlative neuroscience, Part B: Clinical Studies. Elsevier 1966, pp. 350–372.
487. Sano, K., Hiroaki, S. & Mayanagi, Y. Results of stimulation and destruction of the posterior hypothalamus in cases of violent aggressive and restless behaviors. In E. Hitchcock, L. Laitinent & K. Vaernet, Eds., *Psychosurgery*, Thomas, Springfield, Ill., 1972, pp. 57–75.
488. Sawa, M., Ueki, Y., Arita, M., & Harada, T. "Preliminary report of the amygdaloidectomy on the psychotic patients, with interpretation of oral-emotional manifestations in schizophrenics." *Folia Psychiatrician et Neurolgica Japonica* 7 (1954), 309–329.
489. Sayler, A. "Effect of antiandrogens on aggressive behavior in gerbil." *Physiology and Behavior* 5 (1970), 667–671.
490. Schachter, J. "Pain, fear, and anger in hypertensives and normotensives: A psychophysiological study." *Psychosomatic Medicine* 19 (1957), 17–29.
491. Schachter, S., & Singer, J. E. "Cognitive, social and physiological determinants of emotional state." *Psychological Review* 69 (1962), 379–399.
492. Schaffer, N. "Personality changes induced in children by the use of certain antihistaminic drugs." *Annals of Allergy* 11 (1953), 317–318.
493. Schaller, G. B. "Life with the king of the beasts." *National Geographic* 135 (1969), 499–519.
494. Scheckel, C. L., & Boff, E. Effects of drugs on aggressive behavior in monkeys. 1966. Excerpta Medica International Congress Series No. 129, Proceedings of the 5th International Congress of the Colleagium Internationale Neuropsychopharmacologicum. 789–795.
495. Schenkel, R. Play, exploration and territoriality in the wild lion. In P. A. Jewell & C. Loizos, Eds., *Play, exploration and territoriality in mammals*, Academic Press, London, 1966, pp. 11–22.
496. Schenkel, R., & Schenkel-Hilliger, I. *Ecology and behavior of the black rhinoceros*. Parey, Hamburg, 1969.
497. Schou, M. The metabolism and biochemistry of lithium. In S. Garattini & M. N. Dukes, Eds., *Antidepressant drugs*. Excerpta Medica Foundation, Amsterdam, 1967, pp. 80–83.
498. Schusterman, R. J., & Dawson, R. G. "Barking, dominance, and territoriality in male sea lions." *Science* 160 (1968), 434–436.
499. Schwab, R. S., Sweet, W. H., Mark, V. H., Kjellber, R. N., & Ervin, F. R. "Treatment of intractable temporal lobe epilepsy by stereotactic amydala lesions." *Transactions of the American Neurological Association* 90 (1965), 12–19.
500. Schwadron, R. Scaramuzzo gets 15–20 years for manslaughter. *The Times Herald Record*. March 30, 1965.
501. Scott, J. P. "Genetic Differences in the social behavior of inbred strains of mice." *Journal of Heredity* 33 (1942), 11–15.
502. Scott, J. P. "Social behavior, range and territoriality in domestic

mice." *Proceedings from the Indiana Academy of Science 53* (1944), 188–195.

503. Scott, J. P. "Dominance and the frustration-aggression hypothesis." *Physiological Zoology 21* (1948), 31–39.

504. Scott, J. P. *Aggression.* University of Chicago Press, Chicago, 1958.

505. Scott, J. P. Hostility and aggression in animals. In E. L. Bliss, Ed., *Roots of behavior,* Harper & Row, New York, 1962, pp. 167–178.

506. Scott, J. P. Theoretical issues concerning the origin and causes of fighting. In B. E. Eleftheriou & J. P. Scott, Eds., *The physiology of aggression and defeat,* Plenum, New York, 1971, pp. 11–42.

507. Scott, W. G. "The theory of significant people." *Public Administration Review 33* (1973), 208–315.

508. Scott, J. P., Carthy, J. D., & Ebling, F. J. "The natural history of aggression." *Science 148* (1965), 820–821.

509. Scoville, W. B., & Milner, B. "Loss of recent memory after bilateral hippocampal lesions." *Journal of Neurology, Neurosurgery and Psychiatry 20* (1957), 11–21.

510. Sem-Jacobsen, C. W. "Depth-electrographic observations related to Parkinson's disease." *Journal of Neurosurgery 24* (1966), 388–402.

511. Sem-Jacobsen, C. W. *Depth-electrographic stimulation of the human brain and behavior.* Thomas, Springfield, Ill, 1968.

512. Sem-Jacobsen, C. W., & Torkildesen, A. Depth recording and electrical stimulation in the human brain. In E. R. Kamey & D. S. O'Doherty, Eds., *Electrical studies on the unanesthestized brain,* Harper & Row, New York, 1960, pp. 275–290.

513. Serafetinides, E. A. "Aggressiveness in temporal lobe epileptics and its relation to cerebral dysfunction and environmental factors." *Epilepsia 6* (1965), 33–43.

514. Serafetinides, E. A. Psychiatric aspects of temporal lobe epilepsy. In E. Niedmeyer, Ed., *Epilepsy, modern problems in pharmacopsychiatry,* Karger, New York, 1970, pp. 155–169.

515. Servais, J. "Etude clinique de quelques cas de troubles psychosexuels chez l'homme, traites par un inhibiteur de la libido: La methyloestrenolone." *Acta Neurologica et Psychiatrica Belgica* (1968), 407–415.

516. Shrader, R. I., Jackson, A. H., & Dodes, L. M. "The antiaggressive effects of lithium in man." *Psychopharmacologia 40* (1974), 17–24.

517. Shah, S. A., & Roth, L. H. Biological and psychophysiological factors in criminality. In D. Glaser, Ed., *Handbook of Criminology.* Rand McNally, Chicago, 1974.

518. Shainess, N. "A reevaluation of some aspects of femininity through a study of menstruation: A preliminary report." *Comprehensive Psychiatry 2* (1961), 20–26.

519. Shannon, W. R. "Neuropathic manifestations in infants and children as a result of anaphylactic reactions to foods contained in their dietary." *American Journal of Diseases of Children 24* (1922), 89–94.

520. Sheard, M. H. "Behavioral effects of p chlorophenylalanine in rats:

Inhibition by lithium." *Communications in Behavioral Biology* 5 (1970), 71–73.

521. Sheard, M. H. "Effect of lithium on foot shock aggression in rats." *Nature* 228 (1970), 284–285.

522. Sheard, M. H. "The effect of lithium on behavior." *Comments on Contemporary Psychiatry* 1 (1971a), 1–6.

523. Sheard, M. H. "Effect of lithium on human aggression." *Nature* 230 (1971), 113–116.

524. Shuntich, R. J., & Taylor, S. P. "The effects of alcohol on human physical aggression." *Journal of Experimental Research in Personality* 6 (1972), 34–38.

525. Siegel, M. "Crime and violence in America: The victims." *American Psychologist* 38 (1983), 1267–1273.

526. Siegel, D., & Leaf, R. C. Effects of septal and amygdaloid brain lesions on mouse killing. Paper presented at the Eastern Psychological Association. Philadelphia, 1969.

527. Silverman, D. "Implication of the EEG abnormalities in the psychopathic personality." *Archives of Neurology and Psychiatry* 62 (1949), 870–873.

528. Skelton, W. D. "Alcohol, violent behavior, and the electroencephalogram." *Southern Medical Journal* 63 (1970), 425–466.

529. Skinner, B. F. *Beyond freedom and dignity.* Knopf, New York, 1971.

530. Sletten, I. W. & Gershon, S. "The premenstrual syndrome: A discussion of its pathophysiology and treatment of lithium ion." *Comprehensive Psychiatry* 7 (1966), 197–206.

531. Small, J. "The organic dimensions of crime." *Archives of General Psychiatry* 15 (1966), 82–89.

532. Small, J. G., Milstein, V., & Stevens, J. R. "Are psychomotor epileptics different." *American Medical Association Archives of Neurology* 7 (1962), 187–194.

533. Smith, S. W. "Trifluoperazine in children and adolescents with marked behavior problems." *American Journal of Psychiatry* 122 (1965), 702–703.

534. Smolev, S. R. "Use of operant technique for the modification of self-injurious behavior." *American Journal of Mental Deficiency* 78 (1972), 296–305.

535. Sodetz, F. J., & Bunnell, B. N. Interactive effects of septal lesions and social experience in the hamster. Paper presented at the Eastern Psychological Association, Washington D.C., 1967a.

536. Sodetz, F. J., & Bunnell, B. N. Septal ablation and the social behavior of the golden hamster. Paper presented at the Midwestern Psychological Association, Chicago, 1967b.

537. Sommer, R. *Personal space: The behavioral basis of design.* Prentice-Hall, Englewood Cliffs, N.J., 1969.

538. Sommer, B. "Are all women on trial?." *Psychology Today* 18 (1984), 36–38.

539. Sonne, C. "Observations on the symptomatology of insulin poisioning, particularly its psychic effects." *Acta Medica Scandinavica* 34 (1930), 223–233.

540. Sorenson, R. E. Cooperation and freedom among the Fore of New Guinea. In A. Montague, Ed., *Learning non-aggression*, Oxford, New York, 1978, pp. 12–30.
541. Southwick, C. H. Aggressive behaviour of rhesus monkeys in natural and captive groups. In S. Garattini & E. G. Sigg, Eds., *Aggressive behaviour*, Wiley, New York, 1969, pp. 32–43.
542. Southwick, C. H., & Clark, L. H. "Interstrain differences in aggressive behavior and exploratory activity of inbred mice." *Communications in Behavioral Biology 1* (1968), 49–59.
543. Speer, F. "The allergic tension-fatigue syndrome." *Pediatric Clinic of North America 1* (1954), 1029–1037.
544. Speer, F. "The allergic tension-fatigue syndrome in children." *International Archives of Allergy 12* (1958), 207–214.
545. Speer, F. The history of allergy of the nervous system. In F. Speer, Ed., *Allergy of the nervous system*, Thomas, Springfield, Ill., 1970, pp. 3–13.
546. Speer, F. The allergic tension-fatigue syndrome. In F. Speer, Ed., *Allergy of the nervous system*, Thomas, Springfield, Ill., 1970, pp. 14–27.
547. Speer, F. Etiology: Foods. In F. Speer, Ed., *Allergy of the nervous system*, Thomas, Springfield, Ill., 1970c, pp. 198–209.
548. Stafford-Clark, D., & Taylor, F. H. "Clinical and electroencephalographic studies of prisoners charged with murder." *Journal of Neurology, Neurosurgery and Psychiatry 12* (1949), 325–330.
549. Stea, D. "Space, territory and human movements." *Landscape 15* (1965), 13–16.
550. Stedman, J. M., Peterson, T. L., & Cardarelle, J. "Application of a token system in a pre-adolescent boys' group." *Journal of Behavior Therapy and Experimental Psychiatry 2* (1971), 23–29.
551. Stephens, J. H., & Shaffer, J. W. "A controlled study of the effects of diphenylhydantoin on anxiety, irritability and anger in neurotic outpatients." *Psychopharmacologia 17* (1970), 169–181.
552. Stern, J. M., Distribution and binding of 3 H-androgens in neural and peripheral tissues of rats and ring doves: Effects of progesterone and other steroid hormones. Unpublished doctoral dissertation, Rutgers University, New Brunswick, NJ. 1970.
553. Stevens, J. R. "Psychiatric implications of psychomotor epilepsy." *Archives of General Psychiatry 14* (1966), 461–471.
554. Stevens, J. R., Mark, V. H., Ervin, F., Pacheco, P., & Suenatsu, K. "Deep temporal stimulation in man: Long latency, long lasting psychological changes." *Archives of Neurology 21* (1969), 157–169.
555. Stone, C. P. Wildness and savageness in rats of different strains. In K. S. Lashley, Ed., *Studies in dynamics of behavior*, University of Chicago Press, Chicago, 1932, pp. 3–55.
556. Storr, A. *Human aggression*. Atheneum, New York, 1968.
557. Strauss, I. & Keschner, M. "Mental symptoms in cases of tumor of the frontal lobe." *Archives of Neurology and Psychiatry 33* (1935), 986–1005.
558. Strauss, I. & Keschner, M. "Mental symptoms in cases of tumor of

the frontal lobe." *Archives of Neurology and Psychiatry 35* (1936), 572–596.
559. Strecker, E. A., & Ebaugh, F. "Neuropsychiatric sequelae of cerebral trauma in children." *Archives of Neurology and Psychiatry 12* (1924), 443–453.
560. Sturup, G. K. "Correctional treatment and the criminal sexual offender." *Canadian Journal of Correction 3* (1961), 250–265.
561. Sugarman, A. A., Williams, B. H., & Alderstein, A. M. "Haloperidol in the psychiatric disorders of old age." *American Journal of Psychiatry 120* (1964), 1190–1195.
562. Sutherland, H., & Stewart, I. A. "A critical analysis of the premenstrual syndrome." *Lancet 1* (1965), 1180–1183.
563. Sweet, W. H., Ervin, F., & Mark, V. H. The relationship of violent behaviour to focal cerebral disease. In S. Garattini & E. G. Sigg, Eds., *Aggressive behaviour*, Wiley, New York, 1969, pp. 336–352.
564. Takala, M, Pihkanen, T. A., & Markkanen, T. The effects of distilled and brewed beverages: A physiological, neurological and psychological study. Helsinki Publication No. 4, The Finnish Foundation for Alcohol Studies, 1957.
565. Taylor, G. R. *The biological time bomb.* New American Library, New York, 1968.
566. Taylor, D. C. "Aggression and epilepsy." *Journal of Psychosomatic Research 13* (1969), 229–236.
567. Taylor, S. P., & Gammon, C. B. "The effects of type and dose of alcohol on human physical aggression." *Journal of personality and Social Psychology 32* (1975), 169–175.
568. Taylor, S. P., Vardaris, R. M., Ravtich, A. B., Gammon, C. B., Cranston, J. W., Lubetkin, A. L. "The effects of alcohol and Delta-9-tehalydrocannabenol on human physical aggression." *Aggressive Behavior 2* (1976), 193–196.
569. Telle, H. J. "Beitrag zur Kenntnis der verhaltensweise bei ratten, vergleichend dargestellt bei." *(Rattus norvegicus und Rattus rattus.) Zeitschrift fuer Angewandt Zoologie 9* (1966), 129–196.
570. Terrell, M. S. "Response to trifluoperazine and chlorpromazine singly and in combination in chronic 'backward' patients." *Diseases of the Nervous System 23* (1962), 42.
571. Terzian H. Observations on the clinical symptomatology of bilateral partial or total removal of the temporal lobes in man. In M. Balwin & P. Baily, Eds., *Temporal lobe epilepsy*, Thomas, Springfield, Ill., 1958, pp. 510–529.
572. Terzian, H., & Ore, G. D. "Syndrome of Kluver and Bucy reproduced in man by bilateral removal of the temporal lobes." *Neurology 5* (1955), 378–380.
573. Thiessen, D. D., & Dawber, M. "Territorial exclusion and reproductive isolation." *Psychonomic Science 28* (1972), 159–160.
574. Thiessen, D. D., Friend, H. C., & Lindzey, G. "Androgen control of territorial marking in the Mongolian gerbil." *Science 160* (1968), 432–433.
575. Thiessen, D. D., Lindzey, G., & Nyby, J. "The effects of olfactory deprivation and hormones on territorial marking in the male

Mongolian gerbil [Meriones unguiculatus]." *Hormones and Behavior 1* (1970), 315–325.

576. Thiessen, D. D., & Rodgers, D. A. "Population density and endocrine function." *Psychological Bulletin 58* (1961), 441–451.

577. Thompson, T., & Bloom, W. "Aggressive behavior and extinction induced response rate increase." *Psychonomic Science 5* (1966), 335–336.

578. Tilly, C. Collective violence in European perspective. In *Violence in America: historical and comparative perspectives*, U.S. Government Printing Office, Washington D.C., 1969, pp. 5–34.

579. Tinbergen, N. "On war and peace in animals and man." *Science 160* (1968), 1411–1418.

580. Tinklenberg, J. R., & Stillman, R. C. Drug use and violence. In D. N. Daniels, M. F. Gilula & F. M. Ochberg, Eds., *Violence and the struggle for existence*, Little, Brown, Boston, 1970, pp. 327–366.

581. Tintera, J. W. "The hypoadrenocortical state and its management." *New York State Journal of Medicine 55* (1955), 1869–1876.

582. Tintera, J. W. "Stabilizing homeostasis in the recovered alcoholic through endocrine therapy: Evaluation of the hypoglycemia factor." *Journal of the American Geriatrics Society 14* (1966), 126–150.

583. Tobin, J. M., Bird, I. F. & Boyle, D. F. "Preliminary evaluation of Librium [Ro 5-0690] in the treatment of anxiety reactions." *Diseases of the Nervous System, Supplement 21* (1960), 16–19.

584. Toch, H. *Violent man*. Aldine, Chicago, 1969.

585. Torghele, P. R. "Premenstrual tension in psychotic women." *Lancet 77* (1957), 163–170.

586. Traldi, S. "Use of fluphenazine enanthate in chronic schizophrenia." *Folia Medica 53* (1966), 261–277.

587. Travis, L. E., & Dorsey, J. M. "Effect of alcohol on the patellar tendon reflex." *Archives of Neurology and Psychiatry 21* (1926), 613–624.

588. Treffert, D. A. "The psychiatric patient with an EEG temporal lobe focus." *American Journal of Psychiatry 120* (1964), 765–771.

589. Tupin, J. P. "Lithium use in nonmanic depressive conditions." *Comparative Psychiatry 13* (1972), 209–214.

590. Tupin, J. P., & Clanon, T. L. Lithium and aggression control. Personal Communication, 1971.

591. Tupin, J. P., Smith, D. B., Clanon, T. L., Kim, L. I., Nugent, A., & Groupe, A. "The long-term use of lithium in aggressive prisoners." *Comprehensive Psychiatry 14* (1973), 311–317.

592. Turner, E. A. "Bilateral temporal lobotomy for psychomotor epilepsy." *1st International Congress of Neurological Science 2* (1959), 240–241.

593. Turner, W. J. "Therapeutic use of diphenylhydantoin in neuroses." *International Journal of Neuropsychiatry 3* (1967), 94–105.

594. Turns, D., Denber, H. C., & Teller, D. N. "Preliminary clinical study of propericiazine." *Journal of New Drugs 5* (1965), 90–93.

595. Tuttle, W. W. "The effect of alcohol on the patellar tendon reflex."

*Journal of Pharmacology and Experimental Therapeutics* 23 (1924), 163–172.

596. Ulrich, R. E. "Pain as a cause of aggression." *American Zoologist* 6 (1966), 643–662.

597. Ulrich, R. E. "Unconditioned and conditioned aggression and its relation to pain." *Activities Nervosa Superior* 9 (1967), 80–91.

598. Ulrich, R. E., Wolfe, M., & Dulaney, S. "Punishment of shock-induced aggression." *Journal of the Experimental Analysis of Behavior* 12 (1969), 109–115.

599. Urich, J. "The social hierarchy in albino mice." *Journal of Comparative Psychology* 25 (1938), 373–413.

600. Vallardares, H., & Corbalan, V. "Temporal lobe and human behavior. 1st International Congress." *Neurological Science* (1959), 201–203.

601. Valenstein, E. S. *Brain control.* Wiley, New York, 1973.

602. Valzelli, L. "Drugs and aggressiveness." *Advances in Pharmacology* 5 (1967), 79–108.

603. Vasconcellos, J. "Clinical evaluation of trifluoperazine in maximum security brain damaged patients with severe behavioral disorders." *Journal of Clinical and Experimental Pathology* 21 (1960), 25–30.

604. Verheyen, R. Monographie ethologique de l'hippotame [Hippotamus amphibius Linne'] Institute des Parcs Nationaux du Congo Belge. Exploration du Parc National Albert. Bruxelles, 1954.

605. Vonderahe, A. R. "The anatomic substratum of emotion." *The New Scholasticism* 18 (1944), 79–95.

606. Voss, H. L., & Hepburn, J. R. "Patterns in criminal homicide in Chicago." *Journal of Criminal Law, Criminology and Police Science* 59 (1968), 499–508.

607. Vukelich, R. D., & Hake, D. F. "Reduction of dangerously aggressive behavior in a severely retarded resident through a combination of positive reinforcement procedures." *Journal of Applied Behavior Analysis* 4 (1971), 215–225.

608. Walker, A. E. "Murder or epilepsy?". *Journal of Nervous and Mental Disease* 133 (1961), 430–437.

609. Walker, A. E., & Blumer, D. Long term effects of temporal lobe lesions on sexual behavior and aggressivity. Paper presented at the Houston Neurological Symposium on Neural Bases of Violence and Aggression, Houston, Texas: March 9–11, 1972.

610. Wallgren, H. & Barry, H. *Actions of Alcohol.* Vol. I. Elsevier, Amsterdam, 1970.

611. Ward, A. A., Jasper, H. H., & Pope, A. Clinical and experimental challenges of the epilepsies. In H. H. Jasper, A. A. Ward, V. A. Pope, Eds., *Basic mechanisms of the epilepsies*, Little, Brown, Boston, 1969, pp. 1–12.

612. Washburn, S. L. & DeVore, I. Social behavior of baboons and early man. In S. L. Washburn, Ed., *Social life of early man*, Aldine, Chicago, 1961, pp. 91–105.

613. Wasman, M., & Flynn, J. P. "Directed attack elicited from hypothalamus." *Archives of Neurology* 6 (1962), 220–227.

614. Weil, A. A. "Ictal emotions occuring in temporal lobe dysfunction." *Archives of Neurology 1* (1959), 101–111.
615. Weintraub, M., & Barry, D. "Managing the acutely agitated patient." *Drug Therapy* (1979), 99–103.
616. Weischer, M. L. "Uber die antiagressive wirking von lithium." *Psychopharmacologia 15* (1969), 245–254.
617. Wertham, F. *Seduction of the innocent*. Holt, Rinehart and Winston, New York, 1954.
618. Wertham, F., *A sign for Cain*. Macmillan, New York, 1966.
619. Westin, A. F., *Privacy and freedom*. Atheneum, New York, 1967.
620. Whitaker, L. H. "Oestrogen and psychosexual disorders." *Medical Journal of Australia 2* (1959), 547–549.
621. White, G. D., Nielsen, G., & Johnson, S. M. "Timeout duration and the suppression of deviant behavior in children." *Journal of Applied Behavior Analysis 5* (1972), 11–20.
622. Wilder, J. "Problems of criminal psychology related to hypoglycemic states." *Journal of Criminal Psychology 1* (1940), 219–233.
623. Wilder, J. "Psychological problems in hypoglycemia." *American Journal of Digestive Diseases 10* (1943), 428–435.
624. Wilder, J. "Malnutrition and mental deficiency." *Nervous Child 3* (1944), 174–186.
625. Wilder, J. Sugar metabolism in its relation to criminology. In S. Linduer & B. J. Seliger, Eds., *Handbook of correctional psychology*, Philosphical Library, New York, 1947.
626. Williams, D. "The structure of emotions reflected in epileptic emotions." *Brain 79* (1965), 28–67.
627. Williams, D. Temporal lobe syndrome. In P. J. Vinken & G. W. Bruyn, Eds., *Handbook of clinical neurology*, Vol. II. Wiley, New York, 1969, pp. 700–724.
628. Williams, D. "Neural factors related to habitual aggression. Consideration of differences between those habitual aggressives and others who have committed crimes of violence." *Brain 92* (1969), 503–520.
629. Williams, D. R., & Teitelbaum, P. "Control of drinking behavior by means of an operant-conditioning technique." *Science 124* (1956), 1294–1296.
630. Wilson, S. A., *Kinnier, Neurology*. Vol. I. Williams & Wilkins, Baltimore, 1940.
631. Winshel, A. W. "Chlorothiazide in premenstrual tension." *International Record of Medicine 172* (1959), 539–542.

# Index

232

depression (table) 149
Dershowitz 146
Di Mascio 71, 148
Dickey 138
Dilantin 185
disorders producing aggression
   facilitation 73–94
Diuretic 192
Dollard 102
Dopamine 192
drug-induced aggression 61–63
Duncan 60
Dunn 46
Dystonicity 192

# E

EEG. *See* electroencephalograph
Ehrlich 12
Eibl Ebesfeldt 97, 100
Eichelman 150
Elavil 191
electroencephalograph 192
   abnormal 88–92
Ellinwood 63
Ellis 49
emotional immaturity reactions
   54
Encephalization 192
Endocrine Glands 192
Endocrinophathy 192
Endogenous 192
episodic dyscontrol 92–94
Epstein 80
Ervin 15–16, 60, 93, 161–163
Estrogen 193
ethical problems 160–167
Etiology 193

# F

Fabrykant 60
facilitation of aggression 73–94
Falconer 82, 128

fantasy aggression, definition of
   19
fear-induced aggressive behavior
   20 (n)
feeblemindedness. *See*
   Oligophrenia.
female, human, premenstrual
   syndrome and 49–53
Ferracuti 66
Feshbach 97
Flynn 23
Fregly 65
Freud 96, 98, 104

# G

Gammon 65
Gestaut 81
Gibbens 91
Goddard 133
Goldberg 96
Goldstein 103
Gonadotropic Hormone 193
Gordon 147
Gottlieb 56
Gottschalk 49, 185
Gottschalk-Gleser Content
   Analysis Scale 49
Greenwood 61
Gross 89

# H

Hake 119
Haldol 185–186
Haloperidol 186
Harris 52, 168
Harvey 146
Haward 186
Hawke 46
Hayduke 2–4, 21
Heath 28, 31, 132, 135–136
Hediger 173
Heimburger 115, 129, 131
Heino 242–243

# U

Ulrick 34
Uncus 195
Unilateral 195
Urich 181

# V

Valenstein 86, 126, 130, 135
Valium 70, 186–187, 192
Vallardares 128
Valzelli 153
Vaughan 145
violence, definition of 19
Vonderahe 84
Vukelich 119

# W

WAIS. *See* Wechsler Adult
  Intelligence Scale.
Wallgren 64, 67
Ward 162
Wechsler Adult Intelligence Scale
  195

Wechsler-Bellevue Scale. *See*
  Wechsler Adult Intelligence
  Scale.
Weintraub 149–150
Williams 90
Wilson 89
Wolfgang 66

# X

X-Chromosome 195
XX-Chromosome 195–196
XYZ Syndrome 196

# Y

Y-Chromosome 196
Yamamoto 89

# Z

Zeman 86
Zimmerman 185
Zuni 183